Elizabeth, merry christmas 2009
Love from Harris
To extend your 'Gairdenin wisdoms'
xxxx

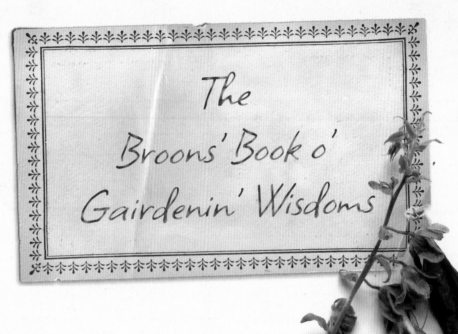

The
Broons' Book o'
Gairdenin' Wisdoms

Published 2009 by Waverley Books Ltd, David Dale House, New Lanark, Scotland ML11 9DJ.

Produced by Waverley Books Ltd, Text © 2009 Waverley Books and D.C. Thomson & Co. Ltd. The Broons logo, The Broons characters and The Broons cartoon strips and The Oor Wullie image (page 154) appear by courtesy of D.C. Thomson & Co. Ltd. and are © 2009 D.C. Thomson & Co. Ltd.

Granpaw's text is by David Donaldson, The Broons scriptwriter, with additional material by Christopher Riches, Catherine Gaunt and Waverley Books.

Design and layout by Mark Mechan.

Selected photographic images are reproduced under licence from Shutterstock.com

Additional photographs are used by permission: The Fortingall Yew © Forestry Commission; The Stronardron Douglas Fir © Lukasz Warzecha. Further additional photographs by Eleanor Abraham, Mark Mechan.

The Beautiful Scotland logo is used with permission.

Additional illustrations are by Peter Davidson and Mark Mechan. Illustrations in 'First Aid For Ailing Plants' (pages 100-101) are from House Plants published by Geddes & Grosset Ltd 1988, used by permission of Time-Life Books, © 1972 Time-Life Books Inc.

Historic illustrations are taken from The Gardener's Assistant: Practical and Scientific. A Guide to the Formation and Management of the Kitchen, Fruit, and Flower Garden by Robert Thompson (published in Edinburgh in 1860) and The Illustrated Dictionary of Gardening: A Practical and Scientific Encyclopaedia of Horticulture edited by George Nicholson (published in London in 1888). Diagrams are from the Geddes & Grosset / Waverley Books archive.

Granpaw would like to thank his pals at the Allotments for their help and also for the advice given by Stuart Syme and Moira Foster from Dundee, and William Tate from Dobbies Garden Centres.

The publishers would like to thank Dobbies Garden Centres for their cooperation.

The publishers acknowledge permission granted by The Auchentogle Bugle to reproduce selected extracts of Gairdener Broon's Gairdenin' Wisdoms.

ISBN: 978-1-902407-98-2

Printed and bound in Scotland by D.C. Thomson & Co. Ltd., West Ward Works, Dundee.

10 - 9 - 8 - 7 - 6 - 5 - 4 - 3 - 2 - 1

Introduction

Hello, a'body.

What rare fun I've had pittin' this gairdenin' book the'gither. Man, it's ta'en me back tae mair memories than I thocht I could bring tae mind. An' no' a' aboot gairdenin' either!

Some o' the memories I canna even tell ye aboot, what wi' ma reputation tae think aboot an' a' that. I was young masel' once upon a time, ye ken. Ma sweetheart Annie Lennox tells me I'm still young … she is tae, even though we'll baith never see eighty candles on oor birthday cakes again. Which reminds me, I must phone Annie aboot oor big nicht oot at the Hortycultooral Institute Denner on Setterday. I aye hae tae phone Annie after eight on a Tuesday, cos that's the nicht her faither's awa' oot at The Bones (that's "dominoes" tae you) an' we can chat in peace while he's awa'.

Oh, aye, what was I speakin' aboot now? Oh, aye, Gairdenin'. A'body should be able tae dae a bit o' gairdenin' … young or auld, able-bodied an' no' sae able. I've had an interest in the land a' ma life, whether it's plantin' oot bonnie floo'ers roond ma cottage, earthin' up the tatties at the allotment, the berries an' the like at The But an' Ben an' some cabbage an' leeks in the back gairden o' 10 Glebe Street. An' ye'd be amazed at whit ye can grow in windae boxes or in yer tenement close on the stairs.

An' of course, for those of ye who have never had the pleasure o' a gairden <u>shed</u>, well, ye'll jist dinna ken whit ye're missin'. It's the perfect place tae get awa' fae the world. The shed can be the place tae hae a fly smoke an' a wee dram, or a place for courtin' bonnie lassies amongst the beddin' plants, or somewhaur tae regale yer grandchildren wi' yer heroic stories aboot the war - that's the Boer War, or a hidey hole for yer Faither's Reserve malt, or workin' on yer auld motorbike ... och, it's like Doctor Whatsit's Tardis machine fae aff the telly.

An' then there's the serious business o' actual gairdenin' ... ye can join me later in the shed an' I'll gie ye a' the tips an' advice I've gleaned ower the years ... what records tae play tae yer geraniums tae cheer them up, how tae mak' yer ingins an' neeps bigger, where an' when tae plant yer tatties an' how tae get rid o' woolly aphids (no, that's no' a description o' ma thermal long johns - they're wee craturs that attack ma roses!).

An' afore ye run awa' wi' the idea that auld Granpaw hasnae a Scooby Doo aboot gairdens, let me tell ye that we Broons come fae a lang, lang line o' famous greenfingered loons. Let me tell ye aboot ma Great-Great-Great-Great Grandfaither "Capability" Broon ...

– Granpaw Broon

Contents

A wee word aboot ma book

I ha' selected a number of gairdein' topics that seem important tae me an' put them in alphabetical order in ma book. It's ma choice an' it micht nae ha' whit ye are lookin' for, but then there are hunners of ither books tae look at - and none of them will tell ye aboot the fun we ha' at the Auchentogle Allotments!

Tae help me, I ha' used two of ma granpaw's auld gairdenin' books, but I cannae aye recall whit I took fae which, sae I say it comes fae Thompson's Gardening Directory, when it could be fae The Gardener's Assistant by Robert Thompson (published in Edinburgh in 1860) or fae The Illustrated Dictionary of Gardening edited by George Nicholson (published in London in 1888).

I looked at ither books and spent a lot o' time at "The Volunteer Arms" takin' the advice o' ma allotment pals, but I didnae seek the advice o' the Auchentogle Hortycultooral Institute or the Editor of "The Bugle".

Gairdenin' Wisdoms

with GAIRDENER BROON

✳✳✳✳✳✳✳✳✳✳✳✳✳✳✳✳✳✳✳✳✳✳✳✳✳✳

HELLO, A'BODY, well, a'body that's readin' this column, that is. An' welcome tae the Heidquarters o' GAIRDEN WISDOM, an' when I say this is the "Heidquarters" o' the gairdenin' fowk in an' aboot Auchentogle, it's no' really a heidquarters as sic, mair like a HINDquarters, mair like a ... a backside I s'pose ... ach, it's actually a SHED. My shed in fact, in the gairden at ma wee hoose. The actual Heidquarters o' the greenfinger brigade hereaboots is EctuAlly the "Auchentogle Hortycultyooral Institute" doon Panloafy Avenue. Hah! Fat lot they ken aboot gairdenin' ... their noses are that far in the air, they'd no' smell a guid load o' manure even if they were staundin' in it. An' talkin' o' which, I got a richt reekin' load o' braw dung fae Jimmy Paterson at the ferm the ither day. Man, whit a rare arrrroma, fair cleared ma tubes. I had tae be firm wi' him when I ordered it, mind ... tellt him strecht, I wanted GUID stuff, nane o' that dung he'd sent me the week afore.

Aye, there's nuthin' I dinna ken aboot gairdenin', nuthin' that's worth kennin' like. As ye'll find oot if ye keep followin' ma column, ye'll see I wiz plantin' oot Pink Fir Aipple tatties lang afore Jim McCall at the Beechgrove Gairden wiz even a twinkle in his faither's e'en. (If ye're readin' this, Young fellah, drap in at The Shed for a wee dram onytime. Bring yer ain bottle this time ... an' nane o' that "Reel Blend" stuff yer auld pal Robbie dishes oot!)

When "The Bugle" editor asked me tae share a' ma gairdenin' secrets wi' you lot ... sorry, readers ... I wiz wantin' tae ca' masel' BROONFINGER (like Greenfinger, ye see) but some smert Alecs at the newspaper thocht it soonded like somethin' fae a James Bond film, an' some even thocht it soonded distasteful like, some'at aboot thin toilet paper if I mind richt ... whit that wiz a' aboot ah've nut a clue.

Now, enough o' that chit chat ... doon tae Broon business. What'll I tell ye aboot this week? Some fascinatin' tip aboot makin' yer tatties swell like neeps, I think. Ach, but wid ye credit that! I've run oota column inches. Ye'll jist hae tae bide yer time 'til next week's 'paper tae find oot whit's whit.

Well, that's a' for the day. I hope ye've learnt some'at useful.

Until next week then. Cheerio the noo. An' mind, unlike yon Geordie beer, ye canna doon this Broon ... ha ha. (It's ane o' ma wee jokes. Get it?) Happy gairdenin' !

Gairdener Broon
x

(That's no' ma real name of course ... it begins wi' "J", but it's secret, actually no, that starts wi' "S". It's J for John, but dinna tell onybody! JOHN Broon. That micht hae been better than Gairdener Broon but some smert erse thocht it soonded like a shipyaird column or a marching tune article. Mind you, John Broon's lot micht hae been better buildin' sheds than ships. They micht still hae been in business like masel'.

As ye'll nae doubt be aware noo, I jist love gairdenin' an' a'thing that goes wi' it. The hard graft, the braw veggies, the bonnie floo'ers, the guid friends, the craic in the shed. Och, I widna miss it for the world. An' I'm a richt lucky auld Broon greenfinger ... luckier than maist ... because I actually have four gairdens. Let me tell ye aboot them.

THE GAIRDEN AT NUMBER 10 GLEBE STREET

Well, really no' sae much a gairden as a back green, better kent by ither fowk as somewhaur tae keep yer bins or hing oot yer washin'. Ower the years I've kent it, it's seen mair changes than the Scottish parliament's front row forwards ... or should that be the scrum??

During the wars, when food was scarce, an' in the dark days afore the supermarket an' the like, Glebe Street gairden was planted oot wi' a' manner o' veg. "Dig for Victory" it was ca'd if I mind richt. Mind you, it wisnae aye an easy crop. Fowk in the close hung their washin' oot on the lines tae the greenie pole above the gairden. Some o' the washin' was "half-washed" at best an' it was a trauchle tae keep the dreeps fae above ruinin' the early tatties. There wiz auld goonies an' long johns an' penters' overalls blawin' aboot in the wind. Some o' that wiz bad enough but dreeps fae auld Tam McDade's shirt oxters wisnae ideal for organic cultivation!! An' talkin' aboot EARLY tatties, ye'd aye tae be up EARLIER than yer ne'ebors tae mak' shair naebody was snafflin' mair than their share o' the "earlies".

But when a' the fowk in yer land lends a hand, it's astonishin' what ye can grow in yer wee tenement plot. An' if a'body uses a bin as a compost heap, that mak's for real re-cycling. An' ye only need one lawnmower a'tween a'body, one spade, one rake an' what have ye.

An' if naebody's a' that fussy aboot vegetables, what better than tae hae a nice bit o' grass that a'body can share. It's aye rare an' sheltered in the back green an' it's a rare place tae sit an' crack wi' yer ne'ebors or share the big barbecue ye can a' lend a hand tae build. Buy some o' thae canvas chairs ye see ootside garages an' fillin' stations tae complete yer wee bit o' ootdoor life.

If ye want tae really brighten up yer back land, plant Virginia Creeper tae cover the back wall o' yer tenement, looking doon on yer barbecue space. It turns a richt bonnie red in the autumn. It'll climb richt up tae the tap floor an' intae yer roof, mind. Watch oot nae burglars climb up it an' in yer windaes mind. Ha ha. Paw Broon climbed up the creeper in number 10 ae nicht when he forgot his keys. We once had a wifie in number 10 we ca'd Virginia Creeper. Virginia McConnell she was ... couldna leave yer front door open for mair than a meenit an' she was in, moochin' a cup o' tea or tae borrow some sugar or a drappie milk. Or some hame-made shortie she'd sniffed oot wi' her big nostrils. A bonnie wumman I remember.

If ye are in a flat an' want yer ain personal bit o' gairden, dinna despair. If yer close has a drappie sunlight at the tap o' the stairs, there's nae end o' things ye can grow in pots richt ootside yer ain front door. An' there's aye windae boxes, dinna forget. A hale tenement wi' windae boxes wi' geraniums looks bonnie ... continental even. Mak's me feel like playin' a puckle o'French tunes on ma accordion.

So ye see, flat living disnae hae tae mean living in black an' white ... or Broon for that matter. Pit some colour intae yer close ... we aye have.

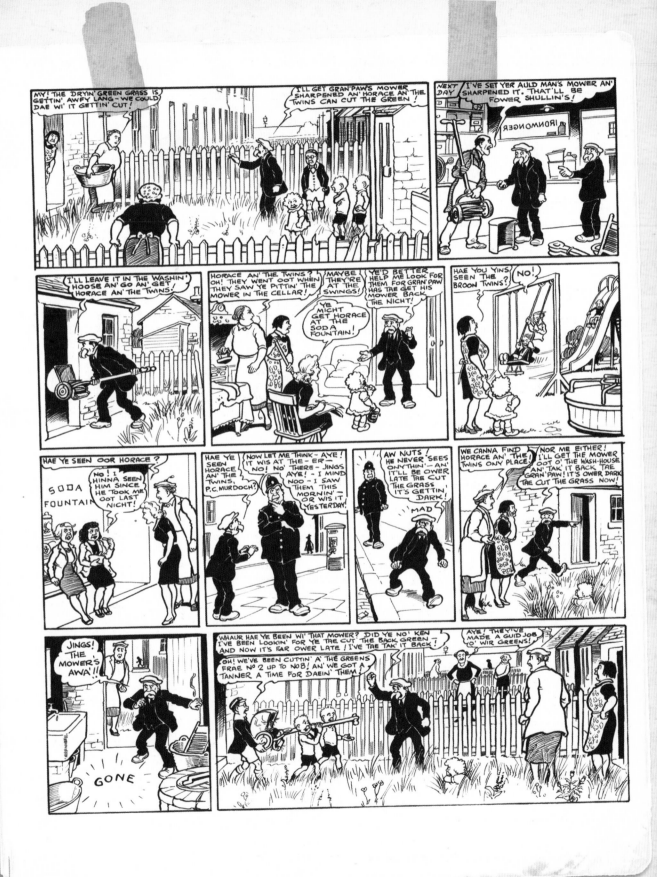

9

THE ALLOTMENT

I ha' an allotment no' far fae "The Volunteer Arms " an' "The Railway Tavern", a grand
location. An' it's a grand big skelp o' ground. I've had it for as lang as I can
remember. It was my faither's afore me. It's on that bit o' land that runs alangside
the auld railway junction line tae what was the colliery at Auchentogle.

An' what grand fowk they are tae, the gairdeners at the allotments. We a' have sheds
on the allotments, oor ain special places whaur we can get a bit o' peace an' quiet
fae the hurly burly o' life. Aye, quiet is the word, except mebbe for Fridays when we
hae oor get the'githers at "The Friday Nicht Allotment Swally Club". Och, a gentle
evenin' really, coupla drams, a fly smoke an' a bit o' braggin' aboot the size o' yer
neeps or how yer sweet peas are fair comin' on. That sort o' thing. An' mair often than
no' there's a bit o' music. There's some fine players amongst us - a fiddler or two,
wi' the accordion an' whoever joins in - The Auchentogle Allotment Association Diggers'
Band no less!

Allotments kinda grew up for thae fowk that had come in fae the coontryside tae live
in the cities an' missed their gairdens an' their ain hame-grown fruit an' veg. Oor
allotments are mair like a wee village, whaur a'body kens a'body else. It's mair like
a social club I s'ppose, or a weekend caravan site withoot the bother o' towin' yer
caravan through a' the traffic that drives fowk tae distraction thae days.

It's mainly veggies I grow masel' here, though there's some that hae richt bonnie
displays o' floo'ers nowadays. Sweet peas on frames is richt popular. Some o' us plant
sweet peas as hedges tae stop ither ne'ebors spying on yer giant leeks or yer marrow
beds. Fowk are aye keekin' in on ane anither, but it's a' hermless fun.

The big difference a'tween yer average allotment an' yer bungalow gairden is, well, how
can I say it, DUNG! Warm, reekin', rich ... tae use Rabbie's words. It's the stuff that
mak's peas the size o' tatties, tatties the size o' neeps an' neeps the size o' fitbas
... or bigger, like fitba players' heids! It is possible tae feed yer finest plots in
suburbia wi' Jimmy Paterson's finest fresh "farmyard fertiliser" of course, but I find
it disnae go doon well wi' yer ne'ebors' teacakes-on-the-lawn gairden parties. I laugh
when I mind Effie Tosh bringin' the vicar an' the ladies fae the choir tae efternoon
tea in her gazebo when auld Fred Nicolson got a "fresh" delivery jist the ither side
o' Effie's privet hedge jist as she brocht oot the finest china an' her angel cakes.
Laugh? I near disgraced masel'. The dung brocht tears tae a glass eye an' brocht the
wee tea an' tiffin tae a spluttering halt ... the wings fell aff the angel cakes I'm
tellt. There's nae sic problems oot at the allotments. We're a' up tae oor oxters an'
wellies in the food o' life.

I generally stop aff at the corner shop on my stroll tae the allotment of a mornin'
for the papers an' rolls an' a pint o' milk an' what have ye. Get the kettle goin' on
the pot belly stove in ma shed an' settle doon in the chair for a roll an' a cuppa an'
catch up on the news an' the fitba in the papers. I'm no' much intae the television
masel'. Radio's fine, like ... I hae a wee wireless in the shed. I like the local
station an' BBC Scotland ... Robbie Shepherd an' the real Scottish stuff. Gets yer feet
tappin'. Like tae hear Phil an' Aly on the box an' fiddle as weel. Man' it's grand tae
hear that stuff inside the shed.

Then it's on wi' the wellies an' oot tae the wee jobs that need daein' aboot the place
-- weedin', plantin', rakin', hoein', shooin' the rabbits awa' an' sic like. An' afore
ye can say "Nicky Tams" it's aboot time for elevenses ... anither cup o' strong tea an'
some ginger snaps dunked in it.

Annie occasionally draps in tae join me for a brew, Annie Lennox, that is, my
girlfriend. Well, she's no' exactly ma girlfriend ... an' yet I s'ppose she is. Mebbe a
girl friend's a better description. Well, sometimes it's mair than that, sometimes no'.
I'm a bit set in ma ways I s'ppose, a bit thrawn, cantankerous. So depending on how I
feel when Annie draps by, I'll gie her a cup o' tea ... or maybe no' ... an' sometimes
I'll offer her ma hand in marriage, an' sometimes I jist offer her a big cabbage.

An' that's life at the allotment. Never a dull moment I can tell ye.

THE BUT AN' BEN

Now, if there was ever a place tae gladden the gairdener's heart, this has tae be it. The But an' Ben. The Broon femily's wee hoosie in the country, the country estate, Grannie's heilan' hame, call it whit ye will. It's jist a wee hoose wi' a big heart, like a guid cabbage.

It's really only one room wi' anither room ben-the-hoose. How we a' get in is a mystery at times. But it's everything tae us Broons, aye has been. There's nuthin' ootside but bonnie countryside an' the few farms jist oota sight. An' as for gairdenin', well! I can tell ye this. There is nuthin' ye canna grow oot here. An' what's mair, withoot ony effort, withoot ony rakin' or plantin', the country gairden is groanin' wi' produce ... overflowing! An' it's a' happening on its ain. It's FREE food. It's a' wild - cherry trees, crab aipples (mak's braw jeely), wild rasps, blaeberies, brambles, wild garlic, mint alang the burn, damsons, plums an' a' manner o' mushrooms (find somebody that kens what they're daein' afore ye try this mind!!)

We still try an' grow veggies in an' aboot the But an' Ben for the pot . . the soup pot's ma favoorite, though some o' the femily like their veg near raw. A' richt if ye hae yer ain teeth. Kail is braw for soup, but we grow lots o' cabbage, leeks, onions, tatties, neeps, pea pods (better for the bairns than i-Pods!).

There is a wee drawback tae a' this country living gairdening oot here. Oor country ne'ebors that's what. An' I dinna mean the local country fowk. They're the salt o' the earth. No, I mean oor furry friends, rabbits an' deer an' the like. The hungriest femilies in Scotland. They'll eat mair than The Broons an' that's sayin' something. No, the rabbit is one femily ye dinna ask back for denner twice. Birds are aboot as difficult tae keep oot, but I find they dinna eat as mony o' ma berries as wid bother me. An' if ye pit oot peanuts in bird feeders an' hing oot a puckle o' fat balls, the bonnie wee feathered fowk are mair than happy wi' that.

An' of course (whisper this), if the rabbits become a real pest, jist trap them an' eat them wi' yer fresh veggies fae the gairden. Rabbit pie is delicious. But dinna let on tae yer weans. We aye tell oor Bairn that it's CHICKEN. For some reason, she wid be horrified tae eat rabbit but will happily eat chicken a' the time. Mind ye, the Bairn has seen Thumper in the "Bambi" film that mony times, it wid be like eatin' her best pal. If ye're squeamish aboot sic things yersel', jist picter thae big rabbitty teeth. They'd eat ye oot o' hoose an' hame an' allotment in twa meenits if ye'd let them.

Keepin' unwanted visitors at arm's length at the But an' Ben disnae aye need fences o' coorse. Scarecrows. That's sometimes worth thinkin' aboot. We've made scarecrows that looked like the ain fae "The Wizard of Oz" an' scary anes like something oot o' "The Wicker Man", but still the brutes get in aboot the greens. Then ae day, quite by chance, we stumbled upon the perfect bird an' rabbit deterrent. Worked a treat. The bunnies took ae look at it an' turned white tail an' ran a' the way tae the tap o' Ben Togle withoot stoppin' or lookin' back. An' ye'll never guess what did it. Dinna mention it tae her mind. It wiz jist oor Daphne leanin' ower the fence. She had ane o' thae face packs on, the stuff that mak's ye beautiful they say, an' she'd her hair in her curlers tae dry oot in the sun. Naebody let on tae Daphne, o' coorse. We jist said how bonnie her hair looked "sun-dried" an' that she should dae it every day tae get that natural look.

There's that muckle tae tell ye aboot gairdenin' at the But an' Ben, it wid fill a hale book on its ain. So I'll say toodle-oo the noo an' awa' an' get mucked in.

MY COTTAGE GAIRDEN

My fourth property (I sound like Lord Broon of Auchentogle) is of course my ain wee garden roond ma cottage. I've stayed aff an' on wi' the femily at Number 10, but it's grand tae hae yer ain front door. No' that I dinna like stayin' the odd nicht at the flat - Maw aye mak's Scotch broth wi' bilin' beef when I come. Lots o' veg an' lots o' beef ... braw! Sticks tae yer ribs.

It's floo'ers I grow in the main in ma wee gairden at hame. I'm a real greenfinger'd dab hand when it comes tae the roses an' gladioli. I can aye impress Annie (she lives jist ower the gairden wa' in the cottage next door) wi' the colour an' size o' ma gladioli. She aye laughs when I tell her that!

Ma wee darlin' The Bairn likes tae come tae the floo'er gairden at the cottage. She's no' sae keen on the allotment really. Gets her bonnie shoes ower mucky she tells me. She's a star wi' the floo'ers an' tak's a great interest when I tell her how tae plant an' the like. Bless her! She's a wee darlin'. The aipple o' ma eye. I mak' her laugh when I ca' her "ma wee sprout". She aye laughs at that ... disnae like sprouts ither. I set aside a wee bit o' the gairden that's jist for her. She helps me rake it oot an' prepare the soil wi' a drappie compost fae the gairden centre. Ye'd laugh if ye saw the twa o' us doon on oor hunkers an' me showin' her how tae mak' holes wi' a big pencil. Then we tak' great care tae drap in nasturtium seeds gently intae the holes. Narsturtiums are easy tae grow an' The Bairn gets fair excited when thay appear like magic oot o' the ground. The wee besom delights in makin' holes for the seeds wi' the stem o' ma pipe when ma back's turned. I think her mother tells her tae plant the pipe itsel' if the truth be tellt. "Plant it DEEP!" she'll likely tell her I imagine.

Annie's anither ane that loves the floo'ers fae the gairden. She's no' sae keen on "Inter Flora" mind. No' the shops that deliver the floo'ers for special occasions I mean. No, she likes them just fine. It's Flora Green she's no' sae keen on. Flora wha bides on the ither side o' my cottage fae Annie's hoose. I'm sandwiched a'tween twa blooms. Ha ha. Dinna let on, but Flora has a wee crush on me. It's a fact. I'm no' sic a bad catch when I hae a guid scrub an' trim ma whiskers. But Annie gets fair worked up when Flora asks me in for a coffee an' tae inspect her pansies. "That WUMMAN!" Annie says. She disnae like tae use strong language ye see. "That WUMMAN ... that Inter Flora!" It's "Interfering" Flora she means, but she gets a' puffed up an' canna speak proper like.

I hae tae admit I've aye been fond o' Roses an' Daisies an' Irises an' Ivys ... there was Rose Humphrey fae Haddington, Rose Robertson an' Daisy Davidson ... Daisy McLaggan ... Iris Tamson ... an' Ivy Gerrard fae the Boolin' Club Social Committee, och, I'm jist pullin' yer leg. Onyway, that was a lang, lang time ago ... must be a least the month afore last.

Well, I think that's mair than enough aboot ma various bits o' gairden ground here an' there. Read on a bit an' find oot for yersel's how tae mak' your gairdens blossom - an' yer love life if it needs a bit o' cultivation. There's nuthin' quite like muckin' in an' muckin' oot in yer wellies tae find oot wha's what an' wha's nut ... if ye see what I mean. I think I'll awa' an' try tae plant a wee seed in Annie's mind. I've aye fancied a Spring waddin', when the daffies are oot an' the bluebells are blanketin' the hale o' the countryside.

GROUP OF SPRING IRIS.
1 IRIS HISTRIO. 2 I. ROSENBACHIANA. 3 I. PERSICA. 4 I. KOLPAKOWSKIANA

The mair I gairden, the mair I learn,
and the mair I learn, the mair I ken how little I ken.

I s'ppose the whole o' life is like that.

Aipples

We've bin eatin' aipples fae thousands o' years - aye, as far back as Adam an' Eve! It wiz the Romans who brocht them tae Britain and there are hunners o' different varieties. Aipples need a cauld winter and so nae problem there!

Mind - if you want aipples, there has tae be anither aipple tree close by for pollination

THE APPLE, termed in its wild state the crab, is indigenous to Britain, and to most warm and temperate parts of Europe. It proves only half-hardy in St. Petersburg, but resists the cold which occurs in the extreme north of the British Isles, and some of its cultivated varieties can be there fruited in tolerable perfection.

The tree forms, in general, a round spreading head, and does not aspire to the height of the pear, yet, under equal circumstances, it acquires a thicker stem. Where the soil is good, and the subsoil not retentive nor liable to become too dry, it will live for hundreds of years. It will succeed in climates too cold for the pear, plum, and cherry; it also blossoms later than any of these – in May, generally a warm period of the season – and thus escapes the frosts which often ruin the crops of the above mentioned fruit-trees, which blossom in April or earlier.

No other kind of fruit-tree is so well adapted for cultivation in the gardens of all classes, and none affords so lasting and so generally useful a supply. The fruit of some of its early varieties is fit for use in July, and that of some later ripening sorts may be kept till that time the following season, and even later. Its usefulness for the dessert, for numerous culinary preparations, in confectionary, and for the production of cider, is so well known as only to need allusion here.

The varieties of the apple are exceedingly numerous, and we may safely state that thousands of them exist nameless, and only known as seedlings in the locality where they originated. Some varieties are cultivated for their rich flavour, others for their peculiar fitness for culinary purposes; some for their size and beauty, others for their late keeping, hardiness and abundant bearing. When we further consider that, with regard to dessert apples, tastes vary greatly – some persons preferring brisk, and others sweet-flavoured apples – that a considerable number of sorts is required for a full succession throughout the year and that different soils and climates require different varieties, it is evident that the number of sorts necessary to be retained in cultivation must be considerable.

FIG. 122. FRUITING BRANCH OF APPLE.

Apple Facts

- The largest known apple was grown in Japan. It weighed 1.85 kilograms (4 lb 1 oz) when it was picked on 24 October 2005.

- Twenty-five per cent of an apple's volume is air, which is why an apple floats.

- It takes the energy from 50 leaves to produce one apple.

- A good apple tree will produce over 100 kilograms of fruit a year.

SOME VARIETIES THAT GROW WELL IN SCOTLAND

EATING APPLES	COOKING APPLES
Beauty of Bath	Arthur Turner
Bloody Ploughman	Beauty of Moray
Cambusnethan Pippin	Bramley's Seedling
Coul Blush	Carlisle Codlin
Discovery	Clydeside
Ellison's Orange	Cox's Pomona
Golden Pippin	East Lothian Pippin
Hood's Supreme	Grenadier
James Grieve	Keswick Codlin
Katy	Lass o'Gowrie
Laxton's Fortune	Lord Derby
Norfolk Royal	Maggie Sinclair
Oslin	Monarch
Peasgood's Nonsuch	Scotch Bridget
Pitmaston Pineapple	Scotch Dumpling
Port Allen Russet	Seaton House
Sunset	Stirling Castle
Thorle Pippin	Tam Montgomery
White Joaneting	Tower of Glamis
Worcester Pearmain	White Melrose

...VILLE BLANCHE.

APPLE, COURT PENDU PLAT.

Some aipples have interesting names an histories – the Bloody Ploughman, grown in the Carse of Gowrie, was named after a ploughman who was caught stealing aipples and shot by a gamekeeper!

If Daphne peels an aipple in a single ribbon an' throws it ower her shoulder, the shape it lands in will be the initial o' her future husband.

19

The Allotment

I've had an allotment for years an' it's a muckle place for growin' veg and learnin' aboot gairdenin', an' much mair as well – but ye'll have tae read "The Bugle" tae find oot mair. Oor Allotment Newsletter is full o' practical advice, an' I have borraed fae it tae help mak this book.

Gairdenin' Wisdoms

with GAIRDENER BROON

✽✽✽✽✽✽✽✽✽✽✽✽✽✽✽✽✽✽✽✽✽✽

TIME TAE WRITE UP ma wee column for The Bugle again. I'm sittin' here in the gairden shed an' ah'm fair excited ah can tell ye. And it's nuthin' tae dae wi' the wee dram I've jist had fae Granpaw's Reserve ... the bottle o' single malt ah keep hidden in ma big floo'er pot.

The Allotment Committee had a letter fae friends in Belgium this week, a wee place jist ootside Brussels ca'd St Brun. Their mayor, B. Russel Sproote, has asked us if Auchentogle wid like tae be twinned wi' THEIR wee toon. The St Brun historian, Fanny Faye Flanders, tells us that hunners o' Auchentogle sojers fought at St Brun on 1st July 1916 during the First World War ... fortunately naebody was badly injured in what was referred to as "an oubreak of WINE FLU" in their local boozer, "Le Brun Koo", apart fae one Private John Broon fae 10 Glebe Street, Auchentogle, who was wrestled intae a local canal by Corporal "Hairy" Gordon o' the Gordon Highlanders fae Inversneckie, who'd consumed six bottles o' the strong local Belgian beer, Neuchateau Brun. (Crivvens! I remember it like it was jist yesterday. It was ma first wash in mair than a month). The pub wisnae ower badly damaged an' the Scots laddies acquitted themselves brawly in the summer offensive, rescuing Mayor Sproote's grandfaither's wine cellar fae the enemy at the Battle o' Pischendoon. Historian Ms Flanders' grannie aye wondered whit had happened tae Private Ranald MacDonald o' Blawearie. She aye kept his photie ... an' Ms Flanders hersel' marvels at how like her ain faither Ranald looked. So ye see, there are a'ready strong links a'tween the twa toons.

Onyway, at the Allotment Friday Nicht Swally, the committee lads unanimously agreed we should accept St Brun's kind proposal an' representatives fae each walk o' life will visit ane anither's toons. It wiz further agreed that the best Auchentogle sprouts be selected as a gift tae St Brun's mayor, tae demonstrate that we are a'ready aware o' their culture and history. It wiz, however, decided efter much heart-searching, that returning the auld photies o' bonnie young Belgian and French lassies that have adorned the walls o' "The Volunteer Arms" since jist efter 1918 widnae be a guid idea ... no' wi' what's written on the back o' maist o' them, that is.

So, it's a' fixed for later in the year. Me an' Provost Alec Donaldson, representin' the local Licensed Trade, will be takin' oot a puckle bottles o' "Auld Auchentogle" 12-year-old an' a case o' Maw Broon's Elderberry Wine tae swap wi' the mayor's offering o' their strong local ale "Trapiste Asnewts" and their famous "Neuchateau Brun", known locally as Le Brun ... and we'll be discussin' a bit o' gairdenin' of coorse. Near forgot that.

I'll need tae brush up on ma singin'. "Mademoiselle frae Armentieres, parley voo ...?"

Gairdener Broon
x

AUCHENTOGLE ALLOTMENT ASSOCIATION

RULES OF ASSOCIATION

1. You can grow vegetables, fruit, and flowers for cutting for yourself and your family's use only.

2. If you sell produce from the allotment, you will be disciplined by the Committee.

3. You must keep your allotment tidy.

4. Don't cause a nuisance to your neighbours. The Committee will consider complaints made to it.

5. You must keep the paths round your allotment in good order.

6. You can build a shed and a greenhouse on your allotment. You can also have a toolbox and cold frames.

7. You should respond to reasonable requests for help from other allotment holders.

8. You must remove everything from your plot when you give it up.

9. You must pay your annual rent promptly to the Committee.

10. You are not allowed to sublet your allotment.

11. The Committee shall rule on all disputed issues.

12. The Committee meets once a month (last Friday) at the Volunteer Arms.

By Order of the Auchentogle Allotment Association Committee

AUCHENTOGLE
ALLOTMENT ASSOCIATION

STARTING YOUR ALLOTMENT

Vegetables need plenty of sun to grow well, so make sure you know the sunniest spots in your allotment. They also need to be grown in well-cultivated, well-drained soil, and demand copious watering throughout the spring and summer. Nearly all vegetables should be grown in a three-year rotation. This means dividing the vegetable garden into three plots and growing different groups of vegetables in each plot each year in a three-year cycle. Rotation helps break the disease cycle and avoids starving areas of the garden of particular trace elements. Here is a typical three-year cycle.

A notable exception to the rotational scheme is the runner bean. These replenish the soil with nitrogen from the air and will feed the ground in this way from late summer to the first frosts. They can be grown year after year in the same spot, so there is every reason to erect a permanent supporting structure, not just temporary bean-poles.

You can actually see the nitrogen nodules on the roots of beans when you pull the roots up at the back of the year

With the limited space in an allotment, it is wise to grow either fast-growing vegetables, like radishes, lettuces, carrots and spring onions; cut-and-come-again vegetables like spinach and purple sprouting broccoli, French beans and runner beans; or permanent plantings like rhubarb, which is virtually trouble-free.

You can make the most of the growing space by sowing catch crops and succession crops. Catch crops of quick-growing lettuces and early carrots can be sown between the rows of slower-growing cauliflowers and Brussels sprouts and lifted before they begin to compete for space. Succession crops can be planted after the main crop is lifted - spinach sown in early spring and picked two months later could be followed by lettuce sown early in summer. Prolong the season by the use of cloches.

Fruit bushes and canes can be grown as well. They will need special care, and will benefit from regular pruning. There are numerous technical manuals to show how to do this.

VEGETABLE ROTATION

YEAR 1	YEAR 2	YEAR 3
Broad beans, peas, celery, chicory, cucumbers, endives, lettuces, radishes, tomatoes, onions, leeks, shallots	Broccoli, brussels sprouts, cabbage, savoy cabbages, cauliflowers, kail, spinach	Beetroot, carrots, parsnips, potatoes, swedes, turnips.
SOWN: early spring & summer; some can be lifted to make way for a second crop.	SOWN: spring, for planting out in summer	SOWN: early spring and summer
DRESSING: manure before sowing	DRESSING: fertiliser & lime	DRESSING: fertiliser
Beetroot, carrots, parsnips, potatoes, swedes, turnips	Broad beans, peas, celery, chicory, cucumbers, endives, lettuces, radishes, tomatoes, onions, leeks, shallots	Broccoli, brussels sprouts, cabbage, savoy cabbages, cauliflowers, kail, spinach
SOWN: early spring and summer	SOWN: early spring & summer; some can be lifted to make way for a second crop.	SOWN: spring, for planting out in summer
DRESSING: fertiliser	DRESSING: manure before sowing	DRESSING: fertiliser and lime
Broccoli, brussels sprouts, cabbage, savoy cabbages, cauliflowers, kail, spinach	Beetroot, carrots, parsnips, potatoes, swedes, turnips.	Broad beans, peas, celery, chicory, cucumbers, endives, lettuces, radishes, tomatoes, onions, leeks, shallots
SOWN: spring, for planting out in summer	SOWN: early spring and summer	SOWN: early spring and summer; some can be lifted to make way for a second crop.
DRESSING: fertiliser and lime	DRESSING: fertiliser	DRESSING: manure before sowing

USEFUL GAIRDENIN' MEASURES

LENGTH

INCHES (IN.)	CENTIMETRES (CM)
1/8	0.3
1/4	0.6
1/3	0.85
2/5	1
1/2	1.3
2/3	1.7
3/4	1.9
1	2.54
2	5
3	7.6
4	10
5	12.7
6	15.2
7	17.8
8	20.3
9	t22.8
10	24.4
11	28
12	30.5

FEET	METRES
1	0.305
1½	0.46
2	0.61
3	0.91
4	1.22
5	1.52
6	1.83
7	2.13
8	2.44
9	2.74
10	3.05
11	3.35
12	3.66
13	3.96
14	4.27
15	4.56
20	6.1
50	15.24
100	30.5

AREA

SQUARE FEET	SQUARE METRES
1	0.09
1½	0.14
2	0.19
3	0.28
4	0.37
5	0.46
6	0.56
7	0.65
8	0.74
9	0.84
10	0.93
10%	1
20	1.86
50	4.65

TEMPERATURES

°F	°C
0	-18
10	-12
20	-6.7
32	0
40	4.5
50	10
60	15.5
70	21
80	26.7
90	32
100	38

LIQUIDS

¼ pint	140 millilitres
½ pint	285 millilitres
1 pint	570 millilitres
2 pints	1.14 litres
3 pints	1.17 litres
4 pints	2.3 litres
1 gallon	4.56 litres

The allotment folk said I should put in these conversion tables tae help them that are a' metric

1 rod = 1 pole = 1 perch = 1/4 chain

100 links = 1 chain

4 pecks = 1 bushel

1 junk = two-thirds of a bushel

36 bushels = 1 chaldron

Auld market measures

a hand of radishes

a pottle of strawberries

a sieve of peas

a bushel of potatoes

a bundle of celery

a half sieve of apples

a punnet of grapes

Animals We Like an' We Dinnae Like

Ye dinnae see many animals in a gairden but that's cos they dinnae wan tae be seen. I love tae have hedgers in the gairden cos they eat insects that would like tae eat ma plants. But there are ither animals that ye dinnae wan tae see near the gairden - at the But an' Ben we seem tae grow veg jist for the rabbits an' deer tae eat.

GROSSET'S FILTERLESS

Good Garden Animals

HEDGEHOGS

One of the gardener's best friends as they eats slugs, millipedes and other insects. Hedgehogs hibernate during the winter and are active in the warmer months of the year. They rest during the day in long grass or in hedges and hunt at night – night-time snuffling noises in the garden are usually made by hedgehogs. To encourage them to stay in the garden, leave part of the garden wild so that they can easily shelter in it during the day. You can also provide a hedgehog nesting box; place the box in a secluded part of the garden for a female hedgehog to build a nest in. About four weeks after birth the hoglets might venture out with their mother and at eight weeks they leave and become independent. Male hedgehogs play no part in bringing up hoglets.

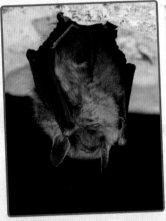

BATS

They fly around in the evening eating midges so are very welcome in any garden. A little pipistrelle bat (the most common in Britain) can eat 3,000 insects in a night! You can provide bat boxes to encourage them to settle in your garden. They are protected animals so once they have started nesting, you will not be able to move them elsewhere.

FROGS AND TOADS

Some of their favourite foods are slugs and snails. A small pond or damp, overshadowed areas of the garden will encourage them to come a settle in your garden.

Dear Gairdener Broon

I have hedgehogs in the garden and I wondered what I should feed them with. I read somewhere that they like bread and milk, but this does not sound right. Can you advise me?

Ye're richt that ye shouldnae gi' them bread an' milk – they'll git diarrhoea. Instead leave 'em a little dry dog food or ye can buy, would ye believe it, food jist for hedgers from pet shops an' gairden centres that contains dried meat, insects, berries, nuts, fruits, cereals an' honey. Mak sure that there is a saucer o' watter as well.

—Gairdener Broon

Try Maw's rabbit casserole in The But an' Ben Cookbook

Annuals an' Biennials

Gairdeners use a' sorts o' special words tae describe different types o' plants. Many of ma favoorite floo'ers are annuals or biennials. I leave it tae Thompson tae tell ye whit the words mean. I jist know that they bring a lot o' colour to the gairden - and tae the hoose.

- You can plant annuals whenever you like from spring onwards — so long as there are at least 12 weeks to grow and flower.

- Always plant annuals in sunny spots in the garden.

- Annuals should not be fed very much; overfeeding will give lots of foliage instead of flowers. They prefer a well-drained soil.

- Hardy annuals need fairly low temperatures to germinate, so they can be sown outdoors early in spring, if the soil is well drained.

- Hardy annuals are easy — just plant the seeds in the ground in the spring and watch them grow (but make sure you follow the instructions on the seed packet, and when the seedlings start growing, keep them free of weeds and thin them out if necessary).

If we planT The DandY Annual will we geT DandY flowers?

SWEET PEA

6D.

AUCHINLECK SEED Co.

AUCHINLECK SEED Co

SWEET PEA

Preparing the seeds

Sweet pea seeds have a hard coat. Before planting, place the seeds on top of a wet piece of absorbent paper and plant them once they begin to sprout. This will speed up germination.

For early flowers

1. Plant into pots in March. Plant two seeds into each pot to a depth of 1 inch.
2. If both seeds germinate remove the second plant so only one plant remains.
3. Once the plants have 3 or 4 pairs of leaves, they will be ready for hardening off outside and then for planting in their final position.
4. Plant each seedling about 5-6 inches apart and nip out the top set of leaves to encourage more growth.
5. Sweet peas need a trellis, poles or netting to climb up.
6. Once flowering starts, pick flowers very regularly to encourage more flowers.

For later flowers

1. Plant the seeds direct into the soil after the risk of frost has passed
2. The follow the instructions as above from (3) onwards.

Ma favoorite annuals
Sweet pea
Love-in-a-mist
Cornflowers
Poached egg plant

Ma favoorite biennials
Wallflower
Sweet William
Honesty
Forget-me-not

Plant biennials this year for floo'ers the next.

ANNUALS All plants which spring from the seed, flower, and die within the course of a year. *Hardy Annuals* are those which require no artificial aid to enable them to develop, but grow and flower freely in the open air. *Half-Hardy Annuals* are those for which our climate is not sufficiently warm, or rather, our summer is not, as a rule, either hot enough or long enough to allow them to grow, flower well, and ripen seed, if planted in the open air. The term 'bedding plants' is applied to many half-hardy plants.

BIENNIALS Plants that occupy two years in the development from seed to the maturation of seed; growing one year, and flowering, fruiting, and dying the next.

Gairdenin' Wisdoms
with GAIRDENER BROON

❋❋❋❋❋❋❋❋❋❋❋❋❋❋❋❋❋❋❋

HERE AH AM AGAIN. Have ye a' had a guid week in yer wellies? Man, what a week it's been for masel'. If ony o' ye were at The Village Show, ye'll hae a wee inklin' o' what ah'm talkin' aboot. Missus Alice Gow's giant marrow … a spectacular example o' guid gairdenin' … an' bad blood!

The Auchentogle judges were fair ta'en by the monstrous marra and it wiz a toss-up as tae whether her exhibit was tae be awarded the gold medal … or wiz her marra tae be pipped for first by Sandy Lawrie's big leek? Of coorse, we'll never ken for sure now as ye'll likely hae read in The Bugle news the ither day.

There hae been muckle mutterings aboot dark an' dastardly deeds followin' the mysterious collapse o' the trestle table which caused Alice's marra tae fa' tae the flair and land on Betty McLeod's wee West Highland Terrier … a lovely wee bitch – nae Betty, that is – her wee doggie. Sadly it burst wide open and leaked a' ower the flair … the marra, no' the dog. Now, there's nae love lost a'tween Sandy and Alice and the woman fair lost her rag and accused Sandy o' skullduggery in the massacre o' her marra. "Deliberate sabotage" were her actual words. However, following a verra thorough investigation by PC Murdoch and Sergeant McDonald, during which it was ascertained that naebody saw a thing, it was their findin' that the hale thing had been caused by a shoogly table leg and that Alice dumpin' Sandy, her then boyfriend, tae marry Erchie Gow efter the war, had little bearing on the said accusations o' foul play.

Eye witnesses hae conflicting reports o' Alice's reaction tae the polis's report. Some say this an' some say that, but The Bugle editor has decided ah'd be wise no' tae mention the brick incident as naebody saw a thing again. And Alice meekly accepted the fact that Sandy's leek got "Best in Show". Well, The Committee could hardly hae pinned the rosette on a burst marra. A' it was fit for by

that time was a guid plate o' soup. It widna hae made a guid photie in the followin' morning's edition o' the paper either.

However, The Committee in their wisdom decided tae award Alice a consolation "Highly Commended" rosette for her marrow … and Chairman reported that The Committee meeting room windae had already been repaired and that Missus Gow can collect her brick ony Tuesday or Thursday nicht efter the meetings … and nae hard feelings.

Happy gairdenin' for anither week – hoe! hoe! hoe!

Gairdener Broon x

SECOND PRIZE

Class: A basket of plenty (mixed vegetables)

Awarded to:

Granpaw Broon

James Wilson
Wilson
Chairman of the Committee

Auchentogle Horticultural Institute

130TH ANNUAL SHOW

Prize Certificate

THIRD PRIZE

Class: Unusual-shaped Vegetables

Awarded to:

Hen and Joe Broon

James Wilson
J. Wilson
Chairman of the Committee

****SCHEDULE***8*

AUCHENTOGLE HORTICULTURAL INSTITUTE
130TH ANNUAL SHOW

The Institute
Panloafy Avenue
Auchentogle

2.00 p.m. Saturday 28 August

The Women's Rural Institute,
Auchentogle Branch will provide teas

SCHEDULE OF CLASSES

No exhibits will be accepted after 10.00 a.m.
Doors open for exhibitors from 8.00 a.m.
All exhibits to be cleared after 4.00 p.m.
Any exhibit not collected by 4.30 p.m. will b
disposed of.

Prizes to be collected from the Secretary at
the show after 3.00 p.m.

SECTION 2 VEGETABLES

2.1 Three onions, from set, globe
2.2 Three onions over 18 in. in
     circumference
2.3 Three onions 12-18 in. in circumference
2.4 Three onions up to 12 in. in
     circumference
2.5 Three turnips, any variety
2.6 Three carrots, long
2.7 Three carrots, stump-rooted
2.8 Three blanched leeks, less than 14 in.
2.9 One blanched leek, more than 14 in.
2.10 Six pods peas
2.11 Three white potatoes
2.12 Collection of potatoes (6 potatoes, at
     least 2 varieties)
2.13 Six tomatoes
2.14 One cucumber
2.15 Basket of Plenty (at least six
     varieties of vegetable)
2.16 One monstrous marrow

SECTION 3 FLOWER ARRANGING

3.1 An arrangement for a busy person
3.2 An arrangement with no flowers
3.3 An arrangement in an old shoe
3.4 The spirit of Auchentogle- arrangement
3.5 A table posy
3.6 An arrangement with ten flowers
3.7 A miniature arrangement 6 in. high
3.8 Arrangement in a jam jar (for children
     only)

MAW BROON'S AIPPLE CHUTNEY

2 1/2 lbs peeled, cored apples
1 1/2 lbs soft brown sugar
1 1/2 ozs garlic
2 teaspoons ground ginger
2 teaspoons peppercorns
2 teaspoons coriander seeds
8 ozs onions
1 lb seeded raisins or sultanas
4 teaspoons salt
1 pint brown vinegar

Chop the aipples, raisins, onions,
an' garlic. Tie the peppercorns
an' coriander seeds in a muslin
bag (mind an' tak' them oot afore
ye pot it). Add the sugar. Mix it
a' weel, put into a pot, add the
vinegar, an' cook for an hour, or
longer, if the aipples still seem
hard. Stir frequently.

This should make aboot 5lbs o'
chutney. Fill dry, hot jars and
screw on lids, or use cellophane
jam covers. Seal jars well and
store in a cool cupboard.

Auchentogle
Horticulural Institute
130TH ANNUAL SHOW
Prize Certificate
FIRST PRIZE
Class: Preserves: Glass Jar Home-made Chutney
Awarded to:
Maw Broon
es Wilson
of the Committee

31

The Bairn's Gairden

I've let The Bairn ha' a wee patch in ma gairden where she can grow some floo'ers. She really likes seein' how they grow - and takin' bunches o' flowers back to Maw so a'body at Glebe Street can enjoy them. I foond these ideas in Allotment Newsletter and they helped me and The Bairn create her gairden. I hope ye find them helpful too!

3d.

mustard & cress
* MEDLEY *

Anchentogle
Horticulural Institute

130TH ANNUAL SHOW

Prize Certificate

FIRST PRIZE

Class: Children's Section: Miniature Garden on a Plate

Awarded to:

Broon Bairn

James Wilson
~~~man~~~ of the Committee

When ye plant seeds, plant them in straight rows or in a clear pattern. Then, when plants begin tae appear, ye'll be able tae see which are the seedlins ye want and which are the weeds, which ye can pull oot.

This year The Bairn planted sunflower, alyssum, nasturtium, love-in-a-mist an' poached egg plant.

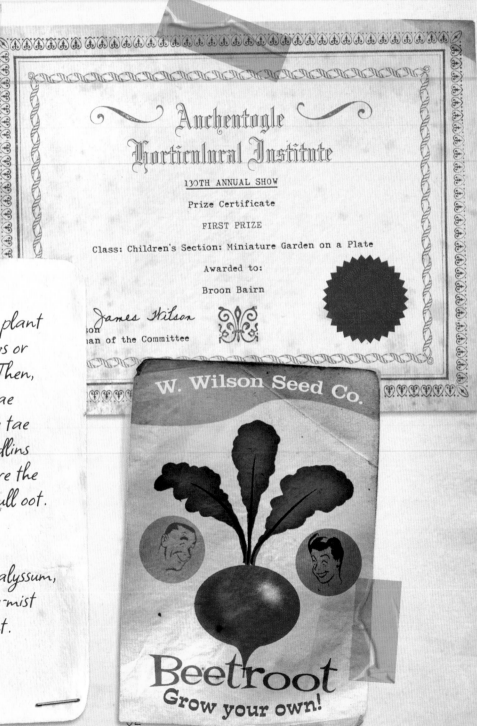

W. Wilson Seed Co.

Beetroot
Grow your own!

INVOLVE THE CHILDREN!

Give over some of your garden or allotment for a children's garden - they'll have fun and learn from it - and you may benefit from extra helpers!

PREPARING A PLOT

You can make a flower garden from seed at any time from March until June. The ideal size plot for a good display from two small seed packets of mixed hardy annuals with giant sunflowers behind is 6 ft. wide by 8 ft. long.

1. The first step is to mark the boundaries of your plot. Make sure that the plot has been well dug over.

2. Push a stick in each corner, stretch a line (strong string) between them tightly and use this as a guide to make a straight groove with a trowel or hoe.

3. Now get ready for seed sowing by preparing the soil. Walk to the middle of the plot and look at your shoes. If a large amount of soil is sticking to them, the ground is too wet for sowing and should be left for a few days to dry out. If very little soil stuck to your shoes, use a rake to break up the lumps, remove large stones, and leave the top 1 in. of soil in a fine, crumbly and level condition.

TECHNIQUE TIP

A common mistake when raking is to pull the soil only towards you so that you end up with a large pile of soil and stones on one side of the plot. The right way is to push the rake backwards and forwards. Push the rake forwards to knock lumps of soil into small pieces, then push backwards and forwards to make it into small crumbs. Start on one side and work across the plot, raking the soil from humps and pushing it into hollows to leave a level surface as you go. Flick stones and bits of weeds towards you so these can be removed on one side of the plot.

4. Now tread all over where you have raked to make sure the plot is nice and firm. Tread on every part of the soil by doing a sort of sideways shuffle. This will show up any soft hollows which you can level by raking once again.

5. Now your plot is ready for sowing.

GROW SOME GIANTS

It is easy to grow flowers taller than a tall man, with yellow flowers the size of dinner plates. These will make a good 'hedge' in a row along the back of your plot.

1. Buy a packet of tall single sunflower seeds.
2. Stretch a string across the plot, 18 in. from the back to mark where the row will grow.
3. Use sticks to mark the positions of the plants, inserting them 12 in. from each end and 2 ft. apart.
4. At the spots marked by each stick make three holes, with a stick or a finger, 1 in. deep. Into each hole drop a seed.
5. After sowing, mark each clump with a stick or label before filling each hole with fine soil.
6. In a notebook make a record of the sowing date and later note when the seedlings first appeared and their height each week until they flower.
7. As they grow taller the sunflower plants will need staking, otherwise they will blow over in the wind. Expect the plant to grow to 6 or 7 ft.

Sunflowers can grow very big - the tallest sunflower was over 25 ft. tall whilst the largest sunflower head was 32 in. across. In warmer countries, sunflowers are grown as a crop by farmers. The plants are harvested for their seeds and to make sunflower oil.

GROWING ANNUALS FROM SEED

In front of the sunflowers, plant a selection of hardy annuals from seed.
1. Read the instructions on the seed packets and follow their suggestions for when to plant.
2. Plant the seeds in rows.
3. Within 8 weeks or so you should start to have some flowers.

Bedding Plants

Bedding plants for colourful summer displays can be planted in the late spring as the weather begins to warm. It does not pay to plant them too early; they may get caught by late frosts. Petunias, fuchsias, busy lizzies, geraniums, lobelias and many more make brilliant shows, often stretching through the summer and into the autumn. Sometimes, though, the colours can be just a little too garish unless cooled by interspersed plantings of silver leaf or pale flowers.

Most summer bedding plants prefer, or even demand, a sunny site. But busy lizzies and begonias are tolerant of a wide range of conditions, including heavy shade. Near the house, or a patio, stocks and tobacco plants (Nicotiana) provide subtle colours and a beautiful scents.

Garden centres sell bedding plants in 'strips' containing between 6 and 12 plants. They will have been grown in greenhouses over the winter. Unless you have a greenhouse and want to grow them from seeds, buying strips of plants is really the only option. Because they have been grown in greenhouses they will require a few weeks in a sheltered spot (ideally a cold frame) outside to 'harden off' before they are planted. Buying the plants each year becomes expensive — and it requires quite a bit of work to plant them out and to water them through the summer (daily in hot weather) — but they are great for a new garden where you need to have some instant colour.

Bedding plants bring lots of colour into the garden or any public park — and even roundabouts. Councils love to use them to provide bright splashes of colour.

Ma favoorite beddin' plants:

African marigold
Alyssum
Begonias
Busy Lizzie
Geraniums
Lobelia

Pansies
Penstemon
Petunia
Snap Dragons
Verbena
Zinnia

BEDDING PLANTS

Why not save some money and grow your own bedding plants if you have space in your greenhouse?

1. Follow the instructions on the packet for the best time to sow between January and April, depending on the plant.
2. Fill a seed tray with potting compost, and then sow the seeds, but not too thickly. Cover the seeds with a thin layer of compost and water the tray.
3. Place the seed tray somewhere warm to help their germination.
4. As soon as the first seedlings appear, make sure the tray receives plenty of light.
5. When the seedlings are big enough to handle, it is time to 'prick out' the seedlings - take an individual seedling and transplant it into a pot on its own or into another tray where the plants can be given more space.Lift them carefully by one of the seed leaves and hold the root end of the plant with a pencil or dibber.
6. When the plants are nearly ready to plant out, harden them off by keeping them in a cold frame or place them outside during the day and take them back inside at night.
7. Plant them out once the risk of frost has passed. When seedlings grown from mixed seeds (say, aubrietia) are ready to plant out, don't just plant the strongest; you will end up with common strains to the exclusion of the rarer and possibly prettier colours.

mind tae get strips o' beddin' plants -

pansies	ⵌ	5
Petunias	|||	3
Lobelia	ⵌ	5
Busy Lizzie	ⵌ |||	7

No, Paw, ye canna use the leaves o' the tobacco plant tae mak baccy, but I did laugh seein' ye try!

Birds in the Gairden

Ah really enjoy seein' birds in the gairden, specially on a winter's day when they are busy feedin' at the bird table (thanks tae Paw's carpentry skills) or in the spring when they are singin' their hearts oot. They dae a lot o' good too, like eatin' pesky insects, but they can be a real nuisance in the vegetable gairden or wi' fruit, so I suggest a few ways of discouragin' them as well.

These are the maist common gairden birds in Scotland - so say the R.S.P.B.

1 Chaffinch
2 House sparrow
3 Starling
4 Blue tit
5 Blackbird
6 Greenfinch
7 Great tit
8 Robin
9 Dunnock
10 Goldfinch

The RSPB (Royal Society for the Protection of Birds) organises a survey of gairden birds every year.

TOP 10 birds at The BUT an Ben

1 Golden eagle
2 GROUSe
3 Red Kite
4 PeeWiT
5 Robin
6 Iten
7 ThRUSh
8 CROW
9 magpie
10 maggie

Auld sparrows are ill tae tame

BIRD SEED

For Aviaries a...

	lb
Mixed Bird Seed	4d
Canary Seed (Best)	7d
Rape Seed	5d
Budgerigar Seed : Mixture	5d
Parrot Seed : Mixture	5d
White Millet Seed	4d
Indian Millet Seed	5d
Red Millet Seed	4d
Hemp Seed	3d
Millet Sprays	2d e...

For Wild ...

	lb
Canary Seed (Small)	5d
Hemp Seed	3d
White Sunflower Seed	3d
Wheat	2d
Chick Food	2d
Shelled Peanuts	5d
Mixed Bird Seed	4d

WINDOW HANGER 6d

SEED HOPPER

PEANUT FEEDER
39-3/-
POST 9d

TITBELL
TITS AND
1-7/6
NUTHATCH
ONLY
POST 9d

SERIES 'A' 10/-
CARRIAGE PAID

The ...
Garden Equipment

A Bird Sanctuary in every Garden

The H.M.B. BIRD GARDEN EQUIPMENT is designed by Mr. H. Mortimer Batten, the well-known ... author, and lecturer, and most of the devices ... bird sanctuary long ...

Our Garden Friends

Feeding the birds

Put a bird table in part of the garden where the birds can use it without being frightened, but where you can easily watch it from a distance without being seen. Ideally you should be able to see the table from a room in the house, so that you can watch the birds from inside during the winter. You may have to try putting it in several different parts of your garden before you find one which the birds really trust.

Keep a record of the different types of birds that visit your bird table. Those you cannot recognise immediately, look up in a book on birds. Watch the different habits of different types of birds, those which chase other birds away, those which have a regular bath, and so on. Experiment with different bird foods, seeds, scraps of bacon rind, to see which the birds like best.
See if you can train birds to come to the table at certain feeding times, always putting new food on the table at the same time each day.

FEEDING TIPS
Birds are not the only animals that would like to eat the food you put out, so:

- Don't put food on the ground or low down. It will attract mice and rats.

- Make sure any food dropped from the table is cleared up.

- Place the table in a position that cats cannot jump on to it. Avoid placing the table close to bushes unless it is a holly bush or some other equally prickly plant.

- Grey squirrels are great climbers, and preventing then getting onto the bird table will challenge your ingenuity. Place baffles on the stake to stop squirrels climbing up.

WHAT TO FEED BIRDS
- Seed mixes There are lots of bird seed mixtures available. Avoid mixes that contain split peas, beans or dried rice as only larger birds will eat them. Some good seeds are: millet seeds, sunflower seeds, flaked maize, pinhead oatmeal.

- Peanuts and crushed peanuts (but not dry roasted or salted).

- Nyjer seeds require a special feeder. Popular with goldfinches and siskins

- Wheat and barley grains only really suitable for large, ground-eating birds — pigeons, doves and pheasants. Their presence will frighten off other birds

- Fat balls, especially in winter. You can buy them or make them: Pour melted suet or lard onto a mixture of seeds, nuts, fried fruit oatmeal (plus cheese or cake), about one-third fat, two-thirds mixture. Mix well and leave to set in a container of your choice.

- Live mealworms are popular with robins and blue tits. You can buy them or rear them yourself. (The RSPB can advise on how do to this.)

- Don't put out milk, margarine, vegetable oils, desiccated coconut, cooked porridge oats, mouldy or stale food or dry biscuits.

Birds dinna like a 'thing salty, so dinnae put oot salted peanuts – better tae eat them yersel'

Making a Bird Table by Paw Broon

Start wi' a very simple bird table. This is nothing mair than a square piece of wood mounted ontae a stake which can be pushed intae the ground, as in ma sketch.

1. The stake should be from 3 to 5 ft. long and 1 in. or 1¼ in. square. Buy a suitable stake from a garden centre. Otherwise buy a 5 ft. length of softwood.

2. Make the top about 9 in. or 10 in. square, cut from a piece of solid plank about ¾ in. to 1 in. thick. Otherwise you can use exterior grade plywood 3/8 in. to ½ in. thick.

3. Make sure that the top of the stake is square. If not, mark around with a try-square and pencil and cut off square with a saw.

4. Drill a hole through the centre of the top and fasten the top to the end of the stake with a brass woodscrew at least twice as long as the thickness of the top. If you find it difficult to screw the screw really tight, remove it and drill a starter hole in the end of the stake.

5. Check that the top is really securely fastened to the stake, and does not wobble.

6. If you think the joint needs to be stronger, cut small triangular-shaped blocks of wood and glue underneath as shown in my sketch.

7. Build a perch on one edge (see my second sketch). You can use pieces of ordinary stripwood for the uprights and a stout twig for the perch, nailing all the parts in position.

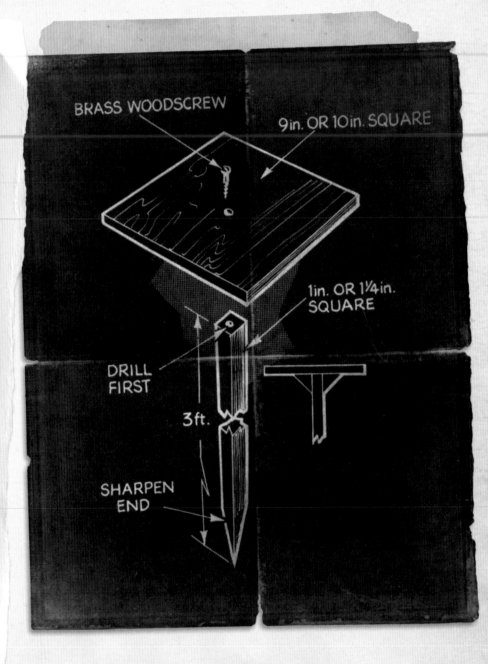

BRASS WOODSCREW

9in. OR 10in. SQUARE

1in. OR 1¼in. SQUARE

DRILL FIRST

3ft.

SHARPEN END

SMALL
PLASTIC DISH

TWIG

PIECES OF
THIN WOOD

½ in. × ¼ in.
BALSA
EDGING PIECES

CUT TO
FIT DISH

8. Add a bird bath. A small plastic or glass dish with a lip about 5 in. × 3 in. is ideal. Do not just stand this on the table because it will blow off. Cut out a rectangle in the table with a fretsaw, into which the dish will fit.

9. To stop bird food being blown off the top of the table, add edging pieces of ½ in. × ¼ in. balsa, glued in place.

10. Clean the table at any time by removing the bath and sweeping old food and dirt out through the hole.

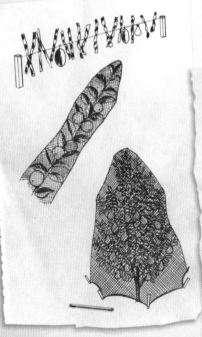

OUTWIT THE BIRDS

While birds do much good by eating harmful pests, they also peck blossom buds in winter and eat the ripe fruit in summer. There are a couple of humane ways to scare the birds away:

Scares: tie strips of kitchen foil to a string stretched across the garden or from tree to tree - or anything which glitters, such as old CDs and lids from tin cans. Cut out life-like silhouettes of hunters (e.g. cats, hawks) and suspend them in mid air on black cotton. Combine movement with noise in various types of simple windmill.

Covers: the only sure way to protect fruits is to cover them up. A few special fruits can be saved by covering them individually with plastic bags. Larger branches can be covered with pieces of netting fastened with string run through the mesh to make a sleeve. A spider-like web of rayon thread can also be bought for draping over trees and bushes.

Spring Tasks

The onset of spring varies across the country; even local variations can be marked. It is not unusual for a warm spell to encourage new growth and spring blooms, only for sharp frosts to recur, killing buds and new sappy wood. As soon as the grass begins to green up and grow again, so do the weeds. Spring is the busiest time for gardeners.

In a good year, spring bulbs will be in flower from January to May, and planting summer bulbs, herbaceous plants and annuals in the spring will ensure a display of flowers lasting into the autumn.

There may be a lot of spring pruning to do. When inspecting frost-damaged plants, scratch the bark away to see if there is life underneath. If the damage is severe, cut back hard into healthy wood. Plants are tougher than you may think. Do not remove a plant until you are sure it is dead: the new season often brings surprises, even to experienced gardeners.

EARLY SPRING

GENERAL MAINTENANCE
- Complete digging and cultivation
- Mulch soil
- Tidy up paths and drives
- Weed borders
- Apply slug pellets (hidden under foliage)

ROSES
- Complete pruning of hybrid teas, floribundas and established miniature roses
- Plant new roses and ensure that the rootstock is below the soil level

HERBS
- Sow chervil, chives, dill, marjoram, parsley and sorrel

VEGETABLES
- Sow broad beans, celery, kohlrabi, parsnips, peas, broad beans, spinach. Carrots under glass in the south
- Plant early potatoes, asparagus, Jerusalem artichokes

FRUIT
- Finish pruning and planting
- Mulch and feed young trees
- Plant strawberry runners
- Deal with pests (e.g. apple scab)

FRUIT
- Remove rhubarb flowers
- Protect bush fruit with nets against birds
- Continue as necessary to spray apples, blackcurrants, pears, strawberries and plums with pesticides, but not while blossoming
- Manure strawberries

MID-SPRING

GENERAL MAINTENANCE
- Mulch beds and borders
- Order seedlings (e.g. dahlias and tomatoes)
- Examine garden for bird damage and net if needed
- Hoe weeds

NEW LAWNS
- Cut the new grass gently to about 2 in

LATE SPRING

GENERAL MAINTENANCE
- Keep slugs under control
- Water frequently if necessary

LAWNS
- Mow at least once a week with blades set low
- Continue to apply fertiliser and weedkiller
- Apply fungicides if required

NEW LAWNS
- Water frequently if necessary

SHRUBS
- Prune early-flowering trees and shrubs after flowering
- Mulch lilacs and remove suckers
- Water newly planted shrubs frequently if necessary

LAWNS

- Rake lawn vigorously and aerate with fork
- Fill hollows with sandy compost or adjust levels below turf
- Reseed worn areas
- Cut with blades set high
- Apply weedkiller and fertiliser

NEW LAWNS

- Rake seedbed and feed soil with pre-seeding mixture
- Sow seed

SHRUBS

- Prune buddleia, hardy fuchsia, hydrangea, ivies, spirea
- Plant rhododendrons and azaleas for spring display
- Propagate by layering, lilac, rhus, wintersweet
- Mulch and prune new shrubs

FLOWERS

- Plant herbaceous plants: acanthus, anemones, asters, campanula, delphiniums, gaillardia, geraniums, hollyhocks, lupins, peonies, phlox, potentillas, red hot pokers, summer flowering bulbs (e.g. gladioli, lilies)
- Sow hardy annuals (e.g. cornflowers) outside, half-hardy annuals under glass (e.g. sweet peas)
- Propagate by taking cuttings from dahlias and chrysanthemums
- Dead-head bulbs after flowering
- Remove dying leaves from bearded irises
- Lift and divide snowdrop bulbs

LAWNS

- Mow frequently, lowering blades further for each cut
- Level humps and trim edges
- Apply weedkillers or grub out dandelions and plantains

SHRUBS

- Plant conifers and evergreen shrubs, pot-grown wall shrubs (e.g. clematis, honeysuckle, jasmine, vines, wisteria)
- Prune forsythias after flowering
- Cut back straggling branches on evergreens (e.g. magnolia, lavender)
- Stop side shoots on fuchsias
- Prune buddleia hard

FLOWERS

- Continue sowing hardy annuals (e.g. asters, sunflowers, stocks) outside, half-hardy annuals (e.g. alyssum, dahlias, phlox) under glass
- Plant out perennials (e.g. hollyhocks, peonies, violas, bedding plants)
- Divide and replant established perennials if necessary
- Dead-head spring flowers (e.g. daffodils)

ROSES

- Feed and hoe in fertilizer
- Apply mulch and weedkiller
- Begin spraying as necessary against black spot, mildew, etc
- Water newly planted roses if necessary

VEGETABLES

- Sow beetroot, broccoli, carrots (main crop), cauliflowers (late summer), onions, peas, winter cabbage
- Plant out late summer cabbages, onions raised under glass
- Finish planting late potatoes

FLOWERS

- Sow biennials (e.g. Canterbury bells, forget-me-nots, foxgloves, polyanthus, poppies, sweet williams, violas, wallflowers)
- Plant out half-hardy annuals (e.g. dahlias)
- Plant lilies and asters
- Lift spring flowers, if necessary, to make room for bedding plants
- Weed alpine beds carefully
- Mulch sweet peas
- Hoe regularly round gladioli and sweet peas
- Dead-head spring flowers
- Support tall herbaceous plants

ROSES

- Watch for pests and diseases (e.g. greenfly and black spot and spray at once if necessary)

VEGETABLES

- Erect canes to support runner beans
- Sow French beans and runner beans
- Plant Brussels sprouts
- Plant out spring cabbage
- Cover early potato shoots with earth to protect against frost

FRUIT

- Water well and feed lightly if fruit is swelling
- Spray against pests, but not on open blossom
- Tie up new growth on blackberries
- Start thinning summer vines and thin out and mulch raspberries

Brambles (Blackberries)

Out at the But an' Ben brambles are great food for free, ye jist need tae spend yer time pickin' them. Ye can grow them in gairdens and allotments and they are easy tae grow (so easy that many gairdeners regard them as weeds).

HOW TO GROW YOUR OWN BLACKBERRIES

If you know someone with a blackberry bush, the easiest way to get your own plant is by propagation. The blackberry is an ideal fruit as it roots easily and grows quickly.

Propagating by tip-layering: July or August are the best months for this. Untie a strong cane and bend it over so that the tip can be buried 6 in. in the soil. Either place a heavy stone or brick across the cane to keep it down or drive a peg into the ground and tie the cane to this. This is called tip-layering. By the autumn the tip will have rooted and may be cut from the mother cane (which will be due for cutting out after fruiting). Next spring lift the young plant carefully and replant in your own fruit garden.

In this case plant the tip in a 5-in. flower pot of soil, buried to its rim in the ground. Then in autumn cut the rooted tip from its mother cane and bring it home in the pot. Keep it in its pot, buried again to its rim in the ground, until the spring when it can be planted out in its permanent fruiting position.

Loganberries and raspberries can be propagated in the same way.

Ah've any number o' braw brambles coming through the fence at the foot o' ma gairden. Mair food for free!

BRICK

42

Bulbs

I always like it when I see the leaves o' the snowdrops coming through the ground at the But an' Ben in January - it may still be the middle o' winter but it's a sign tha' spring will be here a'fore too long.

Bulb tips

- Spring bulbs planted in autumn while the soil is still warm will provide colour from January through to May.

- Plant daffodils in the early autumn. Only lift them if a clump is becoming too dense and requires separating.

- Remove daffodil flower heads after flowering, but let the leaves die back naturally.

- Sometimes *daffodil* is used to describe flowers that have large trumpets and *narcissus* is used to describe flowers with small cups in the centre of the flower (others regard daffodils as yellow and narcissi as white). Botanically both daffodils and narcissi are members of the Narcissus family.

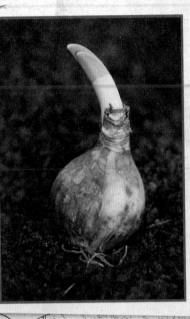

Some daffodil bulbs are almaist as auld as me!

As it is by the action of the leaves that bulbs are formed, it is evident that cutting them off prematurely, or before they naturally decay, must be very prejudicial. Leaves must remain to complete their functions.

THE TULIP, a native of the Levant, appears to have been introduced into Britain about the year 1577, and its culture soon afterwards was enthusiastically pursued both in this country and in Holland. To such an extent has the rage for tulips at times been carried that in 1809 a single bulb of one variety sold at £300, and in 1818 one sort was quoted at £500.

There are lots o' spring-flowering bulbs ye can plant tae bring colour tae the gairden. Ma favoorites are:

Anemones

Bluebells

Crocuses

Daffodils and narcissi

Snake's-head fritillaries

Snowdrops

Tulips

Lots o' places sell bulbs and they are deid easy tae grow, sae have a go!

Daffodils

I wandered lonely as a cloud
That floats on high o'er vales and hills,
When all at once I saw a crowd,
A host, of golden daffodils;
Beside the lake, beneath the trees,
Fluttering and dancing in the breeze.

Continuous as the stars that shine
And twinkle on the milky way,
They stretched in never-ending line
Along the margin of a bay:
Ten thousand saw I at a glance,
Tossing their heads in sprightly dance.

The waves beside them danced, but they
Out-did the sparkling leaves in glee;
A poet could not be but gay,
In such a jocund company!
I gazed—and gazed—but little thought
What wealth the show to me had brought:

For oft, when on my couch I lie
In vacant or in pensive mood,
They flash upon that inward eye
Which is the bliss of solitude;
And then my heart with pleasure fills,
And dances with the daffodils.

William Wordsworth

CYCLAMEN-FLOWERED DAFFODILS
NARCISSUS TRIANDRUS VARS ALBUS AND CYCLAMINEUS

Bulbs - growin' indoors

Ye can also grow bulbs inside. Hyacinths can floo'er for Christmas and mak the hoose smell wonderful. They need grown i' the dark - but Paw was ne'er much good at it!

You'll not be able to grow much on your allotment for Christmas, so why not grow some bulbs for the house? If you buy hyacinth or narcissi bulbs in late August or early September, you will have a collection that should flower in time for Christmas. A bulb is a complete plant packed within a scaly jacket. Inside the jacket are all the leaves folded tightly and in the heart of the leaves is the flower, with everything fully formed but in miniature.

GROWING BULBS IN FIBRE

Plant them in a special kind of compost called bulb fibre, which is available from garden centres. By using bulb fibre, the hyacinths or narcissi can be planted in a container that has no drainage holes.

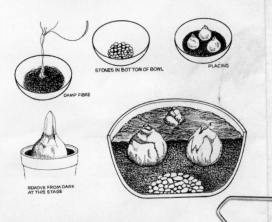

DAMP FIBRE

STONES IN BOTTOM OF BOWL

PLACING

REMOVE FROM DARK AT THIS STAGE

1. Select an attractive, deep container - there may be something like an old glass or china bowl lurking at the back of your china cupboard. It must be deeper than the bulbs and large enough to hold at least three bulbs close together to make a really good display. Suitable bowls can also be bought in gardening centres.

2. First put a layer of small stones in the bottom of the bowl.

3. Next take two handfuls of the bulb fibre and put it in another bowl to be wetted. Pour on enough water for the fibre to soak up until it drips out when you squeeze a handful.

4. Now half fill the first bowl with the wet fibre. Place the bases of the bulbs on this with their sides almost touching. Then put more wet fibre round the bulbs until only their 'noses' are showing.

5. A period in the dark and in the cool helps the bulb to develop its roots and shoot. Put the bowl in a cold, dark cupboard or under a box on the floor in a cold part of the house. It must remain there for at least eight weeks.

6. Do not bring it out before the tops of the leaves have emerged half an inch and when you can feel the hard tip of the flower shoot within them.

7. Take extra care to see that the fibre does not become dry at any stage. When the bowl of bulbs comes into flower, it will be a wonderful display.

8. Add a light surface dressing of pebbles or shells, as this gives a pleasing effect and also helps to conserve the moisture in the bowl.

Pots of daffodils and hyacinths can also be used for display on the landing or on the balcony.

Gairdenin' Wisdoms

with GAIRDENER BROON

❋❋❋❋❋❋❋❋❋❋❋❋❋❋❋❋❋❋❋❋❋❋❋❋❋

It's me again. I'm sittin' here in the allotment shed wi' a mug o' tea and an Abernethy biscuit. Man, what rare it is tae be able tae scribble oot ma stories for "The Bugle" on ma notepad and dunk the biscuit in the tea. The editor tells me I can use e-mail, but that's no' for me ... and onyway, the soggy biscuit micht drip a' ower the keyboard. But, that's enough aboot me. Now, what was I thinkin' tae tell ye aboot the day? Oh, aye the fund-raising event jist last Setterday.

The local gairdeners a' got the'gither tae raise funds tae restore the Floral Clock alangside the war memorial in Victoria Park. It's no' been the same since Albert's Prince had a go at it. I dinna mean Queen Vic's man Albert o' coorse. He's been deid for years. No, I mean Albert Black's big dug Prince, the brute o' a lab that kept diggin' a' the floo'ers oot o' the display when it buried its bones fae Scott the butcher. Well, Prince is a' bones by now and awa' tae the big pooper scooper park in the sky and a'body felt it was safe tae try tae restore the clock tae its floral glory.

The village hall was packed oot at the Bring-and-Buy sale. A'body put in a power o' work. The ladies fae the WRI had made roond cakes like the floral clock itsel', wi' icing floo'ers a' ower the top. Each cake had a real clock inside and the hands o' the clock swept roond the icin' floo'ers just like the real thing. Such a shame that somebody had used alarm clocks for the innards and a' the cakes had tae be ta'en apart tae stop the bleedin' racket when they a' started ringin' and ringin'.

Shugg McDade's plant-yer-ain-tatties packages sellt really well. He'd filled big empty crisp packets wi' aboot a dizzen seed tatties and every bag came wi' a re-used container fae the Chinese Takeaway. Ye'll ken the verra thing ... wee square polythene plasticky boxes that haud the curry or the fried rice. Shugg had filled each ane wi' a guid measure o' Paterson's fermyard manure tae gie the tatties a guid start. Unfortunately, his stall was richt next tae "The Peking Tom's" ain stall, sellin' bags o' prawn crackers wi' a container o' curry sauce as dips. It was easy tae see how some fowk got them baith mixed up.

And wi' lots o' ither things sellin' oot like allotment neeps an' ingins, gairden furniture, ceramic pots and a hale library o' auld gairdenin' books, we raised well ower fower hunner quid for the restoration fund. And when we took aff incidental expenses like a big bouquet o' floo'ers for the lady president, a donation tae The Scouts for washin' up, a coupla shillin's for the ane or twa cases o' lager for the fowk that set up the stalls, 25 fish suppers for a' that helped, a bottle o' sherry for the hallkeeper and a donation to the village hall fund, we cleared oor feet wi' near five pounds left ower.

So there wasnae near enough tae restore the floral clock this year, but Shugg kindly donated a' the seed tatties fowk handed back, so we'll be plantin' oot the clock wi' tatties this year. Of coorse, ye'll no' be able tae see the clock when the tatties grow, but it's aye a start. Anyway, if ye need tae ken the time, ye can jist see the toon hall clock fae the floral clock if ye stand on the park bench.

Until next week,
Aye Yours,

Gairdener Broon
x

THE PLANT WILL GROW & PRODUCE LEAVES—POSSIBLY A FLOWER

BULB

ROOTS WILL TAKE IN WATER

WATER

SMALL PIECES OF CHARCOAL WILL HELP TO KEEP THE WATER CLEAN

One way of growing bulbs is in water – without any soil involved. This is done by using a hyacinth glass, a specially shaped vase made of glass or plastic. The hyacinth glass has a cup on top in which the bulb will fit comfortably. Water is poured into the lower part until it rises up the neck to a point where it is just over a centimetre (half an inch) from the rough base of the bulb when it is placed in the cup. It is important that the bulb does not have its base in the water. This water will need to remain fresh for several weeks, and the way to achieve this is to place two or three pieces of charcoal in the vase, each about the size of half a matchstick. If you do not use charcoal, the water will turn green and the roots may not grow.

GREEN THUMB®

21

Cacti

I dinna ken whit people see in cacti - best place for them is the desert. I once saw a gairden near Glasgow where they were growin' outside, in all that rain! Still, the Twins are keen on them, so here's a bit I found oot aboot them. Thompson says not a thing aboot them. Quite richt.

Cacti come from North and South America. Similar succulent plants such as euphorbias grow in Africa. Other succulent plants can be found elsewhere in hot, dry areas.

1. Opuntia.
2. Cereus.
3. Opuntia streptacantha.
4. Cereus candicans.
5. Mammillaria.
6. Cereus peruvianus monstrosus.
7. Echinocereus electracanthus.
8. Mammillaria.
9. Echinopsis formosa.
10. Echinocactus Visnaga.
11. Cereus peruvianus var.
12. Opuntia candelabriformis.
13. Cereus strictus.
14. Pilocereus senilis.
15. Cereus Tweedii.
16. Cereus chilensis.

Cacti

Cacti are fascinating plants. Because they must often survive for long periods without water, cactus plants develop cylindrical fleshy bodies in which water can be stored. Sometimes they are the only plants that will grow in barren areas, and they would be valuable food for animals if it were not for the sharp spines that cover many of them. This is their protection – and a warning to anyone who handles them carelessly. To deal with deluge or drought, desert cacti have a shallow but very extensive root system to mop up as much water as possible before it evaporates or drains away. As there are few clouds in arid regions, there is no cloud cover to keep in the heat when the sun has gone down: night temperatures in inland deserts can be decidedly chilly, as too can the winters. Cacti do not need high temperatures all the time, and indeed most are happier and more likely to flower if they spend the winter at cool temperatures.

Flowering is definitely to be encouraged. In a tough environment, competition is tough: the plants producing the most spectacular or most enticingly fragrant flowers stand the greatest chance of attracting the insects vital to their reproduction. So it is that cacti produce some of nature's most extraordinary, lavish and vivid flowers.

Forest cacti come from a rather different world, with different demands. Most are epiphytes, living in the branches of trees and storing water in their succulent stems, which, in the less aggressive environment of the treetops, are generally not coated with spines. The most common and popular house plant among these is the Christmas cactus or crab cactus. This produces trailing branches made up of a series of small, nearly triangular segments. Come Christmas, it produces beautiful blooms from the tips of the stems: white, pink, red or purple. That is, it will if it is feeling good-natured, which it will not do if you move it when in bud and if it is not kept in comparatively cool conditions.

A collection of cacti and other succulent plants can be designed to look like a desert landscape. As well as the plants in small pots, you will need a deep tray or dish in which to arrange them, with sand and stones to cover the rest of the surface. A small mirror can be partly buried to be the reflecting water of an oasis. Cacti are not expensive and come in a variety of shapes, from round like a ball, to columnar like a chimney. Some have long sharp spines, others have only soft hairs.

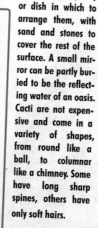

ye canna be too careful!

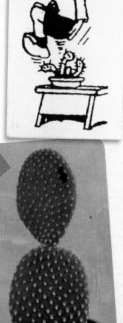

CACTI CARE

POSITION: Desert cacti like to be in the sunniest position possible, summer and winter; forest cacti like bright indirect light.

TEMPERATURE: For most cacti average temperatures in the summer are fine; in winter they should be kept cooler, but not below 40 °F (4 °C), and some, such as Cephalocereus senilis, need 60 °F (16 °C) in winter. Flowering forest cacti should be kept in cool winter temperatures of 55–60 °F (13–16 °C).

WATER: Cacti should be watered well and then the soil allowed to dry out; sink the pot into a basin of tepid water until bubbles cease to rise up from the soil; then drain well. Desert cacti should be kept barely moist in winter. Bring water to budding or flowering forest cacti, as they must not be moved. It is mainly the forest cacti that like humid air; supply by aerial spraying.

FEEDING: Feed once a month in the summer, or when flowering.

PROPAGATION: Usually from cuttings and offsets, or seeds germinated in warmth and humidity.

SOIL: Standard loam-based potting compost, with a third volume of added sharp sand.

PROBLEMS: Overwatering, especially in cold weather can cause rot; lack of water can cause wilting. Prone to common pests, especially mealy bug, red spider mite and scale.

Compost

I'm at ma best when I'm fed well, an' plants are the same. Makin' compost from gairden waste and returnin' it tae the soil, is a green way tae mak' yer gairden greener.

We are all encouraged to recycle as much as possible these days, and using garden and kitchen waste to make compost which will then make the garden grow better is something we all should do.

WHAT IS COMPOST?

Compost is formed by the natural breakdown of organic material into powder-like material called humus. The material is broken down by bacteria, fungi and insects that live in the soil - and to do this they need oxygen (so air needs to get into any compost heap). When organic material breaks down, heat is generated, which is why a compost heap feels warm when it is at work. A compost heap should reach a temperature of 60-70°C (140-60°F), which kills most weed roots and seeds. The resulting humus is formed from six weeks to a year later, depending upon conditions and how the compost has been managed. There's lots of advice on how best to manage your compost heap in books and on the internet. When the compost is ready, it will be sweet smelling, moist and crumbly with no obvious organic matter in it. It can then be spread on the soil and mixed in to give extra food for your plants. This in turn will make the plants grow better and produce more organic waste, which can be used to make more fertiliser. What a virtuous cycle!

WHAT DO I MAKE IT IN?

Compost can be made in specially built containers (ideally with two or three pens, one for new waste, one where the compost is rotting down and one with compost ready to use on the garden). There are also many sorts of plastic compost bins where the rubbish is put in at the top and compost is taken out at the bottom. Plastic bins have the advantage of lids which saves the compost heap from cooling down when it gets wet and from having nutrients washed out.

MAKING LEAF MOULD

All those leaves that fall off the tree in autumn have a use. Collect them up and put them in plastic rubbish bags. Tie the tops of the bags and make a few small holes so that some rainwater can get in. Make a few small holes in the bottom for insects as well. Leave them for a year and more and you will have leaf mould that can be used to mulch and feed your plants. Much more productive than a bonfire!

Aye try tae have a mixture o' plant material in yer compost heap an' not too much o' one thing. Some material, like tattie shaws are no' suitable for composting, and too much grass on the heap isn't a guid idea either.

Juist a reminder o' what you should an' should not put intae your compost:

Composting

GOOD FOR COMPOST HEAPS
Garden waste
Old plants
Grass cuttings
Nettles
Vegetable peelings
Egg shells
Annual weeds that have not seeded
Shredded paper and cardboard
Bark
Tea bags
Coffee grounds
Wool
Animal manure
Wood shavings

BAD FOR COMPOST HEAPS
Woody clippings or branches
Perennial weeds
Diseased plants
Food scraps (they attract rats)
Synthetic fabrics
Eggs
Weeds with seeds
Coal ash
Dog and cat faeces

Dear Gairdener Broon
I have been told that old shoes are good for the compost. Is this true?

Well, dinnae try it wi' auld trainers. Leather shoes will rot doon an' they used tae be buried under peach trees tae mak' em grow. But jist remember that plastic an' rubber disnae rot and will be nae guid for the rubber (hoose) plant either.

—Gairdener Broon

Pee on yer compost tae help it alang.

The Twins wanted a wormery - ye'll find oot aboot that later in the book

Ma granpaw used all sorts o' things on the gairden - Thompson recommends:

Sawdust
Malt dust
Sea weeds
Soot
Blood
Blubber
Horns and hoofs

Bones
Night soil
Guano
(seabird dung)
Cow dung
Pig's dung

Container Gairdenin'

If ye dinnae have a gairden or ye have a patio close tae the hoose, then ye can use containers tae grow a' kind o' things in. I ha' some auld whisky barrels cut in hauf, and whit a fragrant smell there is from the floo'ers ah grow i' them! But ye dinnae need jist tae grow floo'ers. An auld dustbin is good for growing tatties and ye can use other containers for strawberries and lots o' them herbs Maw uses i' her cookin'. Some fowk ha' even used auld cars as containers for their plants, but that's takin' things ower far.

GROWING TATTIES IN A DUSTBIN

1. Drill about a dozen evenly spaced holes in the bottom of the bin to make sure it will drain properly.
2. Put a 2-in. layer of broken crocks or gravel in the bin and cover this with about 6 in. of good potting compost.
3. Place about five seed potatoes evenly over the surface of the compost, sprouts facing upwards.
4. Sprinkle more potting compost onto the potatoes until they are just covered.
5. Water the bin well, but be careful to prevent the compost washing off the potatoes.
6. Position the bin where it will get both sunlight and rain. Make sure it doesn't dry out; water it if necessary.
7. Shoots will appear above the surface after a few weeks. Let them grow about 6 in. high and then add about 4 in. of compost, leaving about 2 in. of the shoots above the surface.
8. Keep checking the bin, adding more compost as the shoots grow through it. Continue until the bin is full. Remember to water the bin if it is dry, and add some fertiliser if the compost isn't rich enough.
9. The potato plants will flower - you can remove these if you like. Small green 'potato apples' may form after flowering; these are poisonous.
10. Once the flowers have faded, there will be some potatoes to harvest, but they will carry on growing until the plants turn yellow and start to die back. You can either harvest a few potatoes or all of them - they won't come to harm by being left in the bin, as long as there is no danger of frost.

GROWING STRAWBERRIES IN A CONTAINER

Plant one of the Everbearing varieties which don't produce many runners. Plant them fairly close together - you can fit up to 10 plants in a container 18 in. long, 9 in. wide and 10 in. deep.

Container Gardening:

Grow radishes in an auld cake tin — but dinna let Maw know!

THE BASICS

The first essential for container gardens is good drainage. Several drainage holes and a layer of crocks or gravel over them will help prevent the most common cause of container plant fatality – root rot.

The soil mix should be moisture-retentive and open. Six parts of good topsoil to one part each of coarse sand and peat is fine for general planting. Alpines and Mediterranean plants will require a sharper, sandier mix, while woodland plants prefer more peat.

Regular watering is essential. Watering is especially important for window-boxes sheltered from the rain. But even in exposed containers, if they are thickly planted, the umbrella of leaves may prevent rain water reaching the soil.

Where the soil is open, a mulch (covering layer) of gravel will increase the decorative effect and will do a very efficient job of moisture retention. This should enable plants to survive irregular watering, although they will only grow vigorously if watered regularly.

When, in subsequent seasons, any perennials or shrubs have matured, they will need feeding. A liquid feed will do, or you can add to or replace the soil.

Old Bottle becomes . . . .
RUSTIC FLOWER POT

THE pretty rustic flower-pots shown in the sketch are nothing but empty bottles in disguise !

Almost any kind of bottles will do for making the flower-pots, and the only other material needed is a pound of plaster of paris and the paint-pot.

Mix up the plaster fairly thick but add a spoonful of sugar to retard setting. With a broad knife cover the bottle with thick plaster, moulding a rough shape resembling a log with stubby branches. The roughness of the bark is easily imitated by stroking the soft plaster with the knife or finger. The branches are formed by pinching the plaster into shape with the fingers.

When the work is thoroughly dry it can be sized and painted in natural colour.

Anyone with a flair for sculpture can mould the plaster into shapes other than logs. Animals and human figures might be attempted.

The concealed bottle holds the water for the flowers, for, of course, plaster of paris is porous by nature.

RUSTIC FLOWER POTS

Cuttin' an' Layerin'

Takin' cuttings tae get new plants is the cheapest way tae add plants tae yer gairden. It takes a bit o' time, mind, for them tae grow, sae ha' patience. Cuttings aren't difficult tae tak'. Follow the text book by a' means, but remember that the best time tae take cuttings is when yer friends or ne'ebors let ye!

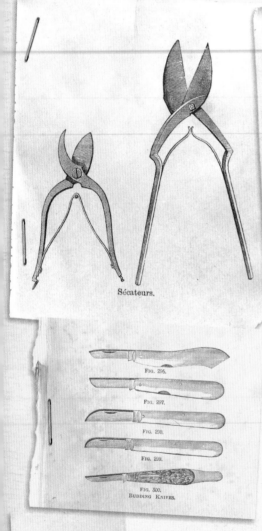

Sécateurs.

FIG. 296.

FIG. 297.

FIG. 298.

FIG. 299.

FIG. 300.
BUDDING KNIVES.

Cuttings from house plants

Tradescantia and busy lizzie (Impatiens) can both be rooted by placing cuttings directly in soil. Strip the leaves from the lower half of the cutting, and with a pencil make a hole for it in the centre of a small pot of soil.

Garden soil may be lumpy or sticky and also may carry pests, weeds or diseases, so you can use instead potting compost sold at garden centres. In fact, these cuttings can be rooted in pure sand or pure peat but when they start growing they will need to be transferred to a compost or soil that contains plant food.

If the base of a planted cutting becomes dry, it will die before roots are formed. The leafy part of the cutting does not like to be in hot, dry air either. There is a method of making sure that both parts of the cutting remain moist. You will need a polythene bag for each pot.

If you get a bag bigger than the pot, stand the pot inside and blow air into the bag until it swells out. Fold and tie the neck tightly. The inflated bag must not touch the cutting at any point. If the bag is about the same size as the pot then put the neck of the bag over the cutting and fix it round the rim of the pot with rubber bands. Two sticks in the soil will stop the bag collapsing and touching the cuttings.

HARD-WOODED CUTTING, EUONYMUS JAPONICUS.

FIG. 274. SOFT-WOODED CUTTINGS PREPARED FOR ROOTING.

You can buy hormone rootin' powder at a gairden centre. This speeds up the rootin' process. Follow the instructions awfy carefully.

Ne'er tak a cuttin' from a plant in full floo'er.

NEW PLANTS FOR FREE!

Taking cuttings is a great way to propagate plants and so increase the plants you have without having to buy new ones. A properly prepared cuttings bed could be worth several hundred pounds at the end of the year; and rooted and potted plants are very attractive presents.

The cuttings bed, perhaps 6 ft. by 3 ft., may be in any hidden corner of the garden or allotment. Simply dig over the chosen area and make it weed free, then mix in a strong proportion of coarse, sharp sand. If you have all your cuttings in one place, they can be kept watered and weed free and can then be planted out into their permanent quarters when they are strong enough to cope.

HARDWOOD CUTTINGS

Take in late autumn after leaves have fallen. Cut a 9 in. long shoot with a sloping cut above a bud and a square cut below the lowest bud. Insert into the soil, with some sand in the base of the hole and the top 1-2 in. showing. Firm well.

SOFTWOOD CUTTINGS

Select a healthy shoot with about four pairs of leaves and cut it from shrub or plant. Cut the shoot diagonally below the bottom pair of leaves, then carefully remove them and the next pair. Make a hole in the compost to the depth of the stripped stem. Insert the stem; firm it in with your fingers and water.

LAYERING

Select a flexible branch of the current year's growth and strip the leaves 30 cm (12 in) from its tip. Make a tongue-shaped cut in the underside of the branch at this point. Gently bend the branch to trail in the soil. Dig a shallow hole beneath the cut and peg it down into the hole with a hairpin. Cover with soil. Firm in and water. Leave to root (up to about a year) then sever from the mother plant and replant elsewhere.

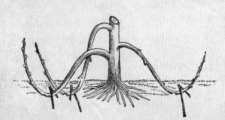

LAYERING BY PIERCING OR NOTCHING.

LAYERING BY TONGUEING OR HEELING.

Diggin'

Diggin' is important for the soil, and it's important that I find ithers tae dae it for me, so I dinna damage ma back. Here's whit the allotment fowk say.

DIGGING YOUR GARDEN SOIL

Digging needs to be done at least several weeks before planting to give the soil time to settle. If the ground contains much clay, it is said to be 'heavy'. Heavy soils should be dug in the autumn and left for the frost to break down the lumps. Do not try to break up the big clods - just leave them lying about. This exposes a bigger area to the cold weather and the freezing will help to break up these lumps. In spring they can be smashed down quite easily with a digging fork. Light, sandy soils can be dug in late winter.

Digging with a spade or fork is seldom done more than once each year, loosening soil which has become hard after heavy rain, snow or hot sun. During digging all weeds and their roots are removed. The best time of the year for digging is between October and March, and never when it is very wet. Most gardeners dig to a depth of 10 in. If the land has not been cultivated before, you will need to 'double-dig'.

During digging, place any weeds you pull out in a tidy heap. Do not burn them or put them in the dustbin, just let them rot. You are bound to turn up grubs and beetles. Most of them are helpful and friendly to the gardener. You will come across earthworms when you dig. They are the gardener's best friend. They live in good soil and make it even better.

After digging, use the rake to level the surface and tidy it up. Use the rake in a 'to-and-fro' motion - walking backwards so that you do not tread on ground already raked. Use the back of the rake to break any large clods of soil. Remove any large stones by drawing them towards you with the rake.

Where soil needs enriching, spread rotted manure, garden compost or partly rotted leaves (leaf mould) over the surface before you start and then mix this with the soil as you dig.

The best fertiliser is your ain shadow

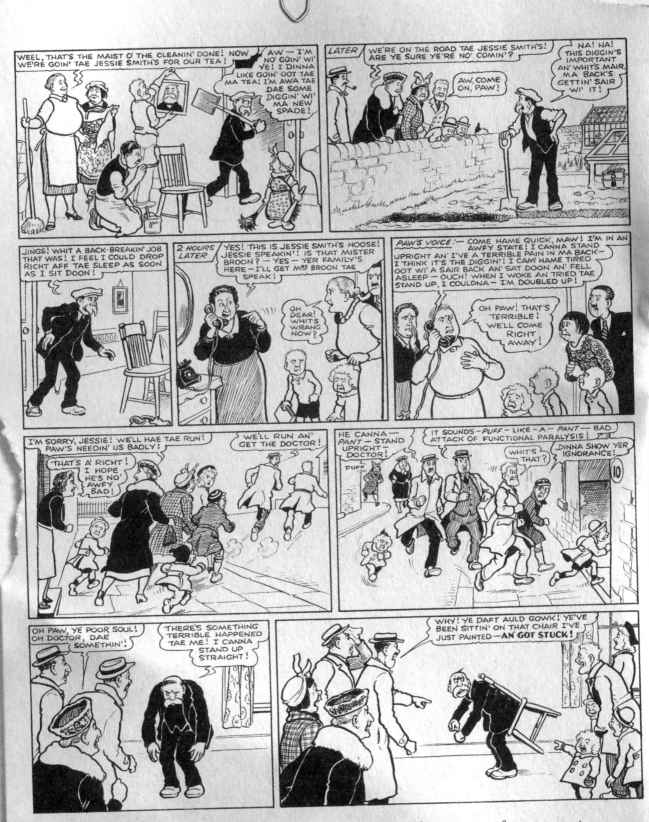

Whit a man needs in gairdenin' is a cast-iron back wi' a hinge in it!

Evergreens

In winter, I like to see some plants wi' their leaves still on, an' that's when evergreens come into their own.

If you want to add a dramatic feature to your garden, you could consider topiary. Grow an evergreen — box and yew are both good plants for this — and then with careful and regular clipping during the summer months, create a special shape. Shaped columns or balls make very eye-catching additions — and then you could always try your hand at something more unusual, and, in time, perhaps you, too, could produce a pair of cyclists!

Try this if ye wish tae see leaves inside during the winter. Gather some beech leaves in nice sprays, discarding those that are shrivelled or no' fully coloured. Lay them under your carpet for a fortnight to get stiff and pressed and they'll last a winter in a vase.

Evergreens

When we talk about evergreens in the garden, we mean plants that keep their leaves over the winter rather than losing them in the autumn and replacing them with new leaves in the spring. Typically evergreens shed and replace leaves throughout the year. Some evergreens will change their leaves every few months, while others will hold onto the same leaves for up to 30 years. Typical evergreens in our climate are conifers and holly. But many plants native to the Tropics are also evergreen and have provided a major boost to the range of evergreen plants that can (at least in some places) be grown here. The great value of evergreens is that they provide foliage to look at throughout the winter, when gardens can look very bare. If you plant a selection of evergreens with different leaf colours (including some variegated plants), they will provide interest throughout the year.

Popular evergreens include: box, ornamental conifers, hebes (those with smaller leaves survive cold weather better), holly, juniper, laurel, Mexican orange blossom (Choisya), rhododendrons and viburnum. There are many exotic evergreens that require some shelter. Take advice locally before considering planting, for example, bamboo, eucalyptus, palm or tree ferns. They provide exotic additions to the garden but need mild conditions to thrive.

Holly is ane o' ma favoorites, an no' jist cos o' its red berries for Christmas (an' fae the birds). There are that many different types o' plants, wi' different leaf colours an' some are variegated. There are e'en anes wi' no prickles on thair leaves.

GROSSET'S FILTERLESS

63

Fertilisers

As well as usin' compost tae mak the gairden grow, there are a' kinds o' fertilisers tae help as well. Here's whit Thompson says:

All substances which, when added to the soil, increase its fertility, may be considered as fertilisers. These may act either directly, by supplying food to plants, or indirectly, by rendering substances already contained in the soil available for the nourishment of plants. The necessity of the application of fertilisers is evident; for as plants withdraw certain elements from the soil, the latter would, in the course of time, become exhausted if no restoration were made.

Fertilisers may be divided into two classes:
1. Organic fertilisers, or those of vegetable and animal origin.
2. Inorganic fertilisers, or those of mineral origin.

Organic fertilisers include all substances of vegetable and animal origin, which have the property of enriching the soil, or of rendering to it substances required by plants for food. All vegetable and animal substances used as fertiliser must undergo decomposition before they become the food of plants, for the roots of these only absorb liquids and gases. This change is generally effected to a certain extent before they are applied to the soil. The results from the decomposition of organic fertilisers are the formation of carbonic acid, ammonia, sulphretted hydrogen, and many other compounds, which are retained in the soil, from which they are taken up by the roots of plants.

Urine forms an exceedingly powerful fertiliser, containing various principles, which, during putrefaction, yield large quantities of ammonia. Urine likewise contains many valuable mineral ingredients of the food of plants. The composition of urine varies in different kinds of animals, and in individuals of the same species, being affected by the age and food of the individual. Human urine is, however, by far the most valuable.

THOMPSON'S GARDEN DIRECTORY

Dinna throw yer tea leaves away – feed them tae yer roses.

Fertilisers

The garden centres have lots of inorganic fertilisers for sale for a whole range of different purposes. Here are a few basics to help you decide what seems best for your needs.

There are three major nutrients that plants require to develop healthily – nitrogen, phosphorus and potassium.

Nitrogen (symbol N) promotes foliage and stem growth. A plant needs large amounts of nitrogen for foliage growth, but with too much the plant will produce too much leaf at the expense of flowers and will become vulnerable to pests and frosts. Too little and the plant will not thrive, with its leaves turning pale green or yellow, first affecting the older leaves.

Phosphorus (symbol P) encourages good root growth, strong stems and healthy crops. It is particularly required by growing seedlings and the ripening of fruit. Too little phosphorus will reduce plant growth and delay fruiting and is indicated by the older plant turning purple.

Potassium (symbol K, from its Latin name, kalium) stimulates general health and disease resistance. If you are using large quantities of nitrogen on leafy plants, you will also need to add potassium as well. Deficiency will lead to a general slowing of plant growth and older leaves will turn a bluish-green and with yellow leaf edges.

The amounts of nitrogen, phosphorus and potassium that any fertiliser contains have to be given on the product. This N–P–K measure will appear in the form: 10, 4, 3. This shows that the fertiliser contains 10 per cent nitrogen, 4 per cent phosphorus and 3 per cent potassium.

COMMON FERTILISERS

Particularly for nitrogen:

AMMONIUM SULPHATE: can make soil acidic.

UREA: up to 46 per cent nitrogen, but some lost as ammonium)

DRIED BLOOD: releases nitrogen slowly as it breaks down

HOOF AND HORN: releases nitrogen slowly as it breaks down

Particularly for phosphorus

SULPHUR PHOSPHATE

TRIPLE SUPERPHOSPHATE: more concentrated than sulphur phosphate

BONE MEAL

ANIMAL MANURE

SEAWEED

Particularly for potassium

POTASSIUM NITRATE, POTASSIUM OXIDE, POTASSIUM MAGNESIUM SULPHATE (sulphate of potash magnesium)

WOOD ASH

There are three further nutrients that plants need in smaller quantities: magnesium (deficiency shown by whitish stripes in leaf veins); calcium (deficiency can cause bitter pit in apples); and sulphur (most needed by legumes, where deficiency shown by yellow appearance and spindly plants).

FERTILISER CAN BE APPLIED IN A NUMBER OF WAYS:

- AS GRANULES OR POWDER: once sprinkled on the ground it will need to dissolve before the nitrogen can get into the soil.

- AS LIQUID FEEDS: gives plants immediate access to the nutrients and its concentration can be well controlled (unlike solid feeds).

- AS SLOW RELEASE FEEDS: sticks or granules that release nutrients very slowly – the sticks used in houseplant pots are a typical example.

How does my garden grow? With silver bells and cockle shells ... an' a wee pickle fertiliser.

AUCHENTOGLE ALLOTMENT ASSOCIATION

Note tae self
- Buy stamp fae letter
- show tae the AAA
lads first

To Anne Strachan & Carole Wilson
Beautiful Scotland
Wallace House,
17-21 Maxwell Place,
Stirling, FK8 1JU
Beautiful Scotland

Dear Anne an' Carole,

I'm writin' on behalf o' the hale toon o' Auchentogle tae ask for the entry forms an' a copy o' the rules o' engagement, tae mak' sure that Auchentogle becomes "Best Bloomin' Toon" (which as a'body kens it already is!).

We're awfy keen tae dae weel. If ye happen tae be passin' this way, we'd be awfy pleased to show ye roond an' if it's a Friday ye can come an' meet some o' the diggers at The Volunteer Arms.

All the best,

Gran...

Gairdenin' Wisdoms
with GAIRDENER BROON

✿✿✿✿✿✿✿✿✿✿✿✿✿✿✿✿

A'BODY IS GETTIN' FAIR EXCITED. We're hopin' tae tak' part in BEAUTIFUL SCOTLAND'S comin' BEST BLOOMIN' TOON competition. As many o' ye will ken, we lost oot tae Pitlochry last year.

The Hortycultyooral Institute sent Alf Tosh and Angus Niven alang wi' oor ain representatives fae the Allotment Friday Nicht Swally Club in a minibus tae Pitlochry tae see whit was sae special aboot the Perthshire toon. Due tae a great "drouth" amongst the travellers efter their journey through the Bankfoot roadworks and a' the hold-ups on the A9, the fact-findin' mission only had enough time for the distillery tours at Blair Athol distillery in Pitlochry and at Edradour afore breakin' aff for lunch at the Moulin Inn bar. The fact-findin' team reported seeing hunners o' bonnie wild floo'ers alang the roadsides whilst the bus stopped for comfort breaks and windae box displays were popular with the tourists that hae tae smoke outside ...ashtrays never looked sae bonnie, accordin' tae Mr Niven.

So, a'body in Auchentogle needs tae pull the'gither tae mak' oor toon look BLOOMIN' marvellous afore the judges appear. The fact-findin' team hae recommended that "Nae Waiting" traffic cones can be planted oot wi' a' manner o' bulbs and the like and the ladies o' the Boolin' Club have offered tae plant oot chamber pots retrieved fae alo' the beds at the Dunroamin Care Home. The "potties" will look braw planted oot wi' tulips on windae ledges in the High Street. Mind an' empty them oot afore plantin', as only rooting compost is allowable by the Bloomin' Toon judges.

Alec McKay is in charge o' wheelie bin decoration and, ye have dozens o' designs tae pick frae. Mind an' talk tae yer ne'ebors, so that we dinna end up wi' the same floo'er patterns on a' the bins in the same street. Variety is what we're lookin' for here.

At the time o' writing, I'm tellt that "The Sunday Post" is takin' a great interest in what I like tae think o' as "Scotland-In-Broon" and maybe hunners o' toons will be competing for THE BEST BLOOMIN' TOON award. The minibus team have already volunteered tae check oot the opposition toons and a list o' guid chippy shops, watering holes and distilleries the length o' the land is being drawn up tae sustain oor fowk during the mammoth task aheid o' them. Best o' BLOOMIN' LUCK tae oor volunteers. Somebody has tae dae it.

We're busy makin' a Sensory Gairden in the toon – We got the idea from the fowk at Braeside Hoose, up the brae at Liberton, in Edinburgh.

A sensory gairden is whaur ye can SENSE what the place is like. It's so that blind fowk an' fowk who cannae see that weel, can picture what's goin' on roond aboot.

They've got a brand new sensory gairden at the front o' their care home for elderly fowk like masel', but who are blind or visually impaired. Braeside Hoose is part o' the Royal Blind charity.

We thought we'd like a gairden like that here in Auchentogle, so we're plannin' a grand water feature wi' a pond an' a waterfall an' a stream ... things ye can hear. There'll be plants wi' rich scents tae stimulate yer sense o' smell an' ither plants ye can touch, an' lots that ye can hear rustlin' in the wind like long grass an' trees. An' I'd fair like tae add some o' thae wind chimes as weel.

Shapes are important tae ... like fancy pavin' ... an' we're even thinkin' aboot a mosaic and some sculptures. Maybe ane o' "Gairdener Broon"!

We'll hae a bit deckin' wi a wooden hoose that sticks oot over the pond so that fowk can sit and SENSE the gairden. Braw!

Gairdener Broon

x

Floo'ers for Cuttin'

I'm no' a dab hand at arrangin' floo'ers, but here are some practical tips.

For cut floo'ers in bowls, fill the bowl wi' sand tae within an inch o' the top, and soak wi' water. The floo'ers stand up nice an' proud, and will keep fresh twice as lang.

Did ye ken, that if you dissolve an aspirin in floo'er water that the life o' the floo'ers will be lengthened?

Add a pinch o' salt tae the water in a vase. This wi' aye keep floo'ers fresh for longer.

If a floo'er has a hard stem, like a rose, split the stem at the bottom to mak it last.

Ne'er mix daffodils wi' ither floo'ers, as daffodils are poisonous tae them.

A plant cannae think, but the wisest man ne'er produces a floo'er.

FLOWER FOOD

There are lots o' floo'ers that are guid for floo'er arranging.
Here are some suggestions fae the WRI ladies:

Alchemilla mollis
Aster
Baby's breath
Brompton stock
Broom
Canterbury bells
Carnation
Chinese lantern
Chrysanthemum
Coneflower
Cosmos
Daffodil
Dahlia
Delphinium
Deutzia
Dogwood
Escallonia
Evening primrose
Flowering currant
Forsythia
Gladioli
Godetia
Golden rod
Guelder rose
Honesty
Iceland poppies
Iris

Kaffir lily
Lilac
Love in a mist
Mallow
Marigold
Michaelmas daisy
Mock orange
Montbretia
Narcissus
Peony
Phlox
Pink
Polyanthus
Red hot poker
Rose
Shasta daisy
Skimmia
Snapdragon
Solomon's seal
Spiraea
Sweet pea
Sweet William
Tulip
Virginia stock
Wallflowers

VICTORIA ASTER.

GLADIOLI

L'ALSACE   MASQUE DE FER

Floo'erin' Plants Through the Year

These suggestions are for general guidance. The plants will be at their best for the months shown. Local conditions can be very variable, so do check before you make any planting decisions. The list gives the common name of the plant, its 'official' name (quite often used in gardening books and plant catalogues) and the type of plant that it is, and covers annuals (including bedding plants), biennials, bulbs and perennials. There is a separate list for shrubs and trees.

JANUARY

Cyclamen	*Cyclamen coum*	bulb
Iris, winter flowering	*Iris reticulata*	bulb
Pansy	*Viola*	biennial
Snowdrop	*Galanthus*	bulb
Winter aconite	*Eranthis*	bulb

FEBRUARY

Crocus	*Crocus*	bulb
Cyclamen	*Cyclamen coum*	bulb
Daffodil	*Narcissus*	bulb
Iris	*Iris stylosa*	perennial
Snowdrop	*Galanthus*	bulb
Squill	*Scilla*	bulb
Violet	*Viola odorata*	perennial

MARCH

Crocus	*Crocus*	bulb
Daffodil	*Narcissus*	bulb
Dog's tooth violet	*Erythronium*	bulb
Elephant ear	*Bergenia*	perennial
Hyacinth	*Hyacinthus*	bulb
Lenten rose	*Helleborus orientalis*	perennial
Violet	*Viola odorata*	perennial
Wallflower	*Cheiranthus*	biennial
Windflower	*Anemone blanda*	bulb

APRIL

Crown imperial	*Fritillaria imperialis*	bulb
Daffodil	*Narcissus*	bulb
Daisy	*Bellis*	biennial
Grape hyacinth	*Muscari*	bulb
Leopard's bane	*Doronicum*	perennial
Lungwort	*Pulmonaria*	perennial
Polyanthus	*Primula*	perennial
Snake's head fritillary	*Fritillaria meleagris*	bulb
Tulip	*Tulipa*	bulb

MAY

Bleeding heart	*Dicentra spectabilis*	perennial
Bluebell	*Endymion nonscripta*	bulb
Columbine	*Aquilegia*	perennial
Feverfew	*Pyrethrum*	perennial
Forget me not	*Myosotis*	biennial
Holewort	*Corydalis*	perennial
Honesty	*Lunaria*	biennial
Iris	*Iris*	perennial
Lily of the valley	*Convallaria*	rhizome
Poppy flowered anemone	*Anemone de Caen*	bulb
Solomon's seal	*Polygonatum*	perennial
Spurge	*Euphorbia*	perennial

Tulip	*Tulipa*	bulb
Water iris	*Iris pseudacorus*	perennial
Wood lily	*Trillium*	bulb

JUNE

Avens	*Geum*	perennial
Beard tongue	*Penstemon*	perennial
Brompton stock	*Matthiola*	annual
Bugle	*Ajuga*	perennial
Candytuft	*Iberis*	annual
Canterbury bells	*Campanula*	biennial
Catmint	*Nepeta*	perennial
Cornflower, perennial	*Centaurea montana*	perennial
Delphinium	*Delphinium*	perennial
Fleabane	*Erigeron*	perennial
Flowering garlic	*Allium*	bulb
Hardy geranium	*Geranium*	perennial
Himalayan blue poppy	*Meconopsis betonicifolia*	perennial
Iceland poppies	*Papaver nudicaule*	perennial
London pride	*Saxifraga umbrosa*	perennial
Lupin	*Lupinus*	perennial
Masterwort	*Astrantia*	perennial
Oriental poppy	*Papaver orientale*	perennial
Peony	*Paeonia*	perennial
Pink	*Dianthus alwoodii*	perennial
Poached egg plant	*Limnanthes*	annual
Virginia stock	*Malcolmia*	annual

JULY

Alyssum	*Alyssum*	annual
Astilbe	*Astilbe*	perennial
Baby's breath	*Gypsophila*	perennial
Begonia	*Begonia semperflorens*	annual
Busy lizzie	*Impatiens*	annual
Californian poppy	*Eschscholzia*	annual
Cape jewels	*Nemesia*	annual
Cinquefoil	*Potentilla*	perennial
Coral flower	*Heuchera*	perennial
Cornflower, annual	*Centaurea cyanus*	annual
Day lily	*Hemerocallis*	perennial
Foxglove	*Digitalis*	biennial
French marigold	*Tagetes*	annual
Godetia	*Godetia*	annual
Gladioli	*Gladiolus*	bulb
Jacob's ladder	*Polemonium*	perennial
Lady's mantle	*Alchemilla mollis*	perennial
Lobelia	*Lobelia*	annual
Love in a mist	*Nigella*	annual
Mallow (annual)	*Lavatera*	annual
Marigold, Pot	*Calendula*	annual

Monkey flower	*Mimulus*	annual
Nasturtium	*Tropaeolum*	annual
Peruvian lily	*Alstroemeria*	perennial
Phlox, annual	*Phlox drummondii*	annual
Prairie mallow	*Sidalcea*	perennial
Shasta daisy	*Leucanthemum maximum*	perennial
Sweet pea	*Lathyrus odoratus*	annual
Tobacco plant	*Nicotiana*	annual

AUGUST

African lily	*Agapanthus*	perennial
Aster	*Callistephus*	annual
Black eyed Susan	*Thunbergia*	annual
Blanket flower	*Gaillardia aristata*	perennial
Carnation	*Dianthus caryophyllus*	perennial
Clarkia	*Clarkia*	annual
Cosmea	*Cosmos*	annual
Dahlia (bedding)	*Dahlia*	annual
Evening primrose	*Oenothera*	perennial
Gladioli	Gladiolus	bulb
Globe thistle	*Echinops*	perennial
Hosta	*Hosta*	perennial
Lamb's ears	*Stachys byzantius*	perennial
Larkspur	*Delphinium*	annual

Livingstone daisy	*Mesembryanthemum*	annual
Loosestrife	*Lysimachia*	perennial
Mexican paintbrush	*Ageratum*	annual
Mignonette	*Reseda*	annual
Montbretia	*Crocosmia*	bulb
Morning glory	*Ipomoea*	annual
Ox eye	*Heliopsis*	perennial
Pansy	*Viola*	biennial
Petunia	*Petunia*	annual
Phlox, perennial	*Phlox*	perennial
Poor man's orchid	*Schizanthus*	annual
Red hot poker	*Kniphofia*	perennial
Slipper flower	*Calceolaria*	annual
Snapdragon	*Antirrhinum*	annual
Spiderwort	*Tradescantia*	perennial
Statice (can be dried)	*Limonium*	annual
Straw flower (can be dried)	*Helichrysum*	annual
Sweet william	*Dianthus barbatus*	biennial
Treasure flower	*Gazania*	annual

SEPTEMBER

Autumn crocus	*Colchicum*	bulb
Autumn lily	*Nerine*	bulb

Herbaceous Pæonies

Violas

PLATE VII.

1

1 Lilium lancifolium album. 2 Lilium lancifolium roseum.

BLACKIE & SON: GLASGOW, EDINBURGH, & LONDON.

Drawn by Mrs Withers.

Bear's breeches	*Acanthus*	perennial
Bells of Ireland	*Molucella*	annual
Chinese lantern	*Physalis*	perennial
Coneflower	*Rudbeckia*	perennial
Crocus, autumn flowering	*Crocus*	bulb
Cyclamen	*Cyclamen hederaefolium*	bulb
Dahlia	*Dahlia*	tuber
Freesia	*Freesia*	bulb
Gayfeather	*Liatris spicata*	perennial
Golden rod	*Solidago*	perennial
Hollyhock	*Althaea*	biennial
Knotweed	*Persicaria*	perennial
Leopard plant	*Ligularia*	perennial
Love-lies-bleeding	*Amaranthus*	annual
Pearl everlasting	*Anaphalis*	perennial
Purple coneflower	*Echinacea purpurea*	perennial
Scabious	*Scabiosa*	annual
Sea holly	*Eryngium*	perennial
Sneezewort	*Helenium*	perennial
Sunflower	*Helianthus*	annual
Sword lily	*Gladiolus*	bulb
Tuberous begonia	*Begonia*	bulb

OCTOBER

Caucasian scabious	*Scabiosa caucasica*	perennial
Japanese anemone	*Anemone japonica*	perennial
Kaffir lily	*Schizostylis*	perennial
Michaelmas daisy	*Aster novi-belgii*	perennial
Pampas grass	*Cortaderia selloana*	perennial
Salvia	*Salvia*	annual
Stonecrop	*Sedum*	perennial

NOVEMBER

Lily turf	*Liriope*	perennial
Pansy	*Viola*	biennial
Violet	*Viola odorata*	perennial

DECEMBER

Christmas rose	*Helleborus niger*	perennial
Cyclamen	*Cyclamen coum*	bulb
Pansy	*Viola*	biennial

Herbaceous Paeonies

1 *Thyrsacanthus Schomburgkianus* 2 *Dendrobium nobile*

CAMELLIAS.
1 *Augustina superba.* 2 *Caryophylloides.*

Fruit

What is fruit?

Botanists, I'm tellt, tak' a fruit tae be that part o' a plant which holds the seed, aither inside (like a grape) or on the surface (like a strawberry). Tae them, runner beans or tomatoes are fruits jist as much as aipples, pears, bananas or oranges. That's no a fruit tae ye or me - a fruit i' sweet an' we eat it in a puddin'. And so rhubarb and raspberries, ane a stalk and ane a berry, are baith fruits tae me. I've written their ain pieces for aipples, brambles, rhubarb and strawberries.

Figs - Control of fruiting

In this northern climate
will not grow into ripe fr
& 8 weeks. After Aug' it
allow buds to flower
Some of the Autumn

damaged tree

RASPBERRIES

Along the banks of the Tay and in the Carse of Gowrie you will see masses of raspberries (and Tayberries) growing in polytunnels that cover the fields there. If farmers can grow raspberries and make money from them, then you can surely manage to grow some in your garden. You can get summer-fruiting and autumn-fruiting varieties. The summer varieties, such as Glen Clova, need to be pruned after fruiting, when you should cut the old wood down almost to the ground. The autumn-fruiting varieties, such as Autumn Bliss, need to be cut back down to the ground in springtime to give fruit in the autumn. The autumn varieties enable you to stretch the taste of summer further. Somehow, eating fresh raspberries in September seems to make them taste even better.

Naming your Fruit

Would you believe that you can name your own fruit? Try this and see. Get some paper and cut out the letters that spell your name – the size needs to reflect the size of fruit you are naming – it works best with apples, pears and plums. Stick the names on the surface of the fruit that faces the sun just before it starts to turn colour. When the fruit is ripe, remove the paper letters and admire your name on the fruit!

CODLIN MOTH AND GRUB (CARPOCAPSA POMONANA).

Summer Tasks

With the bustle of spring receding and the garden filling with colour, the gardener can relax and enjoy the warm summer days. But there is still plenty to do to keep everything looking its best.

When going away on holiday, have somebody check on the garden. Drought is the worst enemy. Mulching helps matters, but thorough watering is essential to promote growth, even if there are summer rains.

This is not the usual time to plant but it can be done (particularly if the plants are container grown), provided the roots are thoroughly soaked beforehand and extra attention is paid to the plants' subsequent welfare.

EARLY SUMMER

GENERAL MAINTENANCE
- Weed, hoe and water as necessary
- Spray against pests and diseases

LAWNS
- Mow once a week in different directions, setting the blades low. If the weather is very hot and dry, leave a fine mulch of clippings on the lawn
- Apply weedkillers and feed

ROSES
- Spray with systemic insecticide to prevent aphids, and spray against black spot and mildew
- Hoe around the bases

VEGETABLES
- Plant broccoli, Brussels sprouts, cauliflowers, marrows, Savoy cabbages, winter cabbages, leeks, outdoor tomatoes
- Stake and pinch out runner beans and tomatoes
- Earth up late potatoes

FRUIT
- Maintain pest-spraying programme
- Check for slug damage. Lay pellets if necessary
- Harvest strawberry crop
- Train fruit trees if necessary
- Prune gooseberries

MIDSUMMER

GENERAL MAINTENANCE
- Continue to weed, hoe and water
- Continue to spray against pests and diseases
- Dead-head and cut flowers

LAWNS
- Mow regularly
- Clip edges with shears
- Apply weedkiller and fertiliser as necessary

FRUIT
- Harvest soft fruit
- Prune currants and raspberries after fruiting
- Summer-prune apples and pears where appropriate
- Train branches as desired
- Spray against pests
- Weed thoroughly around trees and bushes
- Support heavily fruiting plum branches
- Tidy up strawberry beds
- Protect against birds with netting if necessary

LATE SUMMER

GENERAL MAINTENANCE
- Continue weeding, hoeing and watering
- Continue to spray against pests and diseases
- Continue to dead-head and cut flowers
- While on holiday, ask neighbours to pick sweet peas and vegetables, and water occasionally

LAWNS
- Mow and water regularly
- Continue to trim lawn edges
- Continue applying weedkillers as necessary

NEW LAWNS
- Dig over and apply fertiliser to sites for new lawns
- Sow lawn seed a week later

SHRUBS
- Dead-head and prune shoots that have just flowered on shrubs (e.g. deutzia, lilac, philadelphus) to encourage new growth next year
- Dead-head laburnum flowers (poisonous), rhododendrons
- Trim broom with sharp shears to prevent seeding
- Plant out fuchsias
- Propagate by layering young shoots of clematis
- Take cuttings of softwood shoots of cotoneaster, deutzia, fuchsia, hypericum

FLOWERS
- Complete planting out half-hardy annuals grown from seed (e.g. dahlias)
- Set out biennial seedlings in rows
- Support tall annuals with canes
- Dead-head late spring/early summer flowers (e.g. delphiniums, lupins, violas) to encourage a late crop of flowers
- Cut back early-flowering herbaceous plants to just above the ground
- Lift tulips and other spring-flowering bulbs that need to be divided and replanted when leaves turn yellow
- Pinch out main stems of dahlias and chrysanthemums to promote bushy growth
- Water copiously (in the evenings if possible) despite summer rains, especially new and transplanted plants.

SHRUBS
- Continue to dead-head deciduous shrubs
- Clip hedges
- Propagate by layering passion flower, wisteria and shrub roses

FLOWERS
- Continue to dead-head flowers to encourage further flowering
- Support tall plants
- Water well, especially sweet peas and gladioli
- Continue to lift spring-flowering bulbs that need to be stored and replanted
- Plant out perennials (e.g. wallflowers)

ROSES
- Continue to spray against pests
- Cut blooms for decoration and dead-head the rest
- Hoe fertiliser into the soil

VEGETABLES
- Sow beet and lettuce
- Continue to plant broccoli, Brussels sprouts, kail, leeks, cabbage
- Start to lift and store onions and shallots as tops turn yellow
- Water shallow-rooted crops in dry weather

SHRUBS
- Continue to prune shrubs (e.g. wisteria, rambler roses) after flowering
- Propagate rhododendrons by layering

FLOWERS
- Continue dead-heading
- Cut blooms on gladioli and sweet peas
- Disbud chrysanthemums, leaving one flower per stem, to make large blooms
- Order spring-flowering bulbs for autumn planting
- Plant out well-grown perennial seedlings
- s and dead-head
- Continue to spray against pests
- Do not fertilise since this encourages late growth

VEGETABLES
- Sow hardy onions, spinach, spring cabbage, winter lettuce
- Plant winter greens
- Earth up leeks, kail and potatoes
- Crop regularly and dig and fertilise the ground after cropping

FRUIT
- Continue summer pruning of apples and pears where appropriate
- Prune shoots that have borne fruit on peaches, nectarines, cherries, blackberries, loganberries and hybrid berries
- Plant strawberries and rooted strawberry runners
- Support heavily laden plum branches

Gardenin'

Gairdens are no' made by sittin' in the shade, so ye'll need tae dae a bit o' work in them ower the year.

Looking after a garden

Keeping a garden, especially a small garden, in good condition is a simple matter if time is allotted to the task on a regular basis.

Typically, you will need to set aside a few hours a week for garden maintenance – a little more than this in spring and autumn, and a little less in winter. But the time varies according to the nature of your garden – and the time you are prepared to put in.

Gardens with masses of formal borders, rose gardens and rock gardens, lawns and hedges, fruit and vegetable plots, demand an enormous amount of time; gardens with large paved areas, plenty of ground cover to smother weeds, low-maintenance climbers and conifers require much less. In the growing season, from spring on, all gardens must be weeded, hoed and mowed regularly. It is wise to start hoeing early in spring, as soon as new growth appears, before weed seedlings have a chance to establish themselves. But care is needed not to remove desirable seedlings by mistake. It may take considerable time and effort to halt the annual reappearance of perennial weeds in a particular bed, but once this weed-cycle is broken, weeding becomes much simpler

During the summer, frequent watering of container and flower beds is particularly important when it is dry. Lawns relish constant mowing, and this encourages the finer grasses at the expense of the coarser ones. Prune dead or diseased wood, and look out for and treat pests and diseases; fruit and vegetables and roses demand particular attention. It makes sense to leave jobs such as repairing fences, gates, wiring, securing stakes and so on until winter, when there is little else to do in the garden.

The secret of successful garden maintenance is attention to detail. When the weekly chores include such things as removing yellowing leaves and fading flowers from plants, you can be sure the garden is well maintained. Turning a pleasant garden into something even more attractive is much more satisfying; and it is much easier to relax by working in a garden when you can see results at the end of the day.

I've heard fowk say that the're ower many ways tae look efter a wee gairden; the best is tae git a gairdener!

Aye, well, ye might be rich an' famous, but yer gairden disnae care ...

The Gairden Pond

Horace thocht I'd like a pond in ma gairden, but I'd rather ha' a fountain instead. This is whit he foond oot in various books.

PONDS

A pond is really only a hole in the ground filled with water; but if you dig a hole in the garden and fill it with water, all you will get is a muddy mess. In a short time all the water will drain away anyway. What you will need is both the hole and something to keep the water in. But even before that there are things you need to decide upon.

WHAT SIZE POND?

You can make the pond as large as you like, but it has to fit somewhere in the garden, and the bigger it is, the more it will cost. The smallest size of worthwhile pond is around 8-10 sq. ft. Anything smaller will not establish itself like a natural pond, with plant life keeping the water fresh, nor will it hold enough water to provide good living conditions for more than three or four fish.

HOW DEEP SHOULD THE POND BE?

A pond must be deep enough to make sure it does not freeze solid in winter or get too warm in summer. There must be enough depth of water for plants to grow properly. So it must be at least 15 in. deep but need never be more than 30 in.

CATCHING THE SUN

Draw a plan of your garden and work out where the sun falls for about six hours a day, as shown. The best place will be in the morning sun then becoming shaded in the afternoon. Avoid placing your pond under trees or shrubs. Dead leaves falling into the pond will poison the water during the winter. Decide where it fits in with the rest of the garden., The foot of the rockery is one place in a garden where a pond always looks attractive. You should also consider where it can be dug without disturbing the flower beds.

WHAT SHAPE TO MAKE IT?

The shape of the pond can be formal or natural. A formal shape with straight edges is usually a square or a rectangle. A circular or oval shape is best avoided as the shape is more difficult to dig out. More natural shapes are better created using a pre-formed liner as it is more difficult to line an irregular shape. You also need to consider the depth of the pond — ideally with a variable depth to accommodate different types of plants.

WHAT PLANTS TO PICK?

To be healthy, a pond needs a proper balance of plant life. Then, instead of becoming just another stagnant pond, the water stays fresh, fish thrive, and everything living in the pond has a good life.

One type of plant is most important. This is the oxygenating plant, which gives off lots of oxygen. Fish use up oxygen in breathing. Water which is standing rather than running tends to loose oxygen (which is why ponds become stagnant). So oxygenating plants supply the oxygen required in a garden pond. Oxygenating plants live wholly under water. They are planted at the bottom of the pond, growing upwards and spreading out just under the surface.

Some plants, known as marginals, only grow properly in shallow water, say about 3 in. over the top of the soil in their pots. Other plants may need 20 in. or more of water above their soil to grow well. Deeper water plants can take a lot of room. Leaves from a single water lily, for example, may spread over the whole surface of a pond.

AND WHAT ABOUT FISH?

You will need to take advice on the best fish to stock and the number of fish your pond can support, especially when you move beyond just stocking with goldfish. You will also need to find out about feeding them and keeping them at an appropriate temperature — and protecting them against predators, especially the ever-hungry heron.

WILD LIFE

A pond will attract wildlife, and you should soon be aware of frogs and toads, especially if the pond is well planted with marginal plants.

!!Safety First!!
Remember tae keep wee bairns awa fae
the pond unless they are wi' an adult

ANOTHER
POSSIBLE PLACE

N

FLOWER BEDS

LAWN

YOUR
HOUSE

BEST PLACES
FOR A POND

SHADED
BY HOUSE

SHADED
BY TREE

Gairdenin' Wisdoms

with GAIRDENER BROON

✳✳✳✳✳✳✳✳✳✳✳✳✳✳✳✳✳✳✳✳✳✳✳

JINGS, I canna believe a hale week has gone by since I wrote aboot the Best Bloomin' Toon contest. I'm writing this week's column in ma bed as I'm no' feeling a hunner per cent the noo. A' ma ain fault of course, but mair o' that later.

Fowk have been writing in asking aboot hanging baskets and that's what started a' my problems. Maw Broon loves hanging baskets, so I decided tae set up a puckle at the But an' Ben, hingin' them oot fae the guttering. They dinna half look guid when they're established. And mind an' watter the baskets every day. If ye dinna they soon dry oot. I can vouch for this masel' ... I aye like tae get "wattered" once a day at "The Drovers" when I'm oot at the But an' Ben. I ken it mak's me look better and gies me a better colour. The floo'ers are the verra same. Actually, tae let ye intae a secret, I had lined the baskets this week wi' cut-up pairs o' past-their-sell-by-date auld long johns that Dunroamin' Care Home had thrown oot. I was assured they'd been "well-wattered" at times and that they were grand for haudin' the watter. I could well believe that auld towellin' nappies micht be jist as useful. Well, whatever the reason, the baskets fair burst intae floo'er. Absolutely wonderful.

Well, the sun's been oot near a' day and every day this week and I was up and doon the stepladders every ither minute wi' the wattering can. Hangin' baskets are grand for keepin' yer floo'ers high up and oot o' reach o' snails and slugs and the bees jist love tae flit aboot in the blooms. Well, all was goin' jist braw until Thursday efter lunch. I jist couldna resist stickin' ma big nose intae the lovely floo'ery smell. And that's when I came unstuck and that's my gairdenin' tips for ye this week. NEVER stick yer big nose intae yer baskets withoot checkin' for WASPS. And NEVER stand on the tap o' yer stepladders while ye're smokin' yer pipe. A great brute stung me richt on the nose an' I near swallied ma pipe as I crashed doon aff the shoogly ladder. Only the bowl o' the pipe was visible as the stem was stuck richt doon ma throat ... and the pipe was still lit, which wisna daein' ma moustache ony guid at a'. Fortunately I'd only just landed on my dowp when the wattering can landed on ma heid, puttin' oot the pipe. But it wisna a' bad news. I'd spat oot ma false teeth when I got stung an' ma falsers must hae bitten the wasp's heid richt aff. The Bairn found the wasp and the teeth richt inside the basket.

So here I am, sittin' in bed at the But an' Ben nursing a sair backside, nursing ma injured pride, an' nursing a wee single malt (well wattered) an' lookin' oot ower the big lump at the end o' ma nose at the hangin' baskets ootside the windae. Hen's wattering them now ... he disnae need ony ladders at a'. I wish I'd thought o' that afore I took ma tumble.

Chicken an' chips in a basket for this invalid the nicht. An' this basket's no' lined wi' onything fae The Dunroamin' ... jist a bed o' chips.

Cheers the noo —

Gairdener Broon
x

A wasp sting is richt nasty, and bein' oot an' aboot in the gairden, if you get stung, rub a cut onion on the sting.

Hangin' Baskets

If ye want tae brighten up the front door or a balcony, a hangin' basket is the very dab, but tak' care tae read whit I said in "The Bugle".

Hanging Baskets

In spring, garden centres sell a variety of ready-planted hanging baskets, but it is not difficult to prepare your own arrangement. Baskets made of plastic or galvanised wire are easily available, but it is also possible to improvise by using, for example, an old kitchen colander. Hanging baskets can be hung from ceiling hooks, but make sure that the hook is securely fixed, as a basket when it is newly watered weighs quite a lot. Unless you install a pulley system to raise and lower your baskets, remember not to put baskets up too high so that they are a nuisance to water.

The traditional lining of hanging baskets is sphagnum moss, but basket matting or thin layers of grass can also be used with the grass facing inwards and the soil on the outside. If the baskets are to be hung indoors, a polythene lining will be needed to avoid drips.

SUITABLE PLANTS

The colour theme of hanging baskets is very often geranium red, alyssum white and lobelia blue. Variations, however, are very simple. There are all the orange and yellow colours of nasturtiums which thrive well in hanging baskets; there are the petunia pinks and violets, the fuchsia purples, reds and cerises, and the begonia yellows, whites and salmons. There are also all the pretty trailing ferns that wander so effectively over the sides of the basket.

In theory, any plant can be used in a hanging basket, but in practical terms it is best to avoid upright plants that have to be planted at an angle to obtain full nutrition. Trailing plants, such as the fuchsias, petunias and tuberous begonias are suitable, as are smaller flowering plants like miniature roses.

PLANTING

First provide a support for the empty basket — one way is to place it on top of a large empty bucket. Next put in the basket your choice of lining— if you have chosen sphagnum moss, it should have been soaked in warm water for 30 minutes and then squeezed until it is moist and malleable. This lining serves as a container for the soil. If you are planning to use trailing plants, make slits in the lining where you want them to go. The next step is to fill the basket with John Innes Compost, preferably No. 2, then simply place the plants in the compost, about 5 to 6 in. apart, inserting trailing plants from underneath with the roots uppermost. Once the basket is full, soak it well and allow it to drain before hanging it.

WATERING

Plants in hanging baskets get thirsty very quickly and on a really hot day they should be watered both morning and evening. The rising air that warms basket plants makes a hanging basket an ideal container for cacti.

FERNS

The feathery appearance of ferns can enhance a hanging basket and those that produce runners or rhizomes can be trained into an attractive ball shape.

I pit in tae ma hangin' basket a selection o' Pelargoniums (well, I still call 'em Geraniums), Petunias an' Lobelia, red, white an' blue. Ye need tae line the baskets first wi' basket matting ye can buy at a gairden centre or maybe even line them wi' moss.

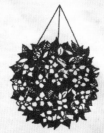

Line the basket with 5 cm (2 in) of moss and 5 cm of compost. Make slits to insert trailing plants.

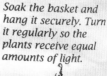

Insert plants about 12 to 15 cm (5 to 6 ins) apart and cover roots with 5 cm of compost.

Soak the basket and hang it securely. Turn it regularly so the plants receive equal amounts of light.

Line the basket with 5 cm (2 in) of moss and add a layer of potting compost. Place the fern in the basket and add more compost round the sides.

To encourage the ball shape, attach the rhizomes or runners round the outside of the basket using U-shaped wires.

Hang the basket in a shady spot and keep the compost damp. Turn the basket occasionally to promote symmetrical growth.

CONVOLVULUS ARVENSIS.

Heather

What wad a gairden be wi'oot heathers, aye an' think o' the hills wi'oot a summer coverin' o' purple. The plant is as Scottish as Rabbie Burns an' whisky.

HEATHERS — by their general aspect, heathers are easily recognized, although the species and varieties comprised in this tribe exceed 500 in number. Their leaves, small, narrow, rigid, and evergreen, possessing considerable elasticity, wave gracefully with the breeze. On the whole heathers constitute an elegant tribe of plants. Although so much of a general aspect is exhibited by the genus, yet there exists in size, form, and colour of flowers, a considerable diversity in the different varieties. The value of the common form (*Calluna vulgaris*) can scarcely be over-estimated for planting on barren hill sides or spaces; it affords excellent shelter for game and food for bees.

From 'Heather Ale'
by Robert Louis Stevenson

From the bonny bells of heather
They brewed a drink long-syne,
Was sweeter far than honey,
Was stronger far than wine.
They brewed it and they drank it,
And lay in a blessed swound
For days and days together
In their dwellings underground.

FLOWERING BRANCH OF ERICA RUBRO-CALYX.

*There's even
a heather that grows tae
the height o' a large shrub or small tree -
'Erica arborea', the Tree Heather.*

FIG. 727. ERICA VESTITA COCCINEA, showing Flowering Branch

fuchentogle
HEATHER HONEY
PRODUCED BY THE WILSON FARM HIVES
Farmer Wilson

Heather in Scotland

AND WE'LL ALL GO TOGETHER,
TO PULL WILD MOUNTAIN THYME,
ALL AROUND THE PURPLE HEATHER.
WILL YOU GO, LASSIE, GO?

Heather has always been important in Scottish country life because it is such a versatile plant, so important that people living in the hills were called 'heather-lowpers'. Heather was used for thatching roofs, making rope and to provide bedding for animals. Inside the home, it was used for stuffing mattresses, making brushes, for dyeing clothes (many of the traditional tartan colours come from heather dyes), as a medicine in the form of heather tea and to make heather ale. And, of course, bees are very fond of the heather flower, producing the wonderfully flavoured heather honey.

Most Scottish heather is purple, but it is the rarer white heather that is a symbol of good luck, and, of course, there is a tradition attached to this. Malvina, the daughter of the Celtic bard, Ossian, fell in love with Oscar, a great warrior. One day she was sitting with her father in the hills when a messenger arrived with the terrible news that Oscar had been killed in battle. He then presented Oscar's last gift, a spray of purple heather. Malvina ran into the hills and where her tears fell, the purple heather turned white and she proclaimed that good luck would come to anyone who found the white heather.
The wild heather or ling (*Calluna vulgaris*) flowers from July through to October.

Nowadys there are lots of other heathers that you can grow in your garden, in all sorts of different colours. Other summer-flowering heathers include bell heather (*Erica cinerea*), Cornish heath (*Erica vagans*), Corsican heath (*Erica terminalis*), cross-leaved heath (*Erica tetralix*) and Dorset heath (*Erica ciliaris*). Another group of heathers flower from November through to March, including *Erica carnea* and *Erica darleyensis*.

WORLD'S TALLEST HEDGE GETS THE CHOP!

WORK IS CURRENTLY UNDERWAY to give Perthshire's famous Meikleour Beech Hedge its ten yearly trim. The hedge has been officially recorded since 1966 as the highest hedge in the world and features in the *Guinness Book of Records*.

The hedge of beech trees is approximately 580 yards long and has an average height of 100 feet, reaching over 120 feet at the Northern end and about 80 feet to the South. The hedge is looked after by the Meikleour Trust. It is cut and measured every ten years using a hydraulic platform and hand held equipment - a complex operation which takes four men around six weeks.

This remarkable hedge was laid out in 1745 by Jean Mercer of Meikleour and her husband, Robert Murray Nairne, probably to denote a boundary. Shortly afterwards he was killed fighting at Culloden. Local folk lore says the hedge was allowed to grow to the heavens as a tribute to his memory.

The very job for Hen - trimming the world's tallest hedge!

Hedges

Picking the right plants for a hedge will depend upon what the hedge is designed to do. Many hedges are grown to mark the boundaries of a garden. If you need privacy in the garden during the summer, plant a deciduous hedge, such as hawthorn or beech (beech will hold on to its dead leaves until spring so offers greater protection). If you want a hedge to give all-round privacy and to be an impenetrable barrier, plant an evergreen such as holly or yew (many evergreen hedging plants are prickly). The evergreen leylandii will grow very quickly to give you privacy, but it must be kept very well trimmed, for it easily grows over 60 ft. high. If the hedge is just to be decorative within the garden, then pick flowering plants such as lavender or rose. If the hedge is designed to shelter the garden from winds you can consider a mixed hedge containing evergreens and deciduous plants to give a more attractive hedge. Here are some suggestions:

DECIDUOUS HEDGES

Beech	Fagus
Blackthorn	Prunus spinosa
Golden privet	Ligustrum
Hawthorn	Crataegus
Hazel	Corylus avellana
Hornbeam	Carpinus

EVERGREEN HEDGES

Box	Buxus
Darwin's barberry	Berberis darwinii
Escallonia	Escallonia
Firethorn	Pyracantha
Golden barberry	Berberis stenophylla
Holly	Ilex
Japanese (or common) laurel	Aucuba japonica
Leylandii	Cupressocyparis leylandii
Portuguese laurel	Prunus lusitanica
Privet	Ligustrum

DECORATIVE HEDGES

Lavender	Lavandula
Oleaster	Eleagnus
Purple leaf sand cherry	Prunus cistena
Rose	Rosa
Rosemary	Rosemarinus
Shrubby cinquefoil	Potentilla
Spindle	Euonymous
Spiraea	Spiraea

A hedge between keeps friendship green

Herbs

Maw uses herbs in her cookin' an' ye can grow lots o' herbs on a balcony or by a windae as well as in the gairden.

Herbs

Every keen cook will want herbs in the garden, but herbs are attractive plants in their own right, and many will claim a place on other grounds. If thyme, parsley, sage, chives, tarragon and so on are required fresh for the kitchen, it makes sense to keep them in a raised container nearby, out of the reach of dogs and cats so that they need not be washed and will taste fresher. Near paths and terraces and places where you may brush past, plant rosemary, lavender, sage and santolina, each of which has a wonderful scent. Each herb has its own quality:

- Lavender hedges are very attractive and can be planted in variety to create an interesting effect.

- Clary sage and angelica are short-lived perennials but create a dramatic effect in a garden with enough space.

- A bed of various thymes is colourful and aromatic, and thyme can be used as an ornamental lawn, as can camomile.

- Dill, fennel and cumin are graceful and valuable for seeds.

There are two general rules to bear in mind about growing herbs. One is to keep cutting them to encourage fresh foliage, except where flowers are desired for petals, decorative value, or the seeds that follow. The other is to keep shrubby herbs like lavender, rue, sage and so on, compact by clipping or pruning them in the spring or after flowering. Herbs generally prefer well-drained soil.

LittLe gardeners

3d

* PARSLEY *

Maw's Herb Vinegar recipe

Wash and dry a good quantity of freshly gathered young shoots of whichever herb you are wanting to flavour the vinegar with, and put them into wide-necked bottles, or jars. Cover with vinegar, seal, infuse for two months, then strain into small bottles, seal, and keep in a cool, dark place.

Pick the herb from the garden on a dry day before the plants begin to flower.

Herbs you could use in this way are mint, tarragon, thyme, dill, rosemary (bruise the rosemary a wee bit first) — really any herb that would be guid an' tasty in a salad dressing or as a marinade.

Grow mint in pots - otherwise it will tak'
ower yer gairden, it's that vigorous.

If ye eat a lot o' parsley, you
can be an auld sage.

HERBS IN CONTAINERS

Many herbs come from hot and dry places, and so enjoy growing in sheltered and sunny spots close to the house or on a balcony. Some will also happily grow inside the house, but you need to make sure that they receive plenty of sun and that the plant pots are as close together as possible and sit on a tray of wet stones (all to increase the humidity around them). Here are some good herbs to try:

Basil (really only works indoors)
Chives
Coriander
Dill
Lemon balm
Mint
Oregano
Rosemary
Sage
Tarragon
Thyme

Parsley is a surprisingly widely used herb given that it is not easy to germinate the seeds. There are many superstitions linked to parsley:

- Parsley only thrives in households were "the mistress is master" or "the wife wears the trousers".

- Never transplant parsley, for it will bring bad luck.

- Between sowing and germination, the parsley seed goes to the devil seven — or even nine — times (hence the long period of germination).

- Only the wicked can grow parsley.

- If a stranger plants parsley, great trouble will befall the household.

- A young woman should sow parsley seed if she wants a baby.

Hooseplants

At Glebe Street inside the flat, there's been tomato plants in the scullery, hyacinths alo' the beds and mushrooms in the lobby press. There's aye been an aspidistra, no that it is 'The Biggest Aspidistra in the World'. A' it takes is a wee bit work and imagination. And floo'ers jist love sunny windae ledges as lang's there's nae draughts. So ye see, flat living disnae hae tae mean living in black and white ... or Broon for that matter.

Keeping House-plants

To keep houseplants well and looking at their best, you have to know their needs. Some thrive in a warm, humid atmosphere where others collapse and rot; some hate being too heavily watered, others can never be given too much water; some need plenty of sunlight and others scorch in it.

LIGHT

Each plant has its own preferred amount of light. For most this is bright indirect light, so a windowsill that receives little or no direct sunlight is ideal.

Although some will tolerate extremely shady conditions quite happily, some light is essential for photosynthesis — the process whereby the plant's leaves absorb the energy provided by light, which is then used by the plant to grow.

Plants that can survive in shade tend to have dark-green leaves, which can make better use of limited light. Variegated plants, which have green leaves splashed or striped with white or cream, need more light. Strong artificial lighting can take the place of natural light.

TEMPERATURE

Standard room temperature is fine for most house plants. Plants placed on a windowsill may need to be protected from the low temperatures that can occur immediately next to the glass in winter; before drawing the curtains at night, remove the plants from the windowsills. Similarly, the sun streaming through glass in summer can cause scorching.

If a plant looks unhappy and starts dropping its leaves in conditions that otherwise seem perfect, this may be due to overwatering, but could also be caused by a draught. The plant may well revive simply by being moved to another, draught-free position.

Starting a House Plant Collection

A good place to start is with four plants that are inexpensive, easy to grow and interesting to watch — the spider plant, indoor ivy, coleus and geranium.

THE SPIDER PLANT

With its long arching green and cream leaves all round the pot, the spider plant does resemble a spider. It grows fast, making thick white roots that soon fill the pot.

The best way to increase the spider plant is to wait until it is big enough to send out arching stems, not leaves, at the ends of which miniature plants will develop. This

unusual habit of reproduction is its way of increasing when growing wild in its native country. The baby plants weigh down the arching stems until they touch the ground and take root.

The spider plant is not fussy about its position indoors. It will grow most quickly and produce well coloured leaves if put on a sunny windowsill and given water every time it begins to dry out. Use any ordinary soil in the pot.

If the tips of leaves go brown, the plant needs more moisture or humidity. If it has pale leaves, it is not getting enough light, or it needs feeding.

INDOOR IVY

An indoor ivy will add height to your collection. The most attractive and popular one has green and cream mottled leaves and its full name is Hedera canariensis. Like other indoor ivies, it prefers a position in good light but out of the hottest summer sun. It needs less water than the spider plant, which means letting it get quite dry between waterings. Try to keep the ivy growing upwards by loosely tying the main stem to a slim cane pushed into the soil.

These two plants plus tradescantia will make an attractive indoor garden together in a bowl, dish or trough. The simplest way to group them is to keep them in their original pots and bury these in peat in the bowl. This makes a neat finish and the dark colour of the peat shows off the green and cream leaves beautifully.

COLEUS

So far we have not introduced bright colours into the house plant collection. The leaves of coleus have all the colours of the rainbow. It is difficult to find two plants with the same leaf patterns and colours. Coleus grows easily and quickly from seed and cuttings, and this is why shops and nurseries are able to sell plants quite cheaply.

It must be in the full light of a sunny window and not in the path of cold currents of air. Coleus plants are mainly available in summer time and it is in winter that they are difficult to keep indoors. Water only when the soil is dry.

As your plants grow, you will probably notice a spiky flower stalk rising from the top of the plant. The flowers it carries are small and uninteresting, and if you allow them to develop it will hinder the future growth of leaves. So pinch out the flower stalk where it arises at an early stage. To get the best from coleus add a few drops of plant food to the water.

If its leaves shrivel and drop, it is too hot and dry, or it is at the end of its season and should be thrown away. If it shows pale coloration or its leaves are reverting to green, it is not receiving enough light, or it may require feeding, or both.

GERANIUMS

Geranium (or, correctly, pelargonium) plants are top value for indoor gardening: they grow quickly and flower freely. In fact they grow so readily that their height must be controlled by cutting back the tallest shoots. This has the effect of causing shoots to grow out lower down and keep the plant bushy.

Rub your fingers against a geranium leaf and you will at once notice the aroma which is released. It is a rather bitter smell — unlike anything else— but not unpleasant.

They grow outdoors in summer, but because they are tender — the stems are soft — they will not survive a cold winter outside, although they will live and flower through most of the year when grown in a pot and kept protected.

There are two main groups of flowering geraniums. First are the zonal geraniums (Pelargonium zonale or Pelargonium hortorum), with characteristic rounded leaves, often marked with rings of colour, and, with enough light, will flower all year. Then there are the regal or Martha Washington geraniums (Pelargonium domesticum or Pelargonium grandiflorum), which have rather fuller petals to the flowers, and leaves that are more triangular and more heavily contoured and serrated; they have a limited flowering season (usually late spring and early summer) and are harder to grow than the zonal geraniums. In addition to these there are also the delightful trailing or ivy-leaved geraniums (Pelargonium peltatum), with their more waxy leaves and large-petalled flowers — perfect for hanging baskets.

Ma advice, jist talk tae yer plants!

Your Garden

Card 8

Aspidistra
or Cast Iron Plant
Aspidistra elatior

The aspidistra is an elegant, spacious plant with rich, dark green leaves with a striking texture. There is a lovely variegated form, with irregular creamy-white stripes following the lines of the veins.

Use a damp sponge to keep the leaves clean and wash them with milk to bring out their shine.

Position: Can be very shady; avoid direct sun light.

Temperature: Standard room temperatures.

Water: Likes plenty of water: water twice a week in summer; in winter keep watering to a minimum.

Feeding: Requires very little feeding: once every other month in summer; do not feed the variegated Aspidistra at all.

Propagation: By root division, or by potting up suckers (shoots growing at the base of the plant).

Soil: Standard potting compost.

Problems: Brown patches on leaves: too much sunlight. Leaves splitting: too much ... common pests.

Your Garden

Card 7

Tradescantia
Tradescantia zebrina

This is an ideal plant for the hanging basket, or for trailing from shelves or mantelpieces. The variegated forms are particularly attractive. All these variegated forms are liable to revert to the original green, and a plant that starts producing all-green leaves should have these removed completely the moment that they appear.

Plants will survive in fairly shady conditions, but they tend to become leggy and dull if starved of light.. When a healthy plant produces tiny white flowers this is notice to take cuttings and to start fresh plants, as it is a sign that the mother plant has finished her span of years and will die as the flowers fade.

Position: Bright indirect light is best, although it will tolerate a fairly shady position.

Temperature: Standard room temperatures are fine, provided winter temperatures do not drop below 50 °F (10 °C).

Water: Water well whenever the soil dries out; use lime-free water for preference.

Feeding: Feed once a month from spring to early autumn, using a mild mix of plant food.

Propagation: From stem cuttings rooted in water, or placed directly in soil.

Soil: Standard loam-based compost.

Problems: Leaves become pale and dry out at the tips: too much sunlight. Plant becoming very leggy: not enough light.

A GROUP OF PITCHER PLANTS.
1. N. VEITCHI.   2. N. BICALCARATA.   3. ALBO-MARGINATA.

Y ur Garden

Card 12

African Violet
Saintpaulia ionantha

The African violet has deep blue clusters of flowers on long, branching stems. The deep-green rounded leaves are usually coated in delicate hairs that give them a soft, velvety sheen. There are now numerous other varieties and hybrids available, in various different colours, sizes and petal shapes. African violets will flower almost the whole year long. The real secret is to water the plant at the base of the pot only: water should not be allowed to touch the leaves, which are highly susceptible to mould.

Position: Bright indirect light.

Temperature: Best kept at around 60 °F (16 °C), i.e. below normal central-heating warmth. Ensure that winter temperatures do not drop below 50 °F (10 °C).

Water: Use tepid water supplied to the base of the pot only; keep the soil damp at all times, but make sure that the plant does not sit in water. African violets like humidity; provide this by placing the pot on a base of wet gravel, not by aerial spraying.

Feeding: Feed with a mild dose of plant food when the plant is growing during the summer. Propagation: From seed in spring; or from leaf cuttings pinned to the soil; or from leaf-and-stem cuttings in soil. Each of these methods requires warmth and humidity.

Soil: Standard peat-based compost.

Problems: Flowers and leaves look unhealthy and develop spotting: too cold and wet, or water.

HOUSEPLANTS - THE DOS AND DONT'S

When you go back home from the allotment, don't forget to look after your houseplants. Here are some reminders of what you should and should not do.

The DOs

- Keep them where they can enjoy plenty of light.
- Keep them where the temperature is steady (not too hot and not too cold).
- Give the leaves a wash occasionally (outside in a shower of rain - or give them a shower in the bathroom).
- Put a couple of drops of liquid feed in the water for the plants during spring and summer.
- Give them less water and feed in winter than at other times.
- Give plants with shiny green leaves (like Ficus and philodendron) a polish with milk or with leaf-shining product.
- Look out for signs of sickness (leaves off colour, drooping or falling) and suspect that cold wet soil is stopping the roots growing. Keep plants warmer and water less often or repot in fresh compost.

24°C maximum temperature for nearly all house plants in ordinary rooms

21°C

18°C

15°C

13°C minimum temperature for delicate types: Aechmea, Aphelandra

10°C begonia, codiaeum, coleus, maranta, peperomia, rhoeo, spathiphyllum

7°C minimum temperature for hardy types: beloperone, Ficus decora, grevillea, Hedera canariensis, hoya, monstera, neanthe, pilea, rhoicissus, sansevieria

2°C minimum temperature for hardy types that do not like warm conditions in winter: aspidistra, billbergia, Cissus antarctica, cyperus, fatshedera, fatsia, Hedera helix, Philodendron scandens, saxifraga, zebrina

Dear Gairdener Broon

I have heard it said that you should wash houseplant leaves with milk to make them shiny. I am allergic to cow's milk, so what do you recommend instead?

Some say usin' the inside of a banana skin does the job, which is fine if ye dinna mind the smell. How aboot buying some o' those artificial plants – tak' them with ye tae the shower an they'll be as good as new!

– Gairdener Broon

DOBBIE'S EXCELSIOR PANSIES
IN CHOICE MIXTURE
Seed. 6ᵈ 1⁄- and 2⁄6 per packet
Plants. 2⁄- per dozen, 3⁄6 per 25,
6⁄- per 50, 10⁄9 per 100, carriage paid

94

Some DON'Ts

- Do not kill your plants with kindness. Water only when drying out.
- Do not add liquid feed in winter when plants are resting.
- Do not place plants close to a hot fire or on the mantelshelf above. Indoor plants do not like fumes from gas fires nor from paraffin heaters.
- Do not keep plants where cold air from a window or door can strike them and cause harm.
- Do not move plants about frequently as changes of situation may upset them.
- Do not be in a great hurry to transfer a plant to a bigger pot. Tap out the root ball and look to see if white roots are filling the compost; if so, move the plant to a larger pot of similar compost.

Tap pot sharply and remove plant as shown (A) and (B). Put two or three crocks and a handful of soil in the bottom of a new pot (C). Place a plant in position, adding fresh soil down the sides (D). Press soil down firmly (E).

1 Weigela rosea. 2 Lapageria rosea.

BLACKIE & SON, GLASGOW, EDINBURGH, & LONDON.

I'm no' auld, I jist need tae be repotted.

95

Landing Gairdenin'

If ye are in a flat and want yer ain personal bit o' gairden, dinna despair. If yer dose has a drappie sunlight at the tap o' the stairs, there's nae end o' things ye can grow in pots richt ootside yer ain front door. I've kent fowk grow grapes, nae less, on the tap landing. Doon alo' on the ground floor, ye'll hae tae be less ambitious - what aboot some grand mushrooms? Unlike Ella Gerrard at Number 8, I widna advise plantin' IVY in yer dose. Hers got oota hand and wiz growin' up through a'body's letter boxes. It wiz like something fae ane o' thae horror movies, things growin' through yer letterbox and alang yer lobbies and under yer bed. Gied me the creeps.

KALANCHOË or FLAMING KATY

This is a succulent with thick, fleshy leaves that bunch up into an irregular, bushy shape no more than about 6 in. high and wide; long stems project from the top of this, bearing clusters of tiny flowers. They are popular around Christmas time, and the flowers will bring a touch of colour to the house for several months. At the end of the season they are usually discarded.

Problems: Drooping leaves, signs of rot: too much water.

BEGONIA REX

Begonia rex comes in a number of forms, with matt-finish leaves in combinations of red, green, brown, cream and green; the leaves are usually a least 6 in. long, heavily contoured and with serrated edges, and form a bold clump of foliage.

Problems: Begonias do not like conditions that are either too hot and dry, or too cold, but overwatering is probably the biggest threat, provoking rot and mildew. Cut back and treat a damaged plant and adjust watering and position.

CHINESE EVERGREEN

A foliage plant with long, mid-green leaves on short stems, but more often met with now in its variegated forms. These introduce cream or white into the leaf markings.

Problems: If the plant is too cold, in a draught, or receives too much water it will begin to drop its leaves from the base and will become straggly, with a scarred trunk. Prone to common pests, especially scale and mealy bug.

Stairwell Plants

The stairs in your close can be dreary places, so why not try some plants to bring a bit of life and colour to the space? There is usually not a great deal of light in the stairs, so you will need plants that can survive without too much light. If you live at the top of the stairs, you may be close to a rooflight that will let in much more light for the plants and gives you greater variety in what you can do – you will even be able to bring plants in flower on to the landing for display – but remember to return them to more favourable conditions as soon as the flowering ceases or when they look unhappy.

When you consider growing plants on the landing, remember that in some buildings fire regulations will demand that landings are kept clear of all obstacles (and this will include any plants). So long as plants are allowed, make sure that they do not cause any obstruction and that they do not irritate your neighbours – you'll not be very popular if you have a holly bush whose prickly leaves keep catching in people's clothes. Also make sure that all the plants sit in saucers that catch water, to avoid any water dripping down the stairs. It's probably best to avoid plants with strong smells – you may think the plant smells wonderful, but not everyone has the same taste – and in the relatively confined space of a stairwell, the smell will be more concentrated than you might expect.

So here are some recommendations: aspidistra or cast iron plant; begonia rex; bird's nest fern; Boston fern; Chinese evergreen (Aglaoema); maidenhair fern; mother-in-law's tongues; spider plant; stags head fern; sweetheart vine.

If you do get some direct sunlight, at the top of the stairs, you can try some flowering plants to provide extra colour, for example, African violet; Chinese jasmine; hoya or wax flower; kalanchoë or flaming Katy; Italian bellflower; tradescantia.

WOULD YOU BELIEVE IT?

A 61-year old granny from Neath in South Wales was threatened with an ASBO for growing two tomato plants in the entrance foyer to her council flat. A council official had suggested that a neighbour had complained that the pesticides and sprays she was using were making her ill – even though she did not use any pesticides on them. On another occasion, she was asked to remove pot plants because they might self combust.

MAIDENHAIR FERN

This is surely one of the prettiest of ferns, with a poetic name to match. It is not difficult to grow but can be sensitive to its position and needs plenty of humidity. Once you have found the right spot for it, leave it there.

Problems: Leaves drying out: needs more water, or, more likely, more humidity. Leaves curling and sickly: too much water. Leaves pale: too much sunlight or needs feeding.

ITALIAN BELLFLOWER

An easy-to-grow flowering house plant with abundant clusters of white or pale-mauve, star-shaped flowers and heart-shaped leaves growing on brittle stems filled with a milky sap. It will flower throughout most of the latter part of the growing year.

Problems: Leaves and flowers wilting and turning brown: too little water. Overwatering will cause rot and collapse.

Looking After Your Houseplants

PLANT FOODS

The soil or compost in which a house plant grows contains a large quantity of minerals and nutrients, but in time, especially if it is growing strongly, the plant will probably have used up most of these nutrients and they will need replenishment.

Houseplant foods are widely available, usually as a liquid solution supplied at the same time as you water the plants. All you do is mix up the food according to the instructions and feed your plants according to their needs. Young or recently repotted plants will not need feeding for six months. Most established plants will need feeding only from spring to autumn; winter-flowering plants may need feeding over winter. 'Slow-release' fertiliser granules provide a steady supply of nutrients over a period of four months or so. This is a useful convenience but will not take the place of more sensitive judgements of a plant's requirements.

SOIL

Commercially produced soil, peat-based and peat-free potting composts should be used for house plants. Composts are either loam-based or peat-based. Loam is a prepared soil rich in decomposed organic material; this is combined with peat, sand and a standard mix of base fertiliser.

PLANT TRAINING

To rear house plants effectively a certain amount of ruthlessness is required: by pruning a plant back hard you will force it to divert its energies into new growth; by pinching out growing tips that threaten to make the plant leggy, you will encourage side shoots and make it more bushy.

HUMIDITY

The dryness of our houses provides one quality that most plants detest, especially those that originate from the steamy atmosphere of the tropical rainforests. There

wick watering

pots can stand on pebbles in water, but the pot must be above water

pots sunk in peat in a trough to keep them cool and moist

above a radiator under a window is a good place for indoor plants—but remember to provide humidity

give big leaves a wash and shine ocasionally

LILIUM
1. pardalinum 2. Leichtlinii

are two solutions: evaporation or aerial spraying.

Because water naturally vaporises at room temperature, it is possible to provide a continual supply of moist air to a plant by keeping the area around its base damp. The easiest way to do this is to stand the pot on a flat tray of gravel that is kept constantly wet; the stones, however, should be large enough so the pot does not actually sit in the water.

Aerial spraying is a more direct method. It involves spraying the plant with a fine mist of water (preferably rainwater). Plastic spray bottles with fine nozzles are widely available and not expensive.

WATERING

The most common threat to house plants is overwatering. Water and the essential minerals dissolved in it are usually taken up by the roots, but these must also have some air. The process whereby the water drains through soil also pulls in air, but if the soil is waterlogged, the roots become swamped and cannot function.

As a rule it is best to water plants thoroughly as occasion demands, removing the excess water that drains through the soil and then leaving them until the next thorough watering. Providing water in dribs and drabs does not meet the plant's changing needs through the year.

In general you should water considerably more in summer than in winter, as in summer the plant is likely to be growing and using up more energy. Also, during warm weather moisture will evaporate from the plant's leaves, and to replace this the plant will draw more moisture up from the roots, a process called transpiration.

Many plants, such as azaleas, dislike water containing lime. This is difficult for anyone living in a hard-water area. Filtering water will remove the lime but also the beneficial minerals. The best solution is to use rainwater, which is soft and ideal for watering or spraying.

Use warm watter on yer plants.
Would ye like a soakin' in cauld watter on a winter's day?

If a hooseplant is poorly, get rid o' it an' buy a new plant.

GOING AWAY?

It's the holiday time of year again. It will no doubt rain on the
allotment while you are away, but what about your houseplants? Here's
some advice on how to avoid returning to a collection of dead plants!

The best solution is to ask a friendly neighbour to come in and water
them while you are away (and hope that they don't over-water the
plants). Failing that, how will you stop the plants drying out?

One way to prevent this is to keep the outside of a pot moist and cool.
Spare pots can be used to make an outer jacket for smaller pots. Fill
the gap between with crumpled wet newspaper or wet peat.

If you have a deep tray or trough on which to stand a number of pots,
it can be filled with wet sand or peat so that moisture will rise up
through the base of each pot to the roots. Be sure to push each pot
down into the wet base to make contact with the compost in the pot or
trough.

The obvious way to keep pots moist - standing them in a bowl of water-
is dangerous because the compost will become saturated and the roots
die. But you can use a bowl of water and lead the water to the pot by
means of a siphon effect. You will need as many strips of thick cloth
as there are pots needing watering. These serve as wicks. The bowl of
water must be higher than the pots - placed on a chair for example,
with the pots grouped around the bottom. Put one end of a wick well
down into the water and lead it over the edge and down to the top of
a pot where it must be buried to stay in place. Do the same for all
the other wicks and pots. Water will be soaked up the wick and travel
slowly down to the pot. This will start more quickly if the wicks are
wetted first. A washing-up bowl of water will keep a dozen pots moist
for a week at least.

Plants lose water faster in bright sun than in the cool shade, so move
items of your indoor garden away from sunny windows for the holiday
period.

A holiday during winter - say at Christmas - is a more difficult time
for indoor plants. A windowsill on a winter's night can be a very cold
place indeed, and plants should be moved to the warmest place in the
house even if the light is poor there.

FIRST AID FOR AILING HOUSE PLANTS

Promptness is the key to curing the various ailments that afflict house plant. If you recognize the symptoms soon enough, most problems will be easy to correct. Even insects are readily dealt with if you discover them before they begin to multiply and spread out of control, attacking one plant after another. Set up a regular inspection schedule. Begin with the foliage, especially the light-coloured new growth, which quickly shows signs of damage or weakness; the brown spots that come from too low a humidity level or too much heat generally start out as very tiny specks. Remember to check the undersides of the leaves where insects are most likely to congregate.

Insects are not as great a problem to plants indoors as they are outdoors, but they can be brought into the house on new plants. If insects appear on established plants, place the plants in quarantine to keep pests from spreading. Most insects can be washed off with soapy water or swabbed away with alcohol. Serious infestations require chemicals, but be careful to follow the directions on the label.

Description	What To Do
 **APHIDS** — Aphids may be green, red, pink, yellow, brown or black. They congregate on soft young tips or the undersides of leaves, and suck out a plant's juices, stunt new growth and cause foliage to die. They secrete honeydew, which becomes a host to sooty black mould.	Pick off and crush any visible aphids, then wash the plant – either dunk it upside down in warm soapy water or swab leaves with a soft soapy cloth. Rinse the foliage with clear tepid water. For serious infestations spray with insecticide.
Leaf edges turn brown, and eventually leaves die and fall off. Cause: too little humidity.	Place the pot on a bed of moist pebbles in a tray or in a larger container with moist moss peat round it or in an enclosed terrarium. Mist the leaves regularly.
Plant appears crowded; roots protrude from the drainage hole in the bottom of the pot or crop out on top of the soil. Plant wilts between waterings or produces only a few small leaves. Cause: plant is too big for its pot.	Repot the plant in a larger container. Spray with a foliar feed to encourage development of new roots in fresh compost.

Description	What To Do
WHITEFLY — Tiny sucking insects that flutter off the leaves when a plant is disturbed. The eggs laid on the undersides of leaves hatch into green larvae that feed on plant sap and do most of the damage. Green leaves turn yellow and drop. Like aphids, they deposit honeydew.	For mild cases, wash the leaves with a strong spray of tepid water, making sure to cleanse the undersides thoroughly. Treat serious attacks with insecticide.
RED SPIDER MITE — Sometimes orange-red, this tiny pest is more usually yellow-green in colour. They feed by sucking sap, causing the leaves to become mottled and pale green in colour. Spider mites live under leaves, spinning white webs that cover the plant. The plants become stunted and die.	Wash small plants at the sink with a strong spray of tepid water; large plants should be wiped with a soft soapy cloth then rinsed with tepid clear water. For serious infestations, spray with insecticide.

Description	What To Do
SCALE INSECTS — Scale insects, which congregate on the undersides of leaves along the main veins, look like oval shells about 3mm (⅛in) long, but their yellowish or greenish brown colour makes them hard to see until the infestation is severe. Scale insects also deposit honeydew.	Gently scrub the scale insects off the leaves, using warm soapy water and a small brush, then rinse. Treat severely infested plants with insecticide.
MEALY BUGS — The soft 6mm (¼in) long bodies of mealy bugs are coated with white powdery wax; they look like bits of cotton clustered under leaves and in crevices on the tops of leaves that are in shade. By sucking sap, they stunt and kill plants.	Dab with a cotton swab dipped in methylated spirits; they will die and fall off. Then wash the plant with warm soapy water and rinse it with clear water. Spray severely infested plants with insecticide.

GROSSET'S FILTERLESS

Description	What To Do
Lower leaves of most afflicted plants turn yellow, and stems become soft and dark in colour; cacti become mushy. Soil stays soggy and green scum forms on clay pots. CAUSE: too much water.	Make sure that the pot's drainage hole is not clogged and do not let the plant stand in water in its saucer for over half an hour. If the soil has become compacted, roots may decay for lack of oxygen; repot the plant. Water only if necessary. Spray with a foliar feed to hasten recovery.
Leaf edges of most afflicted plants dry and curl under, or lower leaves turn yellow with brown spots and fall; cacti and succulents become yellowed. CAUSE: too little water or too much heat.	Water until the excess runs out of the drainage hole in the bottom of the pot; thereafter water as specified for the plant. If the condition persists, move the plant to a cooler location. Spray with a foliar feed to encourage new root development.

Description	What To Do
Yellow or brown patches develop on the leaves of most afflicted plants, or leaves on one side of the plant turn brown; cacti become yellow. CAUSE: too much light; sun scorch.	Move the plant farther from the window so that it will not be subject to so much direct heat, or shield it with a curtain. If the plant is growing under incandescent lamps, move it farther from the bulbs or use lower-wattage bulbs that generate less heat.
Stems of most afflicted plants stretch towards the light source and grow very long; leaves on new stems are pale-coloured and small. On cacti, the new growth looks weak. CAUSE: too little light.	Move the plant closer to a window or to a brighter exposure to get more sunlight. If it is growing under artificial light, shift the plant nearer to the centre of the bulbs, or increase the wattage or number of bulbs used and keep them on longer.

Description	What To Do
Leaf tips turn brown, especially on ferns; leaves or stems appear to be crushed or broken. CAUSE: bruising.	For appearance's sake, use scissors to cut off the damaged sections of foliage, keeping as much of each leaf or stem intact as possible. Move the plant to a more protected location where people are less likely to brush against it.
New growth is rapid but weak and the plant wilts. A white crust of built-up salts develops on the surface of the soil or on the outside of clay pots. CAUSE: too much fertilizer.	Give the plant more light. Fertilize less frequently or at half the suggested concentration. If salts have formed, water the plant thoroughly to dissolve them; then water again in half an hour to wash the dissolved salts through the pot's drainage hole. Scrape salts off the pot's rim and sides.

Description	What To Do
Leaves fade to a pale green and lower leaves turn yellow and drop off. New leaves are small or growth stops. CAUSE: too little fertilizer.	Fertilize more often, especially during the plant's growing season.
Leaves turn yellow and fall off suddenly; the plant tissues appear glassy and translucent. CAUSE: sudden rise or fall of temperature.	Move the plant away from draughts, air conditioners or radiators. When the damage is severe, remove the plant from the pot. If the roots have rotted, discard the plant; if the roots are healthy, prune them back to keep them in balance with the surviving top growth and repot the plant.

GROSSET'S FILTERLESS

101

Bonsai

Maggie thocht I should mention bonsai - she said aboot me bein'
well-placed to 'preciate small auld things...

Bonsai
actual means
'growing in a bowl'

Growing a Bonsai Tree

It is from Japan that we have learned the art of bonsai— the way to grow a tree in miniature. In a container no larger than a soup plate a bonsai tree can live for eighty years and longer. If you could see a bonsai tree of this age it would look as gnarled and twisted as a similar tree of full size on a hillside. It looks like this because the gardener has trained it from the time it was a tiny sapling. Its roots, trunk and branches have been pruned and shaped to keep the tree miniature, but otherwise it has developed like a normal tree. Bonsai is not for someone who quickly loses interest.

A tree that can easily be trained in bonsai form is the evergreen juniper. It is naturally slow-growing, which is an advantage. A deciduous or leaf-dropping tree that can be trained is the maple. In their early years it is possible to train other trees, such as beech and oak, but more difficult to make them into really old specimens.

But you could begin with juniper or maple. A pottery bowl glazed on the outside is suitable for bonsai culture. For compost, gritty soil is better than compost from a bag. Growth must be discouraged with a low food supply. Plant the sapling and firm the soil down well. The soil should be kept just moist.

The secret of shaping the tree is to use soft wire bound in spirals around the stem and shoots just tight enough to bend them into a natural wind-blown formation. As the wood ages it will become fixed in that position and the wire can be removed before it cuts into the tissue. Only some of the shoots can be allowed to remain to make miniature branches. You must decide which ones to pinch out while they are young.

Trees other than the juniper will make leaves larger in proportion than the dwarfed stems and some of these must also be nipped out as buds to improve the proportions of the bonsai.

Not only the shoots and leaves but also the roots must be pruned to balance the growth of a bonsai tree. Once rooted into its container, it should be possible to lift out the complete ball of roots and soil. This can be done each year before new growth starts. Scrape away enough soil to expose the main roots – the thickest ones – and cut these back by about half. This encourages more fine roots to develop instead of thicker taproots. At the same time this allows you to add fresh gritty soil to replace what has been scraped away, which will have given up its goodness to the roots.

A bonsai tree must be kept cool at all times and needs good light and fresh air. In the winter all but the juniper will shed their leaves and rest. Success will depend on attention to detail and application of all you have learned about indoor gardening.

Hooseplants sometimes hae odd names:

Angel wings	Joseph's coat
Bird's nest fern	Kangaroo vine
Cartwheel plant	Lollipop plant
Elephant's ears	Madagascar
Flaming Katy	dragon tree
Flamingo flower	Mother of
Golden shrimp plant	thousands
Grecian vase plant	Piggy tail plant
	Zebra plant

A Japanese gairden is finished
when there is nothing left tae
remove, they say!

Hooseplants - some mair to try

CARE FOR YOUR HOUSE PLANTS

GREEN THUMB®

7 **Flowering Begonia** or **Wax Begonia** *Begonia semperflorens*

Probably the most common of the numerous flowering begonias, *Begonia semperflorens* will produce its red, pink, orange or white flowers almost all year long if given the right conditions.

CARE FOR YOUR HOUSE PLANTS

GREEN THUMB®

13 **Busy Lizzie** *Impatiens wallerana*

There are numerous varieties of the busy lizzie, all with a more or less similar leaf shape and fleshy, succulent stems that are fragile and need to be handled carefully. The flowers grow at the tips of the stems, from the hub around which the leaves at the stem tip radiate; they are usually red, but may also be orange, purple, pink or white, or even 'candy-striped', and can be single or double. Cuttings can be used for propagation at any time of the year.

CARE FOR YOUR HOUSE PLANTS

GREEN THUMB®

7 **Prayer Plant** or **Rabbit's Foot** *Maranta leuconeura*

The prayer plant is a delightful foliage plant with small, soft oval-shaped leaves of grass-green studded with purple-black 'eyes'. It is also known, rather endearingly, as rabbit's foot, for the black markings resemble the tracks of a rabbit. The name prayer plant is said to refer to the way that these plants raise up their leaves in the evening as the light fades.

CARE FOR YOUR HOUSE PLANTS

GREEN THUMB®

13 **Mother-in-Law's Tongue** or **Snake Plant** *Sansevieria trifasciata*

The extraordinary shape of this plant, with its dark-green sword-like leaves, striped with ripples of silvery green, standing tall and bolt-upright, is quite unlike that of any other house plant. It can grow up to 3 ft. high, although they are usually about half this height.

CARE FOR YOUR HOUSE PLANTS

25 **Indian Rubber Plant** *Ficus elastica*

The rubber plant has broad, waxy leaves have an almost perfect elliptical shape, finishing at the tip with a soft point. The shiny surface picks out the ribbed contours of the veins, curving away gently at the leaf margins. Clean the leaves regularly with a damp sponge so that the pores in the leaves do not become clogged up with dust.

103

Gairdenin' Wisdoms

with GAIRDENER BROON

❀❀❀❀❀❀❀❀❀❀❀❀❀❀❀❀❀❀❀❀❀

HI, A'BODY. Have ye had a guid week in yer gairdens? I can tell ye it's been fun and games doon my way this past few days. I've been doon at the allotment a lot ... there's a lot o' allotments there an' whit rare fun we a' have. It's grand tae get the'gither in my shed and swap gairden stories and tips and jokes, and of course on Friday nichts "The Friday Nicht Allotment Swally Club" meets up for a few drams. Man, there's nuthin' better than sittin' back in the auld chair in ma shed an' hae'in a bit o' the "craic". I can never remember what we a' get tae talk aboot, but it aye seems braw fun at the time – politics, gossip, fitba', horsie tips, the price o' mince. You name it, we talk aboot it.

I'd gone doon tae the shed early on Friday as the place needed a wee bit o' a Spring clean and a wee lick o' pent. I got the pentin' overalls on an' looked oot a big pent brush, and then I discovered I'd nae pent. Luckily Willie McLeod, wha's got the shed in the next allotment, had a big tin o' red pent he was willing tae sell me. It was nae lang efter I'd gied him the money and he'd skived aff tae "The Volunteer Arms" that I found out it wisnae pent at a' ... it was a big jar o' beetroot. Ach, I decided it was better than nothing and used it onyway. A rare job it was actually, nice and bright. I'd near finished the roof pentin', when I slipped and fell aff intae the compost heap. It was Annie Lennox, bless her, that found me, ma white overalls covered in red beetroot juice and half the compost heap doon ma back. Of coorse she thought it was blood and thought by the smell o' the compost that I'd had a wee "accident" in ma overalls fae fallin' aff the roof. Once she realised I was okay, she jist stuck the gairden hose up ma trooser legs and turned the cauld water on full blast. Such a wee treasure is oor Annie!

Unfortunately the hose washed the beetroot juice "woodstain" aff the shed and I had tae start a' ower again. Raspberry juice I used this time. I jist trampled a few pund o' rasps in a bucket and pented it a' ower. The berry juice mak's rare dye and a'thing micht hae been okay if it hadna been for the thoosands and thoosands o' wasps and bees and horny gollachs and flies and goodness-knows-what that got stuck in aboot the berries. The shed was literally moving. So it had tae get washed aff tae.

Annie bocht me the real stuff and that should have been the end o' the story, but no, no' me. I had pented the hale jing-bang wi' the wood varnish nearly when I realised I'd pented masel' intae a the tap corner o' the shed roof and couldna get doon withoot standin' on the wet varnish. I was trapped.

Well, Willie McLeod and the rest o' ma pals had gatherd for the swally alo' me, so I thocht it wid be the simplest matter tae shout for help. However, near a'body fae the allotments is as deaf as me. I was hingin' on tae the shed lum and shouted "HELP" at the tap o' ma voice. Oot comes Willie alo' and wi' his hand cupped tae his ear an' what relief I felt, and muttered, "It's YERSELF, WILLIE!" Does he see me? Does he h***! Next thing I hear's his voice driftin' up the lum past ma ear 'ole ... "Broon's playin' silly beggars. I canna see him but I'm sure he shouted HELP ... YERSELF, WILLIE so we'll dae jist that. Now, whaur does the auld rogue keep his best sherry? Here we go, sherry, a'body?"

Needless tae say by the time the varnish had dried, a' the Friday Nicht bottles were dry as well. I near hit the roof – well, I didna actually HIT the roof, that's jist an expression – but I dinna ken best how tae nicely word kickin' Willie richt up the dowp wi' ma tacketty boots, but ye'll get my drift.

'til next week then
Cheers,

Gairdener
Broon
x

Insects in yer Gairden

There are hunners o' different insects in yer gairden - some guid an' some bad. Here's a bit aboot some of the insects ye micht meet. For how tae deal wi' the anes ye dinnae want, look at page 118.

Bees

Auchentogle honey made by bees fae the heather floo'ers on the muirs is ma favoorite thing aboot bees. But there is mair tae bees than honey - some call them "Nature's housekeepers" - let anither Broon ~~tell ye~~ mair, one Mike Broon, Heid o' the National Bee Unit "They are the fabric of life. Everything is interconnected - plants, flowers, bees and pollination. We rely on the bees to be healthy to pollinate the plants so that we have food to eat".

A Bee Visiting a Flower

I ha' this auld book callt 'The Insect World' - they dinnae write like this onymore.

THE HONEY BEE

Bees have long been the little friends of man, and particularly of children who have a sweet tooth, although the honey we take from them is not gathered for our benefit, but is their wise provision for their own needs in a time of scarcity. This honey is the nectar of flowers which is gathered by the bee by means of a slender trunk, something like an elephant's in miniature, which darts into the chalice of the blossom and coiling up, conveys the sweet syrup to its mouth, and from thence it enters a sort of first stomach, called a honey-sac. Here the nectar undergoes a mysterious change, and turns into honey. Every respectable Bee has only one notion, and that is the good of the hive; its own personal desires and feelings, if it has any, do not in the least matter; its whole existence is spent for the welfare of others. The little honey Bee sets us all an example of unquestioning attention to duty without hope of reward. Of course, it takes all sorts to make a world, and sometimes a Bee will take to evil courses, and turn freebooter, robbing honest Bees of the burden they are so unselfishly carrying home to the hive and eating it all up, there and then.

Although they have their faults sometimes, like the rest of us, we can regard Bees as shining examples of hard-working unselfishness, and one cannot but wonder at and admire the perfection of their laws which are made for the welfare of the whole community, and if some poor creatures are martyrs for this great cause, they seem to make the sacrifice most willingly and cheerfully.

A' the honey a bee gathers disnae sweeten its sting.

Ower quarter o' a million floo'ers are needed tae mak' 1lb. o' honey.

Butterflies

Butterflies mak' a summer's day in the gairden - a pity that some caterpillars eat ma veg. It's a bit cool in Scotland for many butterflies, so there are only around 30 different types o' butterflies but many mair types o' moth.

Shrubs to encourage bees

Berberis	Lilac
Broom	Potentiila
Buddleia	Skimmia
Cotoneaster	Spiraea
Daphne	Sumach
Escallonia	Viburnum
Fuchsia	Weigela
Gorse	

Puss Moth
(Cerura Vinula)
Caterpillars June–August
Moths hatch May–June
wingspan 2⅜"–3"

```
WATCH OUT FOR CATERPILLARS!

We gardeners tend to think that caterpillars will eat all our veg, but
many actually eat nettles, bless them. Still, you still need to watch
out for the caterpillars of the Small and Large White butterflies, for
they do cause real problems for any brassica.

FOOD PLANTS FOR CATERPILLARS

Red Admiral: stinging nettles
Small Tortoiseshell: stinging nettles
Painted Lady: stinging nettles, thistles
Large White: nasturtiums, cabbage family
Small White: nasturtiums, cabbage family
Peacock: stinging nettles
Orange-tip: Lady's smock, Honesty
Green Veined White Arabis, Garlic mustard
```

Naturalists, in their hard, unromantic way, call Butterflies and Moths "Lepidoptera" (which means "scale-winged"), because their wings differ from those of other insects in that they are covered on both sides with overlapping scales arranged like the tiles on a roof of a house. It takes a storm to blow the tiles off a roof, unless the jerry-builder has been at work; but the delicate scales of a butterfly rub off with the lightest touch leaving a surface, thin and transparent, like the wing of a Bee. So it is easy to see that the beautiful colouring and velvety appearance are entirely due to the scales.

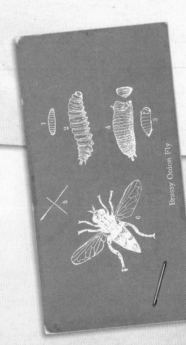

Brassy Onion Fly

106

A selection of plants to encourage butterflies

Bluebells	Lavender
Buddleia	Lilac
Catmint	Marjoram
Cornflower	Michaelmas daisy
French marigold	Phlox
Giant hyssop	Primrose
Heather	Privet
Hebe	Thyme
Honesty	Violet
Honeysuckle	Wallflower

Ye dinna want these craturs in yer gairden:

Ants
Aphids - woolly aphids, black fly, green fly
Caterpillars (kail wirms, grannie wirms)
Cuckoo spit (frog hopper)
Earwigs (hornie-gollach, forkie-tail)
Horseflies (degs)
Leather jackets
Mealy bugs
Midgies!!
Millipedes
Wasps
White fly
Wireworms
Woodlice (slaters)

CATERPILLAR AND CHRYSALIS OF LARGE CABBAGE BUTTERFLY.

If ye see ants on a plant, ye've maist likely got aphids there, for aphids suck sap fae leaves an' then drap a sweet liquid callt "honey-dew" on the plant, which ants love tae eat.

Craneflies or Daddy-long-legs

1, Eggs.   2, Maggot.   3, Pupa-case.
4, Female.

These craturs are guid tae hae i' the gairden:

Bumble bees - they pollinate plants an' rarely sting

Centipedes - they eat vine weevils an' ither insects

Dragon fly (deil's darni()' needle) - their larvae eat midgies!

Earthworms - good for the soil

Ground beetles (clocks) - they eat insect larvae an' slugs

Hoverflies - larvae feed on aphids

Ladybirds (clock leddies, leddy landers)- their larvae eat greenfly an' ither aphids

Ladybirds

Lawn tips

Don't become obsessed with watering your lawn. If you do it will look good for a week or so and then you will have to do it again. If you consider that no lawn has died in Britain for lack of water – indeed grass can survive for up to eight moths without water – it is best not even to start watering. Save your time and save water as well. You can feel virtuous.

The majority of garden chemicals used in Britain are intended to 'improve' lawns. You can spend a lot of time and money trying to produce an immaculate lawn, fit for a bowls championship – but why not rest a little and follow a more organic route. Set the blades on the mower a little higher and leave off the grass box. The cut grass will be used by insects in the lawn and increase its fertility, the grass will look greener and it will feel wonderful to walk across the lawn, gently sinking into the grass. You will also know that your lawn has become a much more varied ecosystem, supporting a wealth of insects – and the animals the feed off them.

A well made and properly kept lawn is always one of the most important features in connection with any garden, especially that surrounding a residence. Where it is improperly levelled and made in the first instance, the defects in the surface caused by holes, or subsidence of the soil in one place more than another, cannot be satisfactorily remedied. The form and extent of the lawn, will, of course, vary in almost every case; the more it covers, the better will be the effect produced, if the work has been well done; and on the other hand, the more prominently will any inequalities be seen. The keeping of lawns, when once established, is work of a routine character, consisting chiefly of mowing, rolling, and sweeping. All of these operations require frequent attention, particularly in the Spring and Summer

In Shank's *Patent Lawn Mower*, manufactured by Alex. Shanks and Son, the sole plate, or ledger blade, has a double reversible edge, and is thus enabled to last longer than most others. This machine is especially recommended in the size worked by a horse, as it is strong in construction, and has a good delivery of grass into the box, and an admirable system of emptying the latter when full.

Ye can weed yer lawn, or jist say it's a gairden

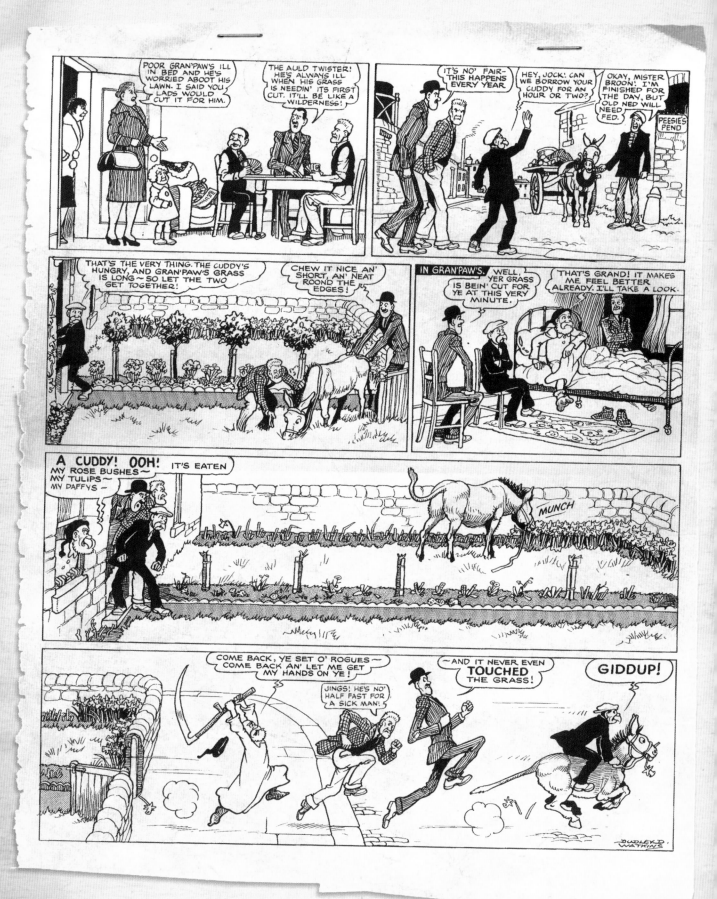

109

Medicinal Plants

Maggie and Daphne tell me ye can grow some plants that can be used tae mak' herbal remedies. I ken that heather tea can calm ye doon, but I like ma medicine tae be a bit stronger!! A'way nettle soup helps the immune system, so try Maw's recipe, aye, an' nettle tea is a painkiller.

Here are a few plant ye can grow and use easily. There are plenty of ither plants, but they're a bit o' bother tae use – tae make evening primrose oil you would need the seeds fae thoosands o' plants an' the allotment wouldna be big enough. There are loads o' books and stuff on the internet on how tae use the plants. I liked ane callt "How tae grow yer own drugs" – an' it's aw proper an' legal.

Onyway, here are some plants that ye can grow at hame – an' many o' them can be grown in pots. Ye can mak' these anes intae relaxin' and soothin' teas, usin' fresh leaves an floo'ers.

lavender	pot marigold (Calendula)	St John's wort (but dinnae tak' if ye are on any pills wi'out checking first wi' yer doctor)
lemon balm		
lemon verbena	rosemary (e'en helps the memory, so they say)	
nasturtium (an' ye can eat the floo'ers an' leaves in a salad)		viola
	sage (but no if ye're pregnant)	camomile (use dried floo'ers)
peppermint		

Ye can grow Aloe vera – the colourless liquid fae the middle of a leaf helps soothe the skin (not the yella stuff from the edge of leaves which used tae be used tae mak' people vomit).

In the gairden and the wild there are ither plants that ye can use once ye've found oot a bit mair aboot them:

cone flowers (Echinacea), elder flowers and berries, rosehips, raspberry leaves, burdock, sticky willy (cleavers), dandelions, chickweed, meadowsweet, nettles and plantain

Jist remember, though, tae tak' medical advice a'fore using any remedy regularly or if ye are already receiving treatment – jist cos it's natural disnae mean it cannae harm ye.

What aboot some grand mushrooms?

Mushrooms

Mushrooms have been cultivated for centuries, traditionally being grown in horse manure and in cellars. Supermarket shelves now stock a range of shapes, colours and sizes of mushrooms. There is the familiar white button mushroom as well as packages of strange, exotic — and expensive — mushrooms. Such mushrooms can be grown at home from kits, available from garden centres and by mail order.

There are two types of kits; one for mushrooms (e.g. white button mushrooms) which grow on the ground, the other for mushrooms (e.g. oyster and shiitake mushrooms and the curious 'lion's mane' mushrooms) which grow on trees.

CULTIVATION INSTRUCTIONS FOR TREE-GROWING MUSHROOMS

Kits consists of spawn-impregnated wooden plugs designed to be inserted into a recently felled (ideally within the previous 3 weeks) deciduous (not laburnum) log. A tree stump could be used instead of a log. If this is done, the mushroom spawn may well benefit the garden by deterring the growth of honey fungus and accelerating decomposition of the stump.

- Drill holes (the size of a plug) in the log, approximately 6 in. apart.

- Gently hammer a plug into each hole.

- Wrap log in plastic and place in a dark moist place at a temperature of 50-77 °F (10-25 °C).

- After a few months, the surface of the log should appear dusted white.

- Remove the plastic wrapping and place outside, sheltered from sun and wind.

- A crop of mushrooms should grow on surface of log.

INSTRUCTIONS FOR GROUND-GROWING MUSHROOMS

Kits consist of a container of compost containing mushroom spawn (equivalent to seed). Best results will be obtained if it is used shortly after purchase.

- Water the compost well.

- Position the container in a place where ventilation is good and the temperature will remain between 50–65 °F (10–18 °C). There is actually no need to keep the container in the dark, but neither do you have to keep it in the light.

- Keep the compost moist but not wet; spray it with water if it seems dry.

- Button mushrooms should appear in four to six weeks. These will grow into larger, flat mushrooms if left for a more few days.

- Harvest the mushrooms by twisting upwards; do not cut. Try not to disturb the surface of the compost.

- One or two further crops should appear over the following weeks.

AN ENCYCLOPÆDIA OF HORTICULTURE.

FIG. 41. AGARICUS MUSCARIUS (FLY AGARIC).

FIG. 43. AGARICUS PROCERUS (PARASOL MUSHROOM).

FIG. 42. AGARICUS GAMBOSUS (ST. GEORGE'S MUSHROOM).

FIG. 44. AGARICUS CAMPESTRIS.

I've heard fowk at The Volunteer Arms talking aboot the mushroom management style at work – keep a'body in the dark an' keep pilin' on the sh***!

Mushrooms

Autumn Tasks

Warm autumn days are the time to begin planting shrubs, herbaceous plants and bulbs. For roots to become quickly established, the soil must be warm and moist.

Grass and weeds will carry on growing despite the leaves falling from the trees. Carry on with regular routine maintenance for as long as it is required; in milder areas, the grass may still need mowing as December approaches.

There is a lot of pruning to be done, and gardens surrounded by deciduous trees will become covered by falling leaves.

By the time Christmas arrives, the garden should have been put to bed for the winter – neat and tidy with tender plants protected against sharp frosts and cold winds.

EARLY AUTUMN

GENERAL MAINTENANCE
- Continue weeding
- Tidy up leaves as they begin to fall

LAWNS
- Mow until end of growing season when grass is dry
- Aerate by spiking and top-dress with sharp sand if soil is heavy
- Re-seed worn patches

MID-AUTUMN

GENERAL MAINTENANCE
- Cover ponds with netting to catch leaves
- Sweep up fallen leaves and save for compost

LAWNS
- Aerate and scarify
- Lay new turves if desired

SHRUBS
- Plant trees, shrubs and climbers in well-prepared ground
- Take hardwood cuttings
- Propagate by layering daphne, fothergilla, witch hazel, etc.

FLOWERS
- Plant autumn-flowering to early spring-flowering herbaceous plants (e.g. Christmas rose, golden rod, pinks, polyanthus, rudbeckia, violas, wallflowers)
- Continue planting bulbs (e.g. anemones, bluebells, crocosmia, crocus, cyclamen, daffodils, fritillary, glory of the snow, hyacinths, kaffir lily, narcissus, nerine, scilla, tulip)
- Sow alpines in a cold frame
- Complete sowing hardy annuals
- Divide and replant overcrowded perennials after flowering
- Lift and store gladioli corms and dahlia tubers

LATE AUTUMN

GENERAL MAINTENANCE
- Complete autumn digging
- Condition the soil if necessary

LAWNS
- Rake off leaves
- Aerate

SHRUBS
- Continue to plant trees and shrubs if weather remains mild; protect less robust species with windbreaks
- Complete hardwood cuttings of aucuba, holly, ivy, laurel, poplar, etc., and put in a cold frame

FLOWERS
- Complete planting perennials
- Continue tidying and cutting back herbaceous flowers
- Remove bedding plants as they fade
- Store (in frost-free place or take indoors or into greenhouse) woodier plants (e.g. fuchsias, geraniums)
- Prune climbing roses
- Complete cuttings

Season of mists an' mellow fruitfulness

SHRUBS
- Main planting season begins
- Take cuttings of hardy shrubs
- Remove dead wood and prune summer-flowering shrubs
- Water newly planted shrubs
- Secure plants against wind damage

FLOWERS
- Plant spring-flowering bulbs (e.g. daffodils, narcissi) in succession
- Plant indoor bulbs (e.g. hyacinths) in pots
- Transplant perennials and biennials sown earlier (e.g. wallflowers)
- Sow hardy annuals
- Cut down perennials after flowering

ROSES
- Continue to dead-head
- Spray regularly against pests and diseases
- Prune climbers and ramblers

VEGETABLES
- Harvest root vegetables
- Plant winter crops (e.g. winter lettuce, spring cabbage) under cloches
- Sow carrots under cloches

FRUIT
- Harvest blackberries as they ripen, then prune and train young growth
- Pick peaches, nectarines, plums and damsons, then prune
- Complete summer pruning of apples and pears
- Check ties and supports
- Plan for new planting later in the season

ROSES
- Prepare new beds for planting
- Take cuttings of floribundas and ramblers

VEGETABLES
- Continue to plant winter crops (spring cabbage, winter lettuce, etc.) under cloches
- Watch out for slug damage to winter vegetables and hoe around them regularly
- Earth up leeks and celery

FRUIT
- Begin planting fruit trees and bushes
- Prune branches that have fruited on gooseberries and summer fruiting raspberry canes
- Continue to pick apples and pears
- Spray peaches against leaf curl

VEGETABLES
- Pick Brussels sprouts and leeks
- Sow broad beans for an early crop
- Cultivate soil after cropping

FRUIT
- Plant all fruit trees and bushes (e.g. apple, blackberry, blackcurrant, cherry, damson, gooseberry, loganberry, nectarine, peach, pear, plum, raspberry, redcurrant, strawberry, vine)
- Prune apples, pears, blackberries and loganberries
- Mulch young trees

Mustard and Cress

Two of the easiest plants to grow at home are mustard and cress. They grow quickly, and the seeds do not need to be planted in soil.

The little plants are ready to cut and eat when only a few days old. The mustard is hot to taste and cress has a mild flavour.

As cress grows faster than mustard, the mustard seed should be sown three days before the cress.

Both kinds of seed can be bought in packets.

1. There is no need for pots and soil, so saucers or food containers made of foil can be used.

   Instead of soil use several thicknesses of kitchen paper or a thin piece of spongy plastic in the bottom of each saucer or tray. This must be soaked with water before the seeds are sown.

2. Shake the mustard seeds gently all over the kitchen paper or plastic. They need to be close together but not touching, and you probably will not need all of the packet. With your fingertip move some of the seeds to spread them evenly.

3. There is no need to do anything more with the mustard except to keep it near a window and make sure the bottom of the saucer does not dry out. In three days the seeds may begin to split.

4. Three days after sowing the mustard, sow the cress in the same way, keeping it equally moist.

5. Then just watch both saucers of seedlings race upwards until they are about 2 in. tall. They should then unfold a tiny pair of leaves.

6. They are now ready to be cut and eaten. Do this with a pair of scissors, and cut each tray of seedlings close to the base of their white stems.

Mustard and cress can be grown in this way at any time of the year. And once you have harvested one sowing, a second crop can be started – but on new material – if you have surplus seeds.

Because the seedlings need to be grown for only a few days – and grown fast – it is not important to keep them close to a window. In fact, mustard and cress will grow in the dark. Try it with a few seeds and compare the difference in growth. Those in the dark grow taller because they are searching for light.

Growing mustard and cress

1 lay blotting paper or spongy plastic in a saucer - add water until soaked

2 sprinkle seed thickly - mustard first, cress three days later, as it soon catches up

3 watch the seeds germinate and push out two tiny leaves, then the stems will grow fast

4 when the mustard and cress are equally tall and the seedling leaves are wide open, you can cut them to eat

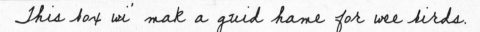

This box wi' mak a quid hame for wee birds.

GROSSET'S FILTERLESS

1. Cut out the following parts, using the dimensions given on the plans.
The Base. A 5 in. x 3 in. rectangle of 3/8 in. exterior grade ply.
Two sides. 5 in. x 2½ in. cut from 3/16 in. sheet balsa.
Two ends. Marked out as shown and cut from 3/8 in. exterior grade ply.
Two roof panels. 5 in. x 3 in. from hardboard.

2. Drill two holes 2 in. apart and 3/16 in. in from the edge at each of the 3 in. long edges of the base, as shown.

3. Use six ¾ in. brass woodscrews to fasten the two ends to the base.

4. Use balsa cement to fasten the two side pieces in place to the ends only (not the base).

5. File the edges of the roof pieces to an angle so that they will fit neatly and use balsa cement to fasten the roof in place.

6. Drill a ¼ in. diameter hole in each end about ½ in. below the circular opening and insert an 8 in. length of ¼ in. dowel to form a perch. Leave 1½ in. of dowel sticking out each end and hold the dowel in place with a dab of balsa cement.

7. The nesting box is best mounted on a stake, just like that used for the bird table. The house can be detached from the base by simply unscrewing the four screws holding the ends. Drill a hole in the centre of the base and fasten to the end of a stake with a 1 in. long brass woodscrew. Then fasten the house back with the four screws.

8. Making the house detachable means that it can easily be cleaned out from time to time.

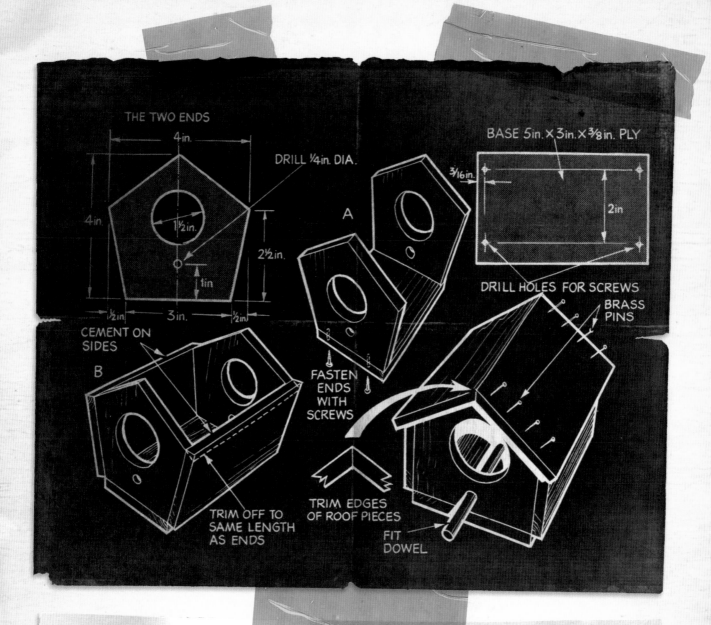

THE TWO ENDS

4 in.

4 in.

DRILL ¼ in. DIA.

1½ in.

2½ in.

1 in.

½ in.   3 in.   ½ in.

CEMENT ON SIDES

A

B

FASTEN ENDS WITH SCREWS

TRIM OFF TO SAME LENGTH AS ENDS

TRIM EDGES OF ROOF PIECES

FIT DOWEL

BASE 5 in. × 3 in. × ⅜ in. PLY

3/16 in.

2 in.

DRILL HOLES FOR SCREWS

BRASS PINS

USING THE NESTING BOX

1. To attract birds, partly fill the inside of the house with straw or dried grass.

2. Try putting the box in different parts to the garden to find a position where birds will adopt it. It is most important that it is not near bushes or any place where a cat could get to the nesting box.

3. The circular cut outs in each end are for the birds to enter and leave the house. You can peep through these from time to time to see if the birds have made a nest.

4. Make a note of the date when the house was first occupied. There will be plenty of false alarms before a pair of birds finally settled in. Keep a record of when the first eggs were laid; when the eggs hatched out, and other happenings in and around the nesting box.

Pests an' Diseases

The Allotment fowk tellt me this is no' aboot human pests but things that can kill yer plants. The treatments were different in Thompson's days.

COMMON PESTS AND DISEASES

Some say that there is a never-ending battle between the gardener and the pests and diseases that want to destroy our plants. There are lots of ways of tackling them, but in recent years many chemicals have been banned, so much more ingenuity is now needed to tackle a number of determined plant infestations.

ANTS

SYMPTOMS
Ants do little direct damage, but they often build nests among the roots of plants. This may make a plant more susceptible to drought.
TREATMENT
Plant lavender, marigolds or chives which ants dislike.
To protect fruit trees, crush some lupin blooms and rub the juice around the base of the tree trunks.
Ants don't like walking over chalk or pepper (especially Cayenne pepper) so sprinkle around plants that ants are attacking.
You can also dust nest with ant killer.

APHIDS

SYMPTOMS
Small oval, usually wingless, insects of various colours (e.g. blackfly, greenfly) massed on the leaves. Leaves often distorted and curled.
TREATMENT
Reduce aphid infestation naturally by encouraging ladybirds, lacewings and hoverflies into the garden by planting suitable flowers.

Also nasturtiums will deter woolly aphids from apple trees, and generally lavender, sage and thyme will deter aphids.
Plant garlic among rose bushes to deter aphids.
Use systemic insecticide at first sign of infestation, and repeat as necessary.

APPLE CANKER

SYMPTOMS
Elliptical cankers on branches, caused by a fungus that eats into the wood, eventually stopping the sap flowing and so killing the branch.
TREATMENT
Cut out infected young growth.
On large branches, cut back and apply a canker paint over the cut to help it heal.

BLIGHT

SYMPTOMS
Brown blotches on leaf indicating fungal growth.
It is most common in warm, humid weather on potatoes, where it passes down into the tubers, causing decay in the crop, and in tomatoes, causing the fruit to go rotten.
TREATMENT
Spray plant with copper fungicide at 14-day intervals.

BLOTCH

SYMPTOMS
Black blotches on flowers.
TREATMENT
Remove affected parts and spray with copper fungicide.

BOTRYTIS (GREY MOULD)

SYMPTOMS

Grey, fluffy mould appears, then the plant rots.

It attacks a wide range of plants, from strawberries and lettuces to sunflowers and pelargoniums. It is most active in damp cool atmospheres.

TREATMENT

Promptly remove affected parts and destroy them. Ensure that there is a good circulation of air. There are now no approved fungicides for the home gardener to use to tackle botrytis.

CABBAGE ROOT FLY MAGGOT

SYMPTOMS

White maggots feeding on roots and stem bases of all brassicas, including kail and turnips.

Leaves turn bluish and the plant dies.

TREATMENT

There are now no approved insecticides for the home gardener to use.

For stemmed brassicas, protect the base of the stem with a card barrier (purchased from a garden centre - or made, for example, from carpet underlay).

For turnips and swedes, grow the plants under garden fleece.

To help protect your plants, regularly earth them up, and ensure the ground is well dug in the autumn.

CANE SPOT

SYMPTOMS

Small, circular purplish fungal spots on raspberry canes, growing to oval white blotches.

TREATMENT

Cut out and burn badly affected canes.

Spraying with a copper fungicide may help. Follow the recommendations on the fungicide.

Plant new raspberries elsewhere in the garden.

Do not plant strawberries where the raspberries were, as their roots will be affected.

CAPSID BUGS

SYMPTOMS

Distorted fruit, flowers and leaves, with small puncture holes.

They attack a wide range of plants.

TREATMENT

Spray fruit trees and bushes with systemic insecticide after flowering. Spray ornamentals at first sign of infestation.

Vegetables normally tolerate capsid attack.

Clear garden rubbish.

CARROT FLY

SYMPTOMS

White maggots tunnel into roots and leaves turn yellow or red.

TREATMENT

To reduce risk, choose seeds that offer some protection. Sow thinly in late May and do not thin out the plants. Harvest before late August.

There are now no approved insecticides for the home gardener to use.

Grow under fleece or use 2-ft. high sheets of clear plastic to protect the rows.

Plant carrots in a different place next year.

CATERPILLARS

SYMPTOMS

Holes eaten in leaves, stems and roots of plants. Many different caterpillar varieties (the larval form of a range of butterflies and moths) can cause problems. In the vegetable garden, brassicas (cabbages, broccoli, etc.) can be particularly affected.

TREATMENT

Some people may wish to endure the damage inflicted by caterpillars to preserve the butterfly. Regularly inspect your plants and remove caterpillars by hand.

Infestations can be controlled biologically using a pathogenic nematode from a specialist supplier.

Otherwise, use a contact insecticide containing pyrethrins.

CHAFER BEETLE GRUBS

SYMPTOMS

Yellow-brown patches on lawn during dry spells in summer.

TREATMENT

Infestations can be controlled biologically using a pathogenic nematode from a specialist supplier.

Otherwise apply a pesticide containing imidacloprid once during the summer months.

CODLING MOTH

SYMPTOMS

Pale pink caterpillars tunnel into ripening apples and pears. They emerge leaving an exit hole.

TREATMENT

Infestations can be controlled biologically using a pathogenic nematode from a specialist supplier.

No specific insecticide is currently available for domestic use.

CORAL SPOT

SYMPTOMS
Die-back of shoots and branches; appearance of pink spots.

TREATMENT
Cut affected shoots back to well below affected area and burn the waste. Paint larger wounds with protective paint. Avoid pruning in damp weather when risk of infection is greater.

CUTWORM

SYMPTOMS
Plants chewed off near ground; root crops burrowed.

TREATMENT
Protect young plants with card collars, pushed a few inches into the soil. Spray plants and surrounding soil with a solution of chilli or garlic, or with water in which dead cutworms have been crushed.

EARWIGS

SYMPTOMS
Holes in leaves and petals of young flowers such as dahlias, clematis and chrysanthemums.

TREATMENT
Earwigs can be trapped in upturned, straw-filled flowerpots. Keeping the garden clear of rubbish reduces the chances of earwig attack.

EELWORMS

SYMPTOMS
Discoloured stems, bulbs and tubers of herbaceous plants, also potatoes and narcissi. Leaves turn yellow and die.

TREATMENT
Difficult to deal with; there are now no approved insecticides for the home gardener to use. Destroy affected plants and leave area fallow for at least three years.

FIREBLIGHT

SYMPTOMS
Leaves of apple and pear (ornamental and edible), cotoneaster, pyracantha and whitebeam turn brown and wilt; cankers develop at base of shoots.

TREATMENT
If the affected plant is small it should be dug up and destroyed. Otherwise, prune out both all infected wood (such wood is stained brown) and several inches of healthy wood below the infected area, applying a suitable garden disinfectant to tools between cuts. Outbreaks of fireblight in Northern Ireland, the Republic of Ireland, the Isle of Man and the Channel Islands must be reported to the authorities; this is no longer necessary in mainland Britain.

GREENFLY see APHIDS

HONEY FUNGUS

SYMPTOMS
Honey-coloured toadstools around the root area of trees and shrubs, with a rim on the stems just below the gills.

TREATMENT
There are no approved fungicides for the home gardener to use. Remove dead and dying plants with as much of their roots as possible, and change the soil. Replant with species which have some resistance to honey fungus - such as clematis, hebe, kerria, lavender, pieris and oak.

LEAF SPOT

SYMPTOMS
Dark spots on the leaves of hellebores and primulas.

TREATMENT
There are no approved fungicides for the home gardener to use specifically for leaf spot, although products containing myclobutanil and penconazole may be effective, as may organic products containing plant and fish oils. Remove and destroy affected leaves.

LEATHER JACKETS

SYMPTOMS
Roots eaten just below surface of the lawn, leaving yellow patches in summer (earlier following mild winters). Small vegetable and flower seedlings also affected.

TREATMENT
Water in late summer or early autumn with pesticide containing imidacloprid. Cultivate soil, where possible, to reduce infestation.

MEALY BUGS

SYMPTOMS
Colonies of white bugs covered in waxy wool around buds of plants in the house, greenhouse or conservatory.

TREATMENT
Ladybirds or parasitic wasps could be introduced to feed on mealy bugs. Alternatively, spray plants with a systemic insecticide containing imidacloprid, thiacloprid or acetamiprid, but check label if using on edible plants. Organic pesticides are also available.

You cannae mix paraffin and water, but if you mix equal amounts o' milk and paraffin, the water will blend in. It mak's a grand insecticide in the garden.

MILDEW

SYMPTOMS
White powdery patches on leaves, stems and buds of many garden plants.

TREATMENT
Thin out foliage to improve air flow around plants. Remove and destroy any infected parts.

Spray with systemic fungicide such as myclobutanil or penconazole, checking the label to determine which is appropriate for the particular plant. Sulphur is also used on some plants.

RED SPIDER MITE

SYMPTOMS
Leaves of a range of plants in the house, greenhouse or conservatory (sometimes also in the garden in hot dry weather) turn bronze and die.

TREATMENT
Introduce Phytoseilus persimilis, the red spider mite predator, for greenhouse plants. Otherwise, spray ornamental plants with a systemic insecticide containing either acetamiprid or thiamethoxam and abamectin. Other products are available for edible plants.

RUST

SYMPTOMS
Rust-coloured blemishes on leaves, stems and tubers of a range of garden plants.

TREATMENT
There are no approved fungicides for the home gardener to use for rust, but products containing myclobutanil may be effective.

GOOSEBERRY SAWFLIES

SYMPTOMS
Gooseberry leaves reduced to a skeleton by greeny-blue caterpillars.

TREATMENT
Spray young larvae with an insecticide containing thiacloprid or pyrethrins.

SCAB

SYMPTOMS
Dark scabs on fruit and leaves of apples and pears.

TREATMENT
Spray with systemic pesticide containing mancozeb or myclobutanil at green bud, white-pink bud and petal-fall stages. Remove affected wood when pruning. Remove fallen leaves from around the tree to prevent re-infection.

SCALE INSECTS

SYMPTOMS
Brown scales on underside of leaves and along stems of a range of ornamental plants and fruit trees. Indoor plants can also be affected.

TREATMENT
Systemic insecticides containing imidacloprid or thiacloprid can be used on ornamental plants (thiacloprid can be used on some fruits, but check the label). Use a winter wash containing plant oils on woody fruit trees and roses in mild dry winter weather.

VINE WEEVILS

SYMPTOMS
Leaf margins of herbaceous plants eaten by adults in scalloped pattern in summer; plants die in autumn if roots attacked by grubs.

TREATMENT
Shake off or remove adult weevils. Encourage wildlife (birds, frogs, toads, etc.) which feed on weevils. Infestations can be controlled biologically using a pathogenic nematode from a specialist supplier. Ornamental plants in containers can be treated with insecticides containing acetamiprid or thiocloprid.

WHITEFLY

SYMPTOMS
Tiny white insects beneath leaves of vegetable and ornamental plants in the greenhouse, conservatory or house. They fly up in clouds when disturbed.

TREATMENT
In greenhouse, introduce the wasp Encarsia formosa; otherwise spray frequently with insecticide containing fatty acids, plant extracts or plant oils at first sign of infestation.

A systemic insecticide containing imidacloprid, thiacloprid, acetamiprid or thiamethoxam may also be suitable, but check the label before buying.

Making a Picnic Table
— by Paw Broon

We use the picnic table at the But an' Ben a lot in the summer - jist mak sure that twa people dinna sit on the same side at the same time, else it micht tip over.

The basic construction of this table is very simple, but there is quite a lot of cutting and trimming of wool lengths. The angled ends of the legs must be cut accurately, for instance, if the table is to stand level. Fig. 1 shows all the wood you need.

1. If you buy finished planed wood for this job, cut the wood to length and then making the table is a simple job of assembly only. All the wood should be cedar (expensive) or pine, which you can get from you local DIY store.

1. Start by assembling the table top. Take three planks, each 4 ft x 5 in. x 1 in. Lay them flat on the ground with about a ¼ in. gap between them.

2. Mark 6 in. from each end, on each side, and connect these marks with pencil lines. This gives the position for two 20 in. x 3 in. x 1½ in. cross pieces which are screwed in place, as shown in Fig. 1 (which is a plan for a table, but the top is the same for the picnic table) using 2¼ in. woodscrews. Drill holes first in the cross pieces to take the screws. This will make the job a lot easier. Remember to make sure that there is a ¼ in. gap between each plank for drainage.

3. Mark out and cut the four legs to the exact dimensions shown in Fig. 2A.

4. Lay all four legs on top of each other to check that they are all exactly the same length and cut at the same angle.

5. Screw the legs in position on the outside edges at each end of the cross pieces on the underside of the table top.

6. Turn the table upright and stand it on a level surface to make sure the legs are true.

7. Take two further planks, 4 ft x 5 in. x 1 in., to be the two bench beams. Fasten one beam across each pair of legs, secured with a single screw to each leg. Lay the planks for the bench tops in place to see if they sit level. This is to check that the two bench beams are parallel. If they are a bit out of line, remove one screw holding the beam, adjust the position of the beam and screw back the beam, using a slightly different hole position.

8. Drill two 3/8 in. diameter holes above and below each screw position on the bench beams. Fit 3/8 in. coach bolts in these holes. Fit a washer between the nut and the inside of the leg, and tighten up the nuts hard.

9. Turn the table upside down and fit the two angle braces cut and trimmed to fit as shown in Fig 2C. Fasten the braces in position with screws.

10. Turn the table the right way up. The last job is to fit the bench planks, 4 ft x 5 in. x 1 in., using two planks on each side. Fit these planks with screws. The holes for these screws must be countersunk so that the screw heads are below the surface of the wood when tightened up.

11. Use a wood preservative or paint of your choice to protect and enhance the look of the table. Follow the instructions given with the treatment you select.

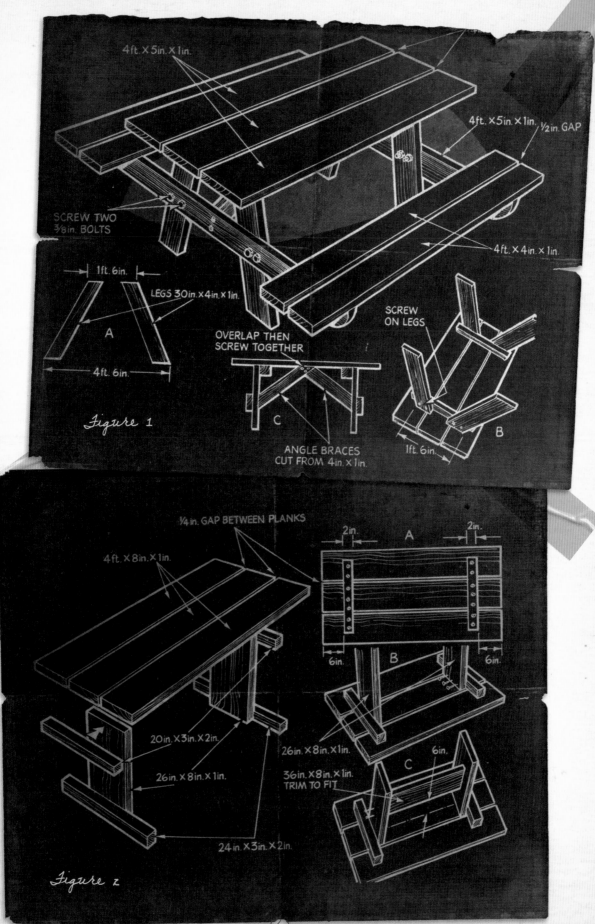

4ft. × 5in. × 1in.

4ft. × 5in. × 1in. ½in. GAP

SCREW TWO
⅜in. BOLTS

4ft. × 4in. × 1in.

1ft. 6in.

LEGS 30in. × 4in. × 1in.

A

4ft. 6in.

OVERLAP THEN
SCREW TOGETHER

C

SCREW
ON LEGS

B

1ft. 6in.

ANGLE BRACES
CUT FROM 4in. × 1in.

Figure 1

¼ in. GAP BETWEEN PLANKS

4ft. × 8in. × 1in.

2in.

A

2in.

6in.

B

6in.

20in. × 3in. × 2in.

26in. × 8in. × 1in.

26in. × 8in. × 1in.

36in. × 8in. × 1in.
TRIM TO FIT

24 in. × 3in. × 2in.

6in.

C

Figure 2

123

AUCHENTOGLE ALLOTMENT ASSO[C]

Plants and Planting

Autumn is the best season for planting, followed by spring, but pot-grown plants can be planted at any time the ground is not frozen or waterlogged. If you plant in summer, though, be sure to water thoroughly and often.

Ideally, your choice of plants should reflect – and establish – the character of different parts of the garden. While it makes sense to use the potential of the garden to the full, restraint is needed when combining plants from different habitats if they are not to look odd. Progress gently from one theme to another, or divide them with a strong feature. When choosing, bear the following points in mind:

- Woodland plants grow well in partial shade and rich soil, while silver-leaved plants respond best to sunshine and good drainage.

- White flowers and golden foliage show up well in shady areas.

- Yellow is a dominant colour and should be used sparingly.

- Evergreens and certain winter-flowering plants will help make the garden attractive right through the winter season.

To achieve a mature look as soon as possible, plant closely using quick-growing plants with slower-growing shrubs. They can be cut to shape or transplanted in late autumn.

MOVING PLANTS

It may be that you have good trees, shrubs or perennials that are in the wrong place. If it is possible to dig up most of the roots, you can transplant even mature shrubs. Deciduous shrubs are best moved in late autumn or early spring when they have no leaves and need little water, so there is less chance of them dehydrating before the roots are re-established in the new site. They may also be moved in winter, provided the ground is not frozen; and you may just be able to transplant in summer, provided you water copiously. Evergreen plants are best moved in early spring, before the new season's growth gets under way. Large conifers, daphnes and brooms are especially difficult to move, but many others can be moved providing you take every possible precaution to ensure the plant does not dehydrate.

HOW TO MOVE PLANTS

1. Dig deep around the roots of the plant, taking care [not to damage] them.
2. Cut long and sinewy roots off cleanly before lifting.
3. When lifting, insert a sack under the root ball to keep it as intact as possible and to minimise damage to the tiny but vital tendril roots. The sack can form a bag around the root ball while you carry the shrub across the garden.
4. Once the shrub is in its new position, insert a stake support if necessary, press the soil down firmly around the roots and water plentifully.
5. Then prune the plant hard to reduce its water needs. If root has been lost during transplanting, lose even more top. If this involves spoiling the shape of the plant, or losing flower buds, strip all the leaves off instead. As a rule, it pays to be severe rather than gentle with pruning, otherwise the plant will dehydrate.
6. In the weeks afterwards, keep the plant thoroughly watered until it is well established.

PLANTING TREES

The roots of the trees from a nursery may have become dry: if so, soak
them in a bucket of water for a few hours. Homegrown trees or bushes
should be dug up with as much soil clinging to the roots as possible.

Dig out a hole wide enough and deep enough for the roots of each plant
to be fully spread out. Don't bend them to fit the hole: always make
the hole fit the roots. Broken roots should be carefully trimmed back
with a slanting cut on the underside.

Planting depth: get someone to hold the tree while you fill in the
soil. The tree must be at the same depth as it was in the nursery.
Fruit trees and some specimen trees from a nursery have been grafted
in which case a bulge can be seen low down on the stem where the top
part (called the 'scion') joins the root part. This bulge is called
the 'union' and should be at least 4 in. above soil level.

Stout stakes: each tree will need for support a stake which should be
driven in before the roots are covered. For a bush-type tree a really
strong stake is necessary - 2 ft. below and above ground. To prevent
rotting it should have been treated with a wood preservative or you
can buy special stakes at garden centres.

Fill in gradually with top soil, covering the roots and working the
soil well in between them and under the main stem with your fingers.
A few handfuls of compost mixed with this soil will help rooting.
Sprinkle some tree fertiliser over the soil as soon as all roots are
covered.

Firm planting: as you fill in, press the soil well down and finally
trample round the tree with your feet to make it really firm. Then
rake it smooth and spread a 2-in. layer of rotted manure, garden
compost or leaf mould or peat around the tree and as far as the roots
extend. This is called a mulch and helps to keep the soil moist during
the first spring after planting. If the weather is very dry, soak the
tree well two or three times during its first spring and early summer.

When the planting is completed, each tree needs to be fastened to its
support. Tie with soft string, wrapping the tree stem with a piece of
sacking and winding the string between tree and stake to make a buffer,
or use a plastic tree tie with a 'buffer' incorporated that can be
adjusted as the trunk grows.

Set oot yer plants efter 4 p.m. - they can then
settle in as the day cools. Avoid settin' plants
a'fore or while the sun is hottest.

Plant Problems

Things dinnae go richt in the gairden a' the time. This may help ye work oot whit's wrang.

PROBLEMS ON LEAVES

LEAVES WITH HOLES

Caterpillars	Most plants; especially trees and shrubs
Gooseberry sawflies	Gooseberries
Earwigs	Dahlias and clematis and many herbaceous plants
Slugs and snails	Lettuces, tulips, delphiniums, sweet peas and many herbaceous and young plants
Pea and bean weevils	Peas and beans
Vine weevils	Pot plants, rhododendrons, clematis, strawberries and vines
Capsid bugs	Apples, currants, roses, chrysanthemums and other ornamentals
Shothole	Cherries, peaches, plums and gages, plus leaved woody plants

DISCOLOURED LEAVES

Red spider mites	Many greenhouse and garden plants such as fruit trees, strawberries, fuchsias, roses, dahlias, violets
Powdery mildew	Many plants, especially strawberries, begonias, Michaelmas daisies and roses
Silver leaf	Plums, currants and many broad-leaved woody plants
Blight	Tomatoes and potatoes
Leafhoppers	Roses and other plants
Honey fungus	Fruit trees, other trees, shrubs
Potato cyst eelworms	Potatoes
Lime-induced chlorosis	Acid-loving plants (including rhododendrons and azaleas), hydrangeas, raspberries and cane fruit
Magnesium & manganese deficiencies	Cane fruits, root vegetables, tomatoes, herbaceous plants, roses, and many others

LEAVES SPOTTED

Apple scab	Apple trees
Leafspot	Many plants

LEAVES DISTORTED

Aphids	Fruit trees, currants and others
Capsid bugs	Roses and herbaceous plants
Leaf-rolling rose sawflies	Roses
Peach leaf-curl	Peaches, almonds, apricots
Whiptail (molybdenum deficiency)	Brassicas
Hormone weedkiller	Many plants, especially tomatoes and vines
Frost	Tomatoes, broad-leaved woody plants

VISIBLE PESTS

Aphids	Almost any plant
Cabbage whiteflies	Cabbages and other brassicas
Glasshouse whiteflies	Tomatoes
Mealy bugs	Many greenhouse and houseplants, especially coleus and orchids
Scale insects	Many greenhouse plants

FUNGAL GROWTH

Powdery mildew	Many plants, including fruit trees, herbaceous broad-leaved woody plants
Rust fungus	Many different plants

PROBLEMS IN STEMS

STEMS EATEN

Aphids	Roses, beans
Scale	Apples, peaches, beeches, horse chestnuts and many other plants
Cutworm	Lettuces and other vegetables

STEMS CRACKED OR WILTING

Witches' broom	Birches, plums and cherries
Cane spot	Raspberries and loganberries
Rose rust	Roses
Scab	Apples and pears
Fireblight	Apples, pears, cotoneasters, hawthorns
Dry rot	Bulbs, corms and tubers
Frost damage	All plants

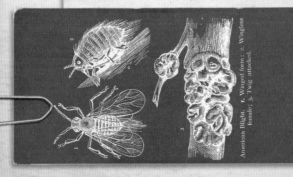

American Blight. 1. Winged form; 2. Wingless female; 3. Twig attacked.

SHOOTS DISCOLOURED

Woolly aphids	Apples, cotoneasters, pyracantha
Mealy bugs	Greenhouse plants, especially succulents and climbers
Bacterial canker	Plums, cherries and gages

VISIBLE FUNGAL GROWTH

Powdery mildew	Many plants
Grey mould (botrytis)	Lettuces, clarkias, godetias and many others
Coral spot	Many trees and shrubs, especially magnolias, acers and currants

VISIBLE PESTS

Brown scale	Old redcurrants and gooseberries

CATERPILLAR OF CURRANT CLEAR-WING MOTH (SESIA TIPULIFORMIS).

PROBLEMS WITH FLOWERS

BUD DAMAGE

Bullfinches	Plums, pears, flowering cherries, forsythias
Caterpillars	Roses, chrysanthemums, apples and others
Apple blossom weevils	Apples

BLOOMS DAMAGED

Earwigs	Herbs, clematis, chrysanthemums, dahlias and other plants
Caterpillars	Greenhouse plants, chrysanthemums
Capsid bugs	Ornamentals
Petal blight	Rhododendrons, cornflowers, chrysanthemums
Grey mould (botrytis)	Flowers grown from seed
Blotch	Delphiniums

PROBLEMS WITH FRUIT

Birds	Ripening fruit
Wasps	Ripening fruit late in the summer
Slugs	Strawberries
Apple sawflies	Apples
Plum sawflies	Plums
Raspberry beetle grubs	Raspberries and loganberries
Pear midge larvae	Pears
Codling moth caterpillars	Apples and pears

BLEMISHES ON FRUIT

Scab	Apples and pears
Capsid bugs	Apples, pears and other tree fruit
Bitter pit	Apples
Stony pit	Old pear trees
Grey mould (botrytis)	Soft fruit, especially strawberries and raspberries
Powdery mildew	Grapes, gooseberries and strawberries
Drought cracking	Apples, pears and plums

PROBLEMS WITH BULBS, CORMS, TUBERS AND ROOT VEGETABLES

ROOTS EATEN

Cutworm	Lettuces
Wireworm	Potatoes
Root fly maggots	Brassicas, onions, beans and carrots
Leatherjackets	Brassicas, other vegetables and ornamentals
Root aphids	Lettuces and ornamentals
Slugs	Potatoes, tulips, daffodils and others
Narcissus fly maggots	Narcissi and daffodils
Onion fly maggots	Onions, shallots and leeks

ROOTS AND TUBERS BLEMISHED

Scab	Potatoes, gladioli and others
Eelworms	Potatoes, daffodils, tulips, hyacinths
White rot	Onions, shallots, leeks
Grey bulb rot	Tulips and hyacinths

A ladybird can eat over 150 aphids (insects that kill yer plants) in a day. Encourage them!

Carrot Fly

Why prune?

All ornamental plants can benefit from pruning – but no pruning is better than pruning that destroys the natural beauty of a plant. Here is some simple guidance.

There are number of reasons to prune a plant:
- To improve flowering or fruiting;
- To remove diseased or damaged branches;
- To thin out dense growth so stopping the loss of lower leaves from shade;
- To train a plant to a particular shape;
- To cut off branches that cause an obstruction;
- To prepare a plant for successful transplantation.

The basic principle of pruning is that the cutting off of a branch will stimulate new buds to develop close to where the cut has been made, leading to a more compact looking plant.

Major pruning for most plants should be done in early spring before new growth has started, except for early flowering plants, which should be pruned after they have flowered, but remember that periodic light pruning can be done at any time and so reduce the need for major pruning.

The knack of pruning is to ensure that the plant retains its natural growing habit, but is just reduced in size. Don't use shears to cut back shrubs unless you want all your plants to look the same.

Wi' careful prunin' an' trainin' ye can change the shape o' trees – particularly fruit trees.

Wavy or Curvilinear Training.

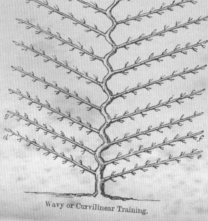

Wavy or Curvilinear Training.

128

PRUNING FRUIT BUSHES AND TREES

Soft fruits: with some, hard pruning means to cut down almost to the soil. For example, immediately after planting you should cut all the shoots on a blackcurrant back to a bud within an inch or so of the soil. All pruning cuts should be made to just above a growth bud. For newly planted blackberries, loganberries and other hybrid berries cut to 9 in. after planting. But with raspberries wait until February or, if you plant later, immediately after planting. Then cut down to a bud 9-12 in. of the soil. For pruning after the first year, check requirements in a book.

With red and white currants, cut each branch back to a bud which points upwards about halfway up. In the case of cordons shorten the last summer's growth (lighter in colour) of the central stem by a third and cut back all sideshoots to half an inch. Gooseberries need to be treated in the same way except that some varieties have a drooping growth. These exceptions should be cut to a bud on the inner side of the shoot.

TREE FRUITS

Curiously, the harder you prune, the stronger a fruit tree will grow. Trees should grow vigorously in their early life to strengthen branches for heavy, future crops. Then, hard pruning with secateurs is the rule. Prune early in the spring following planting. With bush apples cut back the new growth of each main branch by two-thirds (by a half in the case of bush pears). Leave any sideshoots. The pruning you do will also be influenced by the shape of fruit tree you wish. Here are examples of different shapes of tree to meet a range of different growing circumstances.

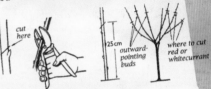

First pruning of a bush apple—where to make the cuts

The first pruning—the harder you prune, the stronger the tree

Climate Change by Horace

Traditionally spring normally starts around 20 March (the vernal equinox when the day and night are the same length).

A recent study said that by 2050 spring in Scotland will begin before Valentine's Day (14 February)! It looked at weather records for Edinburgh, which started in 1775, and plant records in the capital's Royal Botanic Garden, which started in 1850. As average air temperatures rise from global warming, ornamental cherries, peaches and pears, as well as anemones, irises and many perennials, will flower earlier. That might well mean that the insects are out of sync with the flowers — and cause more problems for the bees. Oak trees might suffer from the heat and dry climate.

Dry climate? In Scotland?? - Paw

129

Rhododendrons

If ye ken yer Greek ye'll ken tha' "rhododendron" means rose tree – I ken tha' they ha' grand floo'ers i' the spring an' (maistly) keep their leaves a' year. Wouldnae be wi'out ma rhodis!

RHODODENDRONS.— The value for decorative purposes of this splendid genus is so well known, as to render comment on its merit superfluous; it is enough to say, that common as the rhododendron is in gardens, it is not half as generally cultivated as it ought to be.

The rhododendron, to succeed well, requires to be grown in a light rich soil, readily permeable to moisture, but free from stagnant water; a sandy peat, or heath-mould is the best; but a light, rich sandy loam, mixed with leaf-mould and rotten turf, will answer exceedingly well. Chalk is wholly unsuitable; and in all soils of an adhesive nature, the delicate fibrous roots soon perish. If the soil is naturally unfitted for the growth of the plant, and peat cannot be had, a compost will have to be prepared. This may consist of equal parts of leaf-mould, or other thoroughly decomposed vegetable matter, rotten turf, sandy loam, and sand—the whole thoroughly incorporated, laid in a heap for some months previous to use, and frequently turned. Where plenty of leaf-mould is at command, a greater proportion of that substance may be employed, especially when the loam is not of a very light nature, in which case more sand should be added.

The situation should be moist, and if shady, all the better; but it ought not to be overhung by trees, for these would prove injurious by the drip from their leaves, and by the incursions of their roots, which would not only impoverish the soil, but absorb moisture in enormous quantities to supply the evaporation from the leaves with which they are in connection, and this at the very time when the plants are in the greatest danger of suffering from dryness at the roots— a state which is particularly to be guarded against with this class of plants.

Fancy that!

The *Rhododendron ponticum* is well known as a vigorous grower that can swamp all other vegetation on hillsides and is often now regarded as a weed. But it has another claim to fame. In Ancient Greece, the historian Xenophon described how some soldiers behaved strangely after eating honey from a village surrounded by rhododendrons. It has since been established that honey made from some rhododendrons can produce hallucinogenic and laxative effects. Now, this is the part of the world that *Rhododendron ponticum* comes from, so is considered by some to have been the cause of this effect.

ᵗʰᵉ Auchentogle Bugle

Gairdenin' Wisdoms

with **GAIRDENER BROON**

✦✦✦✦✦✦✦✦✦✦✦✦✦✦✦✦✦✦✦✦✦✦✦✦✦

GALA DAY

HARD TAE BELIEVE it's that time o' year again. And plans are a'ready afoot for the annual Auchentogle Gala Parade. As usual the allotment fowk are enterin' a float in the parade through the toon.

Some o' you readers will remember last year's unfortunate accident, which left a bad taste in some fowk's throats. Ye micht remember we entered a float heaped high wi' Jimmy Paterson's fermyard manure. Braw fresh stuff an' a'... the reek o' the week. It was a' done wi' the best o' intentions, a wee advert for "Organic Fertiliser Trebles Yer Tatties". The horse pu'in' the float in front o' oors drapped a bit o' "organic" o' its ain. Oor horse stepped in it and near skited oot o' its horseshoes, tippin' the hale float ower... a' ower the ladies o' the WRI and their Cake and Candy stall at the side o' the road. It wiz a total disaster. A' that guid stuff was completely ruined – it wiz contaminated wi' hunners o' cakes and cookies and wiz nae langer fit for the tattie plantin'.

However, ye live and learn and this year, bein' "The Year o' The Rhubarb", accordin' tae the Chinese fowk at "The Peking Tom" takeaway, we've decided tae get the loan o' Tam Cowan's big flatbed truck for the weekend. The idea is tae build a rhubarb allotment on the back o' the truck. We'll be usin' 12-inch shuttering a' the way roond the flatbed tae stop the soil fae fallin' aff the larry an' we'll plant the hale thing oot wi' Victoria Rhubarb. The hale committee wiz in agreement a' but Willie McLeod, wha's totally against the idea and is withdrawin' the lend o' his shed for the float. Said he wanted "nae truck wi' rhubarb".

Tam Cowan himsel' has kindly consented tae accompany the float and talk rhubarb a' the way roond the parade. There will be fowk walkin' ahent the float handin' oot rhubarb pies, rhubarb breid, rhubarb crumble, rhubarb cake, rhubarb soor plooms, rhubarb rhubarb, rhubarb stalk wi' a sugery poke for bairns and toilet rolls.

Watch oot for us. Oor float is eleventh in the parade, jist ahent Digger Burnem the undertakers and immediately in front o' "Curl Up an' Dye" the hairdressers... or is that the Funeral fowk's name? I aye get them mixed up.

There are those that think I talk a lot o' rhubarb masel', but that's jist soor grapes ... an' I'm richt fond o' grapes an' a' mind.

Well, 'til next week...

Aye Yours,

Gairdener Broon x

RHODODENDRON
(Jasminiflorum Hyb.)
1. Princess Royal 2. Princess Alexandra

Rhubarb

Dae ye ken that rhubarb is a noisy plant? They say ye can hear it groaning as it pushes its way through the soil!

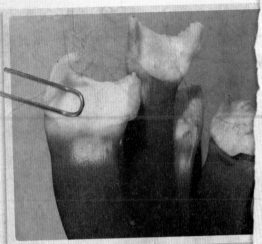

RHUBARB

If there is already a rhubarb bed in the garden, it is quite easy to look after one or two plants in a special way called 'forcing' so that they produce tender stems for pulling early. And this earlier rhubarb tastes better. Start in late December or January. The idea is to cover a plant for protection against the wind and to keep it warmer. Growth starts sooner then and, because it is in the dark, the rhubarb is very pale in colour but more tender to eat. For each plant you will need four strong sticks or plant stakes about 30-in. long and pointed at one end.

1. Drive the stakes 1 ft. into the ground and about 9 in. from the centre of the selected rhubarb plant so that the four sticks form the corners of a square.

2. Fasten the sticks with four bands of string, one close to the bottom, one at the top and the others spaced between.

3. Buy some 18-in. wide black polythene sheeting and you will need one length of about 5 ft. and one of 2 ft. for each plant. Wrap the longer piece of polythene round the outside of the four stakes and strings, and hold in place with four more ties of string. Then put the smaller piece of polythene over the top like a hat and fasten down the edges with a band of string.

4. Obtain from a farm or horse stables fresh strawy manure (which generates heat) or, failing that, plain straw, hay, bracken or leaves. Mound this litter in a heap over the black polythene box. Prevent it from blowing away by putting over the top a square of polythene (any colour will do) and tying bricks to the corners to give it weight.

5. The weather will dictate when the rhubarb will be ready for eating. Look inside about the third week of February to see how it is getting on. Start pulling when the stalks are about 9 in. high. Hold them as low down as possible and twist and pull at the same time.

Dear Gairdener Broon
I'd like to have rhubarb for ma Christmas dinner. How can I grow fresh rhubarb in time for the festivities?

Well, it can be done, but Maw wouldna thank me for it. Ye can 'force' rhubarb tae be early, by lifting a crown (root) of rhubarb in early November, lettin' it lay upside doon fae a week ootside, and then growin' it in the warmth an' the dark. Ye can dae this in a greenhoose or, e'en better, in a warm press, near a hot water tank, for example. Mak sure the soil disnae dry oot – and let yer missus ken aye aboot it.

or ye can use auld drainpipes, as I did!

Rock Gairden

I had a grand rock gairden. Last week fower o' them died. Aye, the auld anes are the best... I once thocht to ha' a rock gairden, but then it didnae feel richt for me. Makin' a rock gairden in the auld sink at ma cottage seemed a better idea.

A trough garden

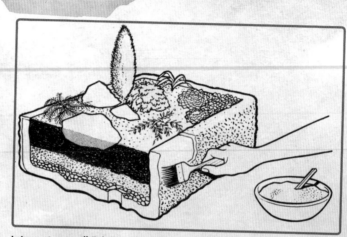

To make a miniature trough garden you need an old stone or ceramic kitchen sink. This popular kind of rock gardening began in the 1920s when a famous rock plant nurseryman was looking for suitable containers in which to grow his plants. He decided the old stone sinks that were being turned out of cottages were just what he wanted. They even had ready-made drainage holes and this set a fashion.

Now, rather than stone sinks, you can still find old glazed sinks which you can make into troughs, but don't try using stainless steel sinks (even without drainers) as they don't have flat bottoms. Alternatively you could make your own trough out of concrete. Glazed sinks can be made to look better by covering them in an imitation stone finish. This is not difficult to do. Just cover it with hypertufa fixed on to it with adhesive. Hypertufa is an artificially made stone and a good imitation of a rock called tufa. Tufa is itself a porous limestone rock formed gradually as water deposits the lime. It is a splendid sort of stone to use for rock plants, especially lime lovers, as it can easily have small holes drilled in it to hold the smaller saxifrages and similar plants.

MAKE YOUR OWN HYPERTUFA

You can produce a fair imitation of natural tufa from a mixture of peat, sand, and cement. One part each of sand and cement to two parts peat will make a tough light porous stone very much like tufa. Mix all the ingredients together first, then add water gradually, mixing it in as you go, until it is wet but fairly stiff in consistency. Spread PVA adhesive over the sink and then spread the stiff mixture of hypertufa over it to the depth of about ¼ in. Make sure you wear gloves when doing this. Leave it to set hard.

POSITION THE TROUGH

A trough is quite heavy, even without anything in it, so decide where it is to stand before you fill it. Otherwise it could be too heavy to move. Do make sure it is level in its final position. Quite apart from the fact that it will look odd if it is not, it will not be evenly wetted when you water it or when it rains. Some plants may then become dry at the roots and die

FILL THE TROUGH

First, cover the base of the inside with crocks, then a layer of coarse peat, or peat-free compost over the crocks.

Although the trough should be well drained, make sure that the compost you use contains enough peat to hold moisture in dry weather.

Press the soil firmly to within 4 in. of the rim of the trough, then add more soil loosely to within about ½ in. of the top, into which the plants will be set. After this you will need one or two small rocks, mainly as decoration, to give the trough an alpine appearance. Next come the plants, some stone chippings to spread over the surface, to help keep the plants' roots cool and moist and also to deter weeds.

There is no need to bury your rocks deeply; about 1 or 1½ in. is quite enough, and they will provide cool soil for some of the plants' roots. Arrange them on the surface temporarily, until you are sure they and the plants are all in the best position before you set them in permanently. The plants must be small, compact and slow growing, and of contrasting shapes. A few of the plants near the edge of the trough can be allowed to spread, carpeting part of the surface and draping themselves over the side, giving a more pleasant and

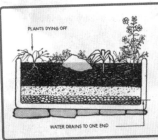

WATER DRAINS TO ONE END

natural appearance. But plants away from the edge must be well behaved, or they will soon overcrowd each other.

The gravel covering of the soil in the trough should discourage slugs, the main pests likely to cause problems in the trough. You may need to use slug pellets around the trough to discourage them.

SOME PLANTS TO CHOOSE FROM

Armeria juniperifolia: a very compact form of thrift, with pink flowers.

Asperula suberosa: a tiny pink-flowered woodruff, flowering off and on from April to autumn, and with silver-grey foliage.

Dianthus freynii: a 2-in. high species with small rose-pink flowers.

Draba rigida: cushion-forming plant with yellow flowers in spring.

Erinus alpinus: purple, white or rose-pink flowers with dark green foliage. not long-lived but should give you self-sown seedlings.

Erodium chamaedryoides: 2-in. high white

or pink heron's bills.

Cushion saxifrages:

- *Saxifraga x apiculata*: yellow flowers
- *Cranbourne*: grey-green foliage and bright pink flowers.
- *Jenkinsae*: grey-green rosettes of leaves and pale pink flowers
- *Saxifraga burseriana*: white flowers in March.
- *Saxifraga grisebachii*: silvery leaf rosettes and spikes of crimson flowers
- *Saxifraga oppositifolia*: purple flowers

Saxifraga cochlearis: dome of tiny silver leaves and white flower.

Sedum album: tiny, chubby leaves with white flowers

Sedum hispanicum: blue green foliage and white flowers

Sedum ewersii: blue-grey leaves and pink flowers.

Sedum spathulifolium: stonecrop with green and silvery white leaves and yellow flowers

Sempervivum: the houseleek, evergreen rosettes with pinkish flowers.

Edraianthus (or *Campanula*) *pumilio*: silver foliage and lavender bells, 2-in. high.

As a carpet plant , grow *Raoulia australis*, with tiny silvery leaves and Mentha requienii, a tiny fragrant mint plant. Also, do not forget to plant at least one small tree – *Juniperus communis var compressa* will do very well.

Roses

When setting new roses, tak' a sod o' grass 6 in. square an' place 'green side doon, broon side up' at the bottom o' the prepared hole. Spread the roots out on this an' finish setting as usual. Your rose trees will thrive!

Growing Roses

Roses offer tremendous value as garden flowers. Modern hybrids give a long flowering season, lasting well into autumn; they are good for cutting and displaying, and the scented varieties are wonderfully fragrant.

There is now a vast range of different colours available, but combining too many together in the same bed, or even in the same garden, can be garish. It is better to choose a theme involving just a few complementary colours.

Where there is room, the older species can be charming, and many gardeners prefer the traditional varieties to the new hybrids. Hybrid teas and floribundas should be grown alone in their own bed or border. You could plant wallflowers as bedding plants through the winter, but, in summer, nothing should detract from the showiness of the roses.

Roses need a great deal of attention, and rose-growing is a surprisingly labour-intensive activity. Almost without exception, they require a lot of sunshine. But they also need regular mulching, feeding and spraying against pests if they are to provide the best display. It helps if you choose disease-resistant varieties, but you still need to spray from early in the season against attacks by aphids, blackspot and mildew.

All roses should be pruned annually to maintain their shape and keep them flowering profusely. Climbers and ramblers should be pruned after flowering; hybrid teas and floribundas in February or March. In the milder areas, you can prune in your own time. But if you do prune before early spring, avoid cutting back hard before sharp frosts; the new sappy growth encouraged by pruning may die back.

The blooms of hybrid teas must be dead-headed as soon as they wither, by cutting off just above a strong shoot. This encourages another blooming later in the season. Later in the year, dead-head the flowers a little more gently. With floribundas, you can afford to be much more ruthless in dead-heading, cutting off the entire flowering head just below the first bud.

PRUNING ROSES

Hybrid teas
Remove any dead branches, weak shoots and stems that cross. Cut back remaining stems by about two-thirds. Do not prune harder unless growing for exhibition.

FLORIBUNDAS

Again, remove any dead wood, weak shoots and crossing stems but cut back the remaining stems much less severely than for hybrid teas, pruning to above the topmost leaf. Always cut into the previous year's growth and not older wood.

STANDARDS

Prune back to outward-pointing buds in the previous year's wood. Floribunda blooms are pruned less hard than hybrid teas, as above. Cut for a good, open shape, removing dead and diseased wood and weak shoots.

O my Luve's like a red, red rose,
That's newly sprung
in June.

A rose-bud by my early walk

A Rose-bud by my early walk,
Adown a corn-enclosed bawk,
Sae gently bent its thorny stalk,
All on a dewy morning.
Ere twice the shades o' dawn are fled,
In a' its crimson glory spread,
And drooping rich the dewy head,
It scents the early morning.

That's Rabbie for ye.
I need say nae mair.

ROSES.
1. Souvenir de la Malmaison (Bourbon). 2. General Jacqueminot (Hybrid perpetual).

BLACKIE & SON, GLASGOW, EDINBURGH & LONDON.

137

Some samples of vegetable seed

cabbage

pumpkin

sweet corn

beetroot

pea

Buying seedlings and containerised plants saves time and effort, but you are limited to the garden centre's range of best sellers, and specimens are often less than perfect. Seedlings and bedding plants tend to be very expensive too. With seeds, you have an almost unlimited choice, and they are relatively cheap.

Seeds need moisture, air and warmth to germinate. Follow the instructions on the packet and do not sow too thickly. Eventually you will have a crop of young seedlings, but there are some points to consider:

* Hardy annuals need fairly low temperatures to germinate, so they can be sown outdoors early in spring, if the soil is well drained.

* When planting outside, press down on the soil after sowing so that the seed can grow on firm ground.

* Vegetables need to be grown fast in rich soil if they are to be tender. Vegetable seeds are usually sown in greenhouses or heated frames where they can be kept warm during the early stages of growth, or they may be sown outside late in the spring when the weather has started to warm. If sown outside too early, vegetable seeds grow slowly and become tough.

* Like vegetables, half-hardy annuals need relatively warm conditions to germinate.

* You don't need to use all the seed in the packet. What seed you don't use should be kept somewhere cool and dry so that it can be used at another time.

* When transplanting seedlings, hold them by their leaves rather than their stems, which are very fragile.

* Make sure you have the right equipment for growing seeds.

BIRTH OF A PLANT
LEAVES
SEED (FOOD STORE)
STEM
LATERAL ROOTS
MAIN ROOT (TAP ROOT)

Glebe Street School

Name: **Horace Broon**
Biology experiments

DO THIS EXPERIMENT AT HOME

GROWING A BROAD BEAN SEED
A broad bean seed grows quickly in the warmth of a room rather than in the garden outside where the ground may be cold. Record the progress of the seed in a table and draw your plant when it starts to produce leaves.

Equipment needed
Broad bean (Vica faba) seed
Small plant pot
Soil or potting compost

INSTRUCTIONS

1. Fill the pot halfway and place the seed on the surface.

2. Cover it with more earth to 1 inch from the top.

3. Stand the pot in a saucer, then add water gradually until a little runs out of the bottom into the saucer. Pour this away.

4. It will take about two weeks for the seed to split and start growing. It may take longer, but be patient.

5. Whenever the soil feels dry, add more water.

6. A green point will soon break the surface and start to grow quickly.

7. It will need plenty of light if it is to stay green. If you take it to the side of the room away from the window it will bend towards the light in a day or two and at the same time become paler green and grow faster.

Aye plant mair seeds than ye need plants. They used tae say:
Ane fae the rook, ane fae the crow,
Ane tae die an' ane tae grow.

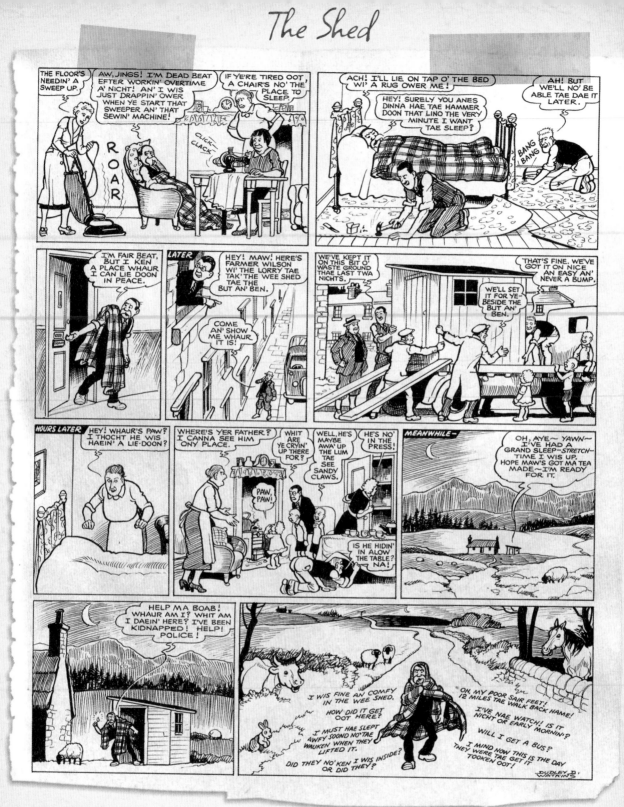

A roof repairin' hint. Leaks are easy tae locate fae the inside o' the shed. Specks of light or draps o' watter are sure indications o' leaks, but tae locate them fae the ootside is tricky unless ye push straws or wee sticks through the faulty material before clamberin' ontae the roof tae remedy the trouble.

Gairdenin' Wisdoms

with GAIRDENER BROON

✤✤✤✤✤✤✤✤✤✤✤✤✤✤✤✤✤✤

JINGS, IT'S BEEN CHUCKIN' IT DOON in Auchentogle this past week. Never seen rain like it. Talk aboot "cats an' dogs"? This was mair like "horses an' coos". There's no' a lot tae actually report this week, except tae say no' a lot's been happenin' on the gairdening home front. Naebody was even oot wi' their watterin' cans ... no' needed wi' a' this rain. I was sittin' in ma shed during ane o' the worst doonpours readin' "The Sunday Post" and the rain was batterin' aff the corrugated roof. Sounded like somebody was trying to drill richt through. But not a drap came through and I was as snug as a bug wi' the wee cast iron stove on. And what was even better, was the knowledge that naebody wid come tae visit and disturb me in that weather.

My shed is ma wee special place. If ye dinna hae a shed o' yer ain, think aboot it. Ye'll never regret gettin' ane. But get a guid ane. An' ye dinna hae tae spend shedloads o' dosh tae get ane.

When I first inherited the allotment fae ma ain faither a' thae years ago, there was a shed here that had seen better days. It was a' shoogly, the watter jist poured through the roof and there was mair things growin' oot the walls than there wiz growin' in the allotment itsel'. And talk aboot draughty!? If ye can imagine what it wid feel like wearin' yer kilt withoot drawers tae clad yer hurdies an' somebody stuck a garage airline up yer Ancient MacDonald, that's how draughty it felt. I tried patchin' the leaky roof wi' tarry

pent, but the rain jist washed it doon through the cracks an' ye needed an umbrella tae jist sit inside tae keep the black tarry rain aff yer napper. Mind you, havin' said a' that, I had the maist waterproof brolly in the toon wi' a' the tar that wiz on it.

Well, onyway, ae nicht during a thunderstorm, the hale thing jist fell doon aboot ma ears. Unfortunately it wisnae jist MY ears it fell roond aboot. Annie Lennox wiz in the shed at the time an' a'. I was doon on bended knee askin' for her hand in marriage, when suddenly the walls jist vanished and there we were, baith richt oot in the open in a' that rain. Fair cooled her ardour ... and her new hairdo and twin set. If only I'd had the new shed that very nicht! Och, well, I'm still hopin' ... and ye canna rush thae things efter a'.

Richt there and then, doon on ma knees, wi' the rain trickling doon ma drawers, I decided tae build a brand new Granpaw Broon Supershed ... and I did. Dae ye want tae ken how I did it? I'm sure ye do, but ye'll need tae buy next week's "Auchentogle Bugle" for The History o' The Shed Part 2. Ha ha. Actually, this wisnae my idea. The Bugle editor said it was a marketing ploy tae get ye tae read next week's newspaper.

But here's something ye micht be interested in. If ye canna wait tae find oot what happens in Part 2 next week, ye'll find me in "The Volunteer Arms" in the snug efter the Dominoes on Tuesday and I'll tell ye a' aboot it tae yer face, for a wee dram or twa.

'til next week then, folks ... or at "The Volunteer" on Tuesday nicht, of coorse.

Aye Yours,

Gairdener Broon

x

Look efter the wid and locks on yer shed – or ye'll end up wi' a door ye canna open!

Shrubs an' Trees Through the Year

JANUARY

Common name	Latin name	Type
Bodnant viburnum	*Viburnum bodnantense*	shrub
Flowering cherry	*Prunus subhirtella 'autumnalis'*	tree
Flowering peach	*Prunus davidiana*	tree
Laurestinus	*Viburnum tinus*	shrub
Winter jasmine	*Jasminum nudiflorum*	shrub
Winter-flowering heather	*Erica carnea*	shrub
Winter-flowering heather	*Erica darleyensis*	shrub
Wintersweet	*Chimonanthus*	shrub
Witch hazel	*Hamamelis mollis*	shrub
Golden barberry	*Berberis stenophylla*	shrub
Gorse	*Ulex europaeus*	shrub
Japanese rose	*Kerria japonica*	shrub
Korean spice viburnum	*Viburnum carlesii*	shrub
Ornamental pear	*Pyrus*	tree
Pieris	*Pieris*	shrub
Purple leaf sand cherry	*Prunus cistena*	shrub
Rosemary	*Rosmarinus*	shrub
Skimmia	*Skimmia*	shrub
Star magnolia	*Magnolia stellata*	shrub

FEBRUARY

Common name	Latin name	Type
Daphne	*Daphne mezereum*	shrub
Flowering cherry	*Prunus subhirtella 'autumnalis'*	tree
Hazel	*Corylus avellana*	tree
Japanese mahonia	*Mahonia japonica*	shrub
Laurestinus	*Viburnum tinus*	shrub
Lily of the valley bush	*Mahonia 'charity'*	shrub
Winter jasmine	*Jasminum nudiflorum*	shrub
Winter-flowering heather	*Erica carnea*	shrub
Winter-flowering heather	*Erica darleyensis*	shrub
Wintersweet	*Chimonanthus*	shrub
Witch hazel	*Hamamelis japonica*	shrub

MARCH

Common name	Latin name	Type
Almond	*Prunus dulcis*	tree
Camellia	*Camellia japonica*	shrub
Dogwood	*Cornus*	shrub
Flowering cherry	*Prunus subhirtella 'autumnalis'*	tree
Flowering currant	*Ribes sanguineum*	shrub
Forsythia	*Forsythia*	shrub
Japanese quince	*Chaenomeles*	shrub
Japanese rose	*Kerria japonica*	shrub
Kilmarnock willow	*Salix caprea 'Pendula'*	tree
Oregon grape	*Mahonia aquifolium*	shrub
Shrubby willow	*Salix alba*	shrub
Star magnolia	*Magnolia stellata*	shrub

APRIL

Common name	Latin name	Type
Almond	*Prunus dulcis*	tree
Bridal wreath	*Spiraea arguta*	shrub
Camellia	*Camellia japonica*	shrub
Flowering cherry	*Prunus*	tree
Flowering crab apple	*Malus*	tree
Forsythia	*Forsythia*	shrub

MAY

Common name	Latin name	Type
Ash	*Fraxinus*	tree
Bird cherry	*Prunus padus*	tree
Broom	*Cytisus*	shrub
Clematis	*Clematis*	climbing
		shrub
Cotoneaster	*Cotoneaster*	shrub
Deutzia	*Deutzia*	shrub
Firethorn	*Pyracantha*	shrub
Hebe	*Hebe*	shrub
Horse chestnut	*Aesculus*	tree
Lilac	*Syringa*	tree
Mexican orange blossom	*Choisya ternata*	shrub
Prickly heath	*Pernettya*	shrub
Purple leaf sand cherry	*Prunus cistena*	shrub
Rhododendron	*Rhododendron*	shrub
Spiraea	*Spirea*	shrub

JUNE

Common name	Latin name	Type
Broom	*Genista*	shrub
Clematis	*Clematis*	climbing
		shrub
Cross leaved heath	*Erica tetralix*	shrub
Deutzia	*Deutzia*	shrub
Escallonia	*Escallonia*	shrub
Guelder rose	*Viburnum opulus*	shrub
Hawthorn	*Crataegus*	tree
Hebe	*Hebe*	shrub
Honeysuckle	*Lonicera tatarica*	climbing
		shrub
Laburnum	*Laburnum*	tree
Lilac	*Syringa*	shrub
Mock orange	*Philadelphus*	shrub
Orange ball tree	*Buddleia globosa*	shrub

Rock rose	*Cistus*	shrub
Senecio	*Senecio Brachyglottis*	shrub
Weigela	*Weigela*	shrub

JULY

Bell heather	*Erica cinerea*	shrub
Butterfly bush	*Buddleia davidii*	shrub
Cinquefoil	*Potentilla*	shrub
Common jasmine	*Jasminum officinale*	shrub / climber
Cornish heath	*Erica vagans*	shrub
Corsican heath	*Erica terminalis*	shrub
Cross leaved heath	*Erica tetralix*	shrub
Dorset heath	*Erica ciliaris*	shrub
Heather (ling)	*Calluna vulgaris*	shrub
Lavender	*Lavandula*	shrub
Lavender cotton	*Santolina*	shrub
Rose	*Rosa*	shrub
St. Dabeoc's heath	*Daboecia cantabrica*	shrub

AUGUST

Bell heather	*Erica cinerea*	shrub
Californian lilac	*Ceanothus*	shrub
Cornish heath	*Erica vagans*	shrub
Corsican heath	*Erica terminalis*	shrub
Cross leaved heath	*Erica tetralix*	shrub
Daisy bush	*Olearia*	shrub
Dorset heath	*Erica ciliaris*	shrub
Escallonia	*Escallonia*	shrub
Fuchsia	*Fuchsia*	shrub
Heather (ling)	*Calluna vulgaris*	shrub
Himalayan honeysuckle	*Leycesteria*	shrub
Hydrangea	*Hydrangea*	shrub
Laurel magnolia	*Magnolia grandiflora*	shrub
Lavender	*Lavandula*	shrub
Myrtle	*Myrtus*	shrub
Periwinkle	*Vinca species*	shrub
Plumbago	*Ceratostigma*	shrub
Rose	*Rosa*	shrub
Rose mallow	*Hibiscus*	shrub
St. Dabeoc's heath	*Daboecia cantabrica*	shrub
Sumach	*Rhus typhina*	shrub

SEPTEMBER

Bell heather	*Erica cinerea*	shrub
Cinquefoil	*Potentilla*	shrub
Cornish heath	*Erica vagans*	shrub
Fuchsia	*Fuchsia*	shrub
Heather (ling)	*Calluna vulgaris*	shrub
Himalayan honeysuckle	*Leycesteria*	shrub
Hydrangea	*Hydrangea*	shrub
Hypericum	*Hypericum*	shrub
Laurel magnolia	*Magnolia grandiflora*	tree
Rose	*Rosa*	shrub
Rose mallow	*Hibiscus*	shrub
St. Dabeoc's heath	*Daboecia cantabrica*	shrub
Virgin's bower	*Clematis*	climbing shrub

OCTOBER

Castor oil plant	*Fatsia japonica*	shrub
Cinquefoil	*Potentilla species*	shrub
Cornish heath	*Erica vagans*	shrub
Fuchsia	*Fuchsia*	shrub
Heather (ling)	*Calluna vulgaris*	shrub
Hydrangea	*Hydrangea*	shrub
Hypericum	*Hypericum*	shrub
Laurel magnolia	*Magnolia grandiflora*	tree
Rose	*Rosa*	shrub
Rose mallow	*Hibiscus*	shrub

NOVEMBER

Bodnant viburnum	*Viburnum bodnantense*	shrub
Flowering cherry	*Prunus subhirtella 'autumnalis'*	tree
Hebe	*Hebe*	shrub
Winter jasmine	*Jasminum nudiflorum*	shrub
Winter-flowering heather	*Erica carnea*	shrub
Winter-flowering heather	*Erica darleyensis*	shrub

DECEMBER

Flowering cherry	*Prunus subhirtella 'autumnalis'*	tree
Fragrant viburnum	*Viburnum fragrans*	shrub
Japanese mahonia	*Mahonia japonica*	shrub
Laurestinus	*Viburnum tinus*	shrub
Mahonia	*Mahonia bealei*	shrub
Winter jasmine	*Jasminum nudiflorum*	shrub
Winter-flowering heather	*Erica carnea*	shrub
Winter-flowering heather	*Erica darleyensis*	shrub
Wintersweet	*Chimonanthus*	shrub
Witch hazel	*Hamamelis mollis*	shrub

Shrubs

Whit is a shrub? Here's whit ma auld dictionary said.

Ma favourite shrub has tae be the Daphne, wi' its spring flowers (ye'll come an' do ma weeding noo, won't ye, Daphne). Thompson particularly mentions twa Daphnes, ane a shrub an' ane for the rock gairden. Here's whit he says…

SHRUB, *n.* A drink or liquor of lemon-juice, spirit, sugar, and water.

SHRUB, *n.* A low, dwarf tree: a woody plant with several stems from the same root; and so **SHRUBBERIED, SHUBBERY, SHRUBBINESS, SHRUBBY, SHRUBLESS**

DAPHNE CNEOREUM – 1 ft. Trailing. Leaves small. Flowers small but numerous; very sweet-scented; rose-coloured or white; April and May, and frequently again in the autumn. Highly ornamental. peat soil and a shady situation.

DAPHNE MEZEREUM – 3 to 5 ft. Flowers small but numerous, and very ornamental, pink, sweet-scented; January to March. There is a variety with white, and another with red flowers. Seeds. The plant, it may be remarked, is poisonous.

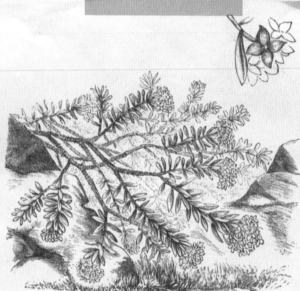

DAPHNE CNEORUM, showing Habit and Detached Cluster of Flowers.

Looking after shrubs

Many shrubs respond well to being pruned, which both encourages new growth and ensures that the shrub remains an appropriate size for its position in the garden.

In cutting back shrubs, aim not to trim evenly all round, but to thin out, leaving plenty of long stems to give shape.

If a philadelphus, for instance, has dozens of stems, remove the oldest and thickest ones from the centre, and also damaged and diseased wood; younger stems can be 'pattern pruned', which involves cutting back lead shoots, where stronger side shoots have developed.

Although most shrubs are pruned immediately after flowering, they can in fact be pruned at many other times of year, provided they are pruned sensitively. Most shrubs can be pruned throughout their dormant period, from late autumn to early spring, though you should not prune sappier shrubs too hard in late autumn as they may die back from their wounds in the frost. Roses, for instance, should only be pruned very lightly unless long and straggly and prone to wind rock.

Do not be afraid of pruning hard if a plant is vigorous. Honeysuckles, for instance, can be dealt with very firmly; once you have removed the tangled growth, the shrub will quickly show new buds in the growing season.

Slugs an' Snails

Ye can mak' a rare slug trap wi' a sooked-oot orange. Cut the oranges in half, sook oot the juice, an' pit them face doon. The slugs crawl under, an' ye can scoop them away wi' a trowel in the mornin'.

Wee heaps o' bran placed aroond yer gairden will attract the slugs. Hunners can be dealt with.

Slugs and snails can be a real menace in the garden. Their delight in eating lettuce and any precious young seedlings is well known. In fact, however, they are a bit more picky than you might like to think. Among the plants they dislike are those with strongly smelling foliage, such as geranium, plants with glossy, hairy or waxy leaves, and plants which are tough and bitter. The following are among flowering plants that are usually slug resistant: aquilega, crocosmias, ferns, foxgloves, hellebores, hydrangeas, lavenders, potentillas, roses and sedums, while in the vegetable garden they are less keen on chicory and sprouting broccoli, for example.

This still leaves a lot of plants under threat, so what can you do to protect yourself against slugs and snails? There have been many suggestions over the centuries:

- Lay bands of grit, sharp sand or other abrasive materials around plants, as they dislike rough surfaces.

- Sink a cup into the ground close to the plants you wish to protect and pour in some beer. They like the smell and will crawl in only to discover that they cannot get out again.

- Place some large leaves, e.g. rhubarb leaves, on the ground near the plants in the evening. Next morning you will find large numbers of slugs, which can then be disposed of.

- Grow a few sacrificial plants, such as lettuce, in a border in the hope that slugs will just spend time eating them rather than the other plants. You will regularly need to remove the slugs from the plants.

- Water in the morning rather than the evening.

- Encourage natural predators by planting trees and bushes to entice thrushes, by building a pond to attract frogs and toads, and by leaving an area of the garden wild to attract hedgehogs.

- Plant sage and thyme near your vegetables as they don't like the smell.

- Sprinkle soot, wood ash or salt on the ground near the plants you wish to protect.

- Be very controlled in using slug pellets as they are dangerous to hedgehogs, cats, dogs and small children.

Whereas slugs and snails are real pests, be very considerate to worms who do great work in the garden, helping to aerate the soil. They also help material to rot in a compost heap and one variety of worm (the tiger or brandling worm) can be used in a domestic worm composter. Feed the worms household waste (but not meat, fish, rice, pasta, cheese or baked beans, for example) and a liquid compost will be produced. Find out more about wormeries on the internet or from a garden centre.

I wouldna add tae ma friends anyone wha needlessly steps on a worm

the only guid snail shell is an empty ane!

Soil

Look at yer ne'ebors gairdens to see whit grows well, for that'll show ye whit thrives in the local soil.

As gardens are generally formed where the ground has been under cultivation, and where trees or hedges are frequently on the site, the growth of these should be observed. If the oak or elm thrive well, there is every probability that the soil is capable of being adapted for a garden; and where the common hawthorn makes vigorous shoots, there fruit-trees, such as the apple, pear, plum, and cherry, will also succed, and, indeed, we may say, all other fruit-trees likewise, so far as the soil is concerned.

Types of Soil

To get the best out of your plants, you need to know what type of soil you have. There are many plants which simply will not grow in particular soil conditions.

Some gardeners accept the soil as it is, and choose plants suited to the conditions. Gardeners with very acidic soil, for instance, may plant acid-loving shrubs like azaleas and rhododendrons; those living on chalky soil, on the other hand, may grow plants that thrive on alkaline soil, such as climbing clematis and hebe.

There are plants to suit almost every condition of soil, but there is no necessity to accept the soil as it is. Almost all soils can be adapted and improved to enable a much broader range of plants to flourish. Even if the soil cannot be changed to suit a particular plant, you could plant it in imported soil in a raised bed or container.

HEAVY SOIL

The main problem with heavy clay soil is that it is made up from fine particles that lump together very tightly. Roots can make little headway in this soil, while the rich supply of nutrients is locked up out of reach within the lumps. Moreover, water tends to accumulate in the soil, making it wet and cold. Heavy clay soil takes a long time to warm up in the spring, and during droughts it will set rock-hard and crack into wide fissures.

The solution to these problems is to open up the mix by introducing large particles of coarse aggregate or sharp sand as the soil is forked over. Thorough cultivation of the soil by double digging in late autumn or winter also helps. Adding bulky organic matter is often recommended, but by itself, this can make the soil even more retentive of water.

CLAY SOIL

This withstands drought well but can be rather heavy, acid, badly aerated and poorly draining. However, plant growth is usually good. Improve the soil by adding well-rotted compost to increase the humus content and open up the structure.

CHALKY SOILS

These can vary from heavy to light and are usually alkaline and lacking in humus. They are also very free draining. Improve by adding good compost or by green manuring. Such soils will only support lime-tolerant plants; grow others in imported soil.

LOAM SOIL

Loam soils can be either heavy or light according to the mineral content. Well aerated and free draining, loam soil is always an asset, and when it is about 60 per cent sand and 30 per cent clay – a medium loam – it is pretty near ideal. The remaining 10 per cent is mostly humus and lime, and the only improvement needed is to add manure annually if the lime content is high, less often if the loam is acidic. A little lime is usually needed in acidic loam if you want to grow plants that prefer alkaline conditions. This is the best type of soil for a gardener to have as growth is usually good, but weeds will flourish along with plants so you will have to be vigilant and diligent.

SANDY SOIL

Sandy soil is gritty to the touch and often lacking in organic matter. It warms up quickly in spring and drains freely. The problem is, it drains a little too freely, allowing nutrients, especially potash and lime, to be washed out of the soil. It also dries out rapidly in drought conditions. You will need to dig in well-rotted organic manure and compost to improve sandy soil significantly, while in summer you may need to lay a mulch of compost around plants to help trap moisture. Feed with nitrates and potash.

146

Glebe Street School

Name: Horace Broon
Biology experiments

DO THIS EXPERIMENT AT HOME

TESTING THE SOIL

Clay soil feels sticky and can be moulded almost like putty;
sandy soil feels dry and crumbles in the fist; loamy soil crumbles
but keeps its shape and leaves a dark stain on the skin. In this
experiment you will test soil from three different places.

Soil Sample 1 The Allotment
Soil Sample 2 Granpaw's gairden
Soil sample 3 The But an' Ben

Dig a few trowelfuls of soil, down to a depth of 8 in. or
so.
Mix up the soil thoroughly and place a handful in a jam-jar
three-quarters full of water.
Shake the jar vigorously and leave to settle for about 40
minutes.
You should be able to see a number of distinct layers, with the
coarsest sand and gravel at the bottom; fine sand above that;
clay above that; and, floating on the surface of the water,
organic matter.

Repeat this procedure with the other soil samples and compare
your results.

Winter Tasks

Though the garden can retain interest throughout the year, the winter months do involve less work for the gardener. Continue checking plants against weather damage.

There are usually plenty of bright, sunlit days, however cold they may be, and light is at its clearest. Deciduous trees, bare of leaves, show structure. This is the best time to prune them, before the sap begins to rise. Take care not to walk on the soil after heavy rains as the resulting compaction will then have to be corrected.. Whatever the type of soil, cultivation in winter is desirable to improve aeration and to expose pests to the birds; robins are not being especially friendly when they see a fork in action – they just know a good thing when they see it.

EARLY WINTER

GENERAL MAINTENANCE
- Fork over beds when frost-free
- Tidy garden, including sweeping up leaves
- Protect stand-pipes and taps against frost

FRUIT
- Check stored fruit and for wind damage to ties and stakes
- Prune vines, fruit bushes and trees when weather is mild
- Complete root pruning
- Grease-band fruit trees to protect against infestation

MIDWINTER

GENERAL MAINTENANCE
- Continue planting and ordering seedlings
- Check garden structures

LAWNS
- Continue aerating, rake out moss and remove dead leaves

SHRUBS
- Mulch azaleas, rhododendrons, camellias, etc., if not already done
- Ensure young shrubs are protected against frost
- Brush heavy snow off branches to prevent them snapping under the weight. Conifers can be permanently misshapen in a heavy snowfall.

LATE WINTER

GENERAL MAINTENANCE
- Service gardening equipment

LAWNS
- Brush with a birch broom on dry days to remove worm-casts
- Dress with fine sand
- Repair edges
- Continue preparing for spring seeding by raking soil to fine tilth

SHRUBS
- Begin planting in mild weather
- Prune hard summer-flowering clematis

FLOWERS
- Plant (in mild weather) anemones, lilies, buttercups, primroses
- Sow hardy annuals under glass till late in season if weather is mild
- Divide large clumps of perennials
- Sprinkle rock garden with slug pellets
- Prepare ground for sweet peas
- Dig beds for annuals and biennials

LAWNS
- Check for badly drained areas and remedy
- Prepare areas to be sown in spring
- Service lawn mower

SHRUBS
- Continue planting when ground is frost-free and not waterlogged
- Prune shrubs after flowering for bushy summer foliage, particularly elder and sorbaria
- Ensure shrubs are secured against strong winds
- Mulch azaleas, rhododendrons, camellias, etc.

FLOWERS
- Hoe tulip beds and spray with insecticide
- Check bulbs and corms in store

ROSES
- Prune lightly to prevent wind rock
- Continue planting when ground is not waterlogged or frost-bound

VEGETABLES
- Check vegetables in store and discard anything rotten
- Dig over sites for next season's runner beans
- Order seeds

FLOWERS
- Plant lilies, antirrhinums, etc., provided soil is not waterlogged or frost-bound
- Divide perennials
- Check chrysanthemums for waterlogging and aerate with a fork if necessary; also check them for grey mould and spray with fungicide if necessary
- Complete dead-heading of hardy herbaceous plants
- Bring indoors bulbs (e.g. hyacinths) for flowering

ROSES
- Continue planting if weather permits

VEGETABLES
- Order seeds
- Sow (in mild areas) early vegetables (e.g. broad beans, peas)
- Plant rhubarb; cover with straw and manure
- Check stored vegetables and discard anything rotten

FRUIT
- Continue spraying
- Continue pruning
- Continue to check ties and stakes
- Check stored fruit and discard anything rotten

ROSES
- Continue planting if weather permits

VEGETABLES
- Sow early peas and beans when weather is mild; put carrots and parsnips under cold frame
- Plant shallots in shallow drills

FRUIT
- Continue pruning except during frosts

If Winter comes, can
Spring be far behind?
Yes, a long way...

Strawberries

Nae dout God could ha' made a better berry,
but nae dout God ne'er did!

FRUIT OF FRAGARIA CHILENSIS.

Several species, indigenous to various parts of the world, have given rise to numerous varieties. The strawberry will grow in any good garden soil. Tenacious soils do not suit the strawberry, unless ameliorated by such means as have been pointed out in the chapter on soils. Ground that is apt to get very dry from the effects of only ten days' or a fortnight's drought is not suitable, on account of the enormous quantity of water that will be necessary; and if once the plants begin to flag for want of moisture, the crop will be all but lost. A soil that is naturally somewhat moist, but not too wet answers well; and, where the land has admitted of irrigation, we have seen heavy crops produced every year.

FRAGARIA VESCA (WILD STRAWBERRY).

PLANTING The best time for this operation is as soon as the plants are well rooted. If the ground, on account of crops, or owing to other circumstances, cannot be got ready for planting in summer, then it should be done early in the autumn, whilst the ground is warm enough to encourage the plants to strike good roots before winter; or, if this cannot be done, the operation had better be deferred till plants are about to start fresh growth in spring, in February or March, according to the season and the state of the weather. When the ground is ready for planting, furrows should be drawn with a hoe, as if for sowing pease. The plants ought to be carefully taken up with balls, laid on a hand-barrow, and planted with a trowel. The proper distance between the rows varies according to the nature of the soil and the habit of the plant. In planting the roots with the ball of earth should be placed as deep as they can be without covering the heart of the plant. Water must be plentifully given at first, but afterwards sparingly, until the plants have taken root.

CULTIVATION After the plantation has been completed, the ground should be kept clear of weeds, and the surface stirred. From the time the blossoms begin to appear till the fruit is ripe, the ground should never be allowed to become dry. The plants, when in full foliage and active growth, evaporate a large amount of moisture in dry weather. Watering over the tops is not sufficient in hot weather. In some soils, it is necessary to flood the whole surface of the ground repeatedly, so that the water may reach the lowest roots. The leaves should never be allowed to flag, for if permitted to do so they will never perfectly resume their functions, even if afterwards supplied with an abundance of moisture, and from being unable to digest it properly, the fruit will be of bad flavour.

GATHERING Strawberries should be gathered if possible when dry, but not when heated by the sun. For dessert, they ought to be gathered with the calyx, and just as much of the stalk below it as is sufficient to lay hold of it. Those intended for preserving are taken without the calyx.

NEW STRAWBERRY PLANTS FROM OLD

Many strawberry plants produce long cord-like shoots called runners. At intervals of a few feet along these runners there are joints and from each joint leaves and roots grow. It is not difficult to obtain new plants, therefore, by rooting the plantlets which form on the runners. As strawberry plants need replacing every four years or so, getting free replacements is a great boon. The early summer-fruiting types of strawberry start to produce runners in June; some perpetual types have few or no runners, but those that do, produce them later in the summer. In all cases the secret of success is to get new plants rooted as early as possible.

GROWING ALPINE STRAWBERRIES

Alpine strawberries are descended from those growing wild on the slopes of the Alps. The berries are smaller than normal but they have very good flavour. They do not always produce runners but can be grown from seed. Plant the seeds in a tray and keep in the greenhouse. In mid-May move the tray of seedlings to a warm, sheltered corner of the garden to accustom them gradually to outdoor conditions. At the end of May or early in June plant the alpine strawberries a foot apart in a moist and slightly shaded part of your fruit area. Berries should be ready for picking by late summer or early autumn. Next year they will be ready sooner.

The quickest home-grown variety is the perpetual strawberry. Plant these in March, April or early May. Perpetual strawberries produce more than one crop during the latter part of the summer and autumn. Select a piece of ground in a sunny part of your garden for the bed. The plants should be spaced 18 in. apart, with 30 in. between rows so that there is space to walk. Do not forget that strawberries must not be planted at the edge of the bed - they need at least 10 in. in every direction. Water each plant with a full watering can.

If after a week no rain has fallen, water again. No more watering is necessary but it is wise to keep an eye on the strawberry bed. Dry soil soon kills a young plant and the berries will need plenty of moisture to swell them. In a really hot, dry summer, water well every four or five days.

Remove weeds with a hoe or by hand. When you see the first flower buds, carefully nip these off with the nails of your first finger and thumb. When the second lot of blossom appears you can leave it to 'set' fruit. When the berries begin to swell, lay pieces of polythene close to the crown to prevent earth splashing the fruit when it rains. Birds are as fond of strawberries as you, so you will have to protect your plants with netting.

Sweet-smellin' Floo'ers

Maw loves the smell o' floo'ers. Plant some o' these in yer gairden!

Fragrant Garden flowers

Here are some suggestions of plants that will make your garden smell beautiful – and many of them are shrubs, so you will enjoy the smell every year.

Azalea	*Rhododendron*	shrub
Brompton stock	*Matthiola incana*	annual
Buddleia	*Buddleia*	shrub
Buffalo currant	*Ribes odoratum*	shrub
Daphne	*Daphne*	shrub
Fragrant viburnum	*Viburnum farreri*	shrub
Golden barberry	*Berberis stenophylla*	shrub
Honeysuckle	*Lonicera fragrantissima*	shrub
Lavender	*Lavandula*	shrub
Lilac	*Syringa*	shrub
Lily of the valley	*Convallaria majalis*	perennial
Mexican orange blossom	*Choisya ternata*	shrub
Mignonette	*Reseda*	annual
Mock orange	*Philadelphus*	shrub
Myrtle	*Myrtus communis*	shrub
Night scented stock	*Matthiola bicornis*	annual
Oleaster	*Elaeagnus*	shrub
Rose	*Rosa species*	shrub
Sweet alyssum	*Lobularia maritima*	annual
Sweet pea	*Lathyrus odoratus*	annual
Sweet william	*Dianthus barbatus*	biennial
Tobacco plant	*Nicotiana*	annual
Verbena	*Verbena*	annual
Violet	*Viola odorata*	perennial
Witch hazel	*Hamamelis mollis*	shrub
Wintersweet	*Chimonanthus praecox*	shrub

"Sweet William" will dae well onywhere, – even an auld bucket!

The language of flowers

From the 19th century onwards flowers were thought to have particular meanings. While the red rose as a symbol of love is now a universal symbol, many flowers have been given many meanings — and, sometimes, in different cultures they have been given different meanings. Here are some examples:

Daisy - innocence

Fennel - strength

Heather - solitude

Lilac - first love

Lily of the valley - return of happiness

Marigold - grief or jealousy

Rose - beauty

White chrysanthemum - truth

Cultivate the garden for the nose, and the eyes will take care of themselves.

- Robert Louis Stevenson

Gairdenin' Wisdoms

with GAIRDENER BROON

❋❋❋❋❋❋❋❋❋❋❋❋❋❋❋❋❋❋❋❋❋❋❋

STOP PRESS!!! The Big Stooshie

Well, wha'd hae believed it? What a stramash there's been in an' aboot the gairdenin' fowks this week. If ye read ma "Garden" column last week, ye'll ken I invited onybody that felt like it tae drap in tae "The Volunteer" on Tuesday nicht tae find oot how I pit ma new shed the'gither. Well, "The Bugle" editor wis no' pleased... not a bit, nae pleased at a'. He read whit I'd written in the column an' said I was tryin' tae cash in on ma position as the paper's columnist. I was fair dumbfoonert. Imagine the editor actually readin' the newspaper. I thocht he was a REAL journalist. Far as I was aware, he's spent the last thirty years drinking in "The Volunteer" every workin' day o' the week and it's a'body else in the office that pits the newspaper tae bed, so tae speak. Of coorse, I probably underestimate the popularity o' ma wee column and it's maist likely the only thing he bothers tae read and check. He was bilin' mad as weel aboot fowk comin' tae speak tae me at the boozer and then mebbe no' buying "The Bugle" at a' that week. So he decided tae appear at the snug bar in the Volly on the Tuesday jist tae see if onybody DID in fact turn up. And did they no' jist... in their droves!!

Willie McLeod ma freend fae the allotments is on the same dominoes team as masel' on a Tuesday nicht and he'd nae sooner gone oot on a double-six tae pit Bert Michie's smug lot fae "The Anchor" oot o' the local medal when the pub's door near cam' aff its hinges as what looked like the hale gairdenin' population came poorin' intae the pub. It was like Hampden Park comin' oot.

Whit a stooshie. The pub regulars couldna get near the bar for ma freends ordering me drams. Ye see, I'd promised tae spill the beans aboot how I built my allotment shed for a few wee "nippy sweeties" and the guid fowk were payin' their entrance fees as it were. Some o' the aulder crowd couldnae afford tae buy drams and some like Lizzie Small had brocht me bags o' their hame-grown vegetables. Well, in the general stramash, afore I could spill the beans aboot ma shed, Lizzie, no' being sae nifty on her pins and gettin' jostled aboot wi' the crowd, spilled mair than her beans (runner beans that is. Awfy tasty they are). Lizzy went heid ower high heels an' spilled her hale bag o' veg richt next tae the pool table. Fowk wiz skitin' aboot on a' thae rollin' tatties an' neeps an' ingins. There wiz arms an' legs birlin' a' way an' fowk daein the splits and tumblin' cap-ma.

Tam Auchterlonie had jist pit 50 pence in the pool table, when ower it went an' a', wi' a' the snooker ba's addin' tae the rest o' the stuff rollin' aboot the flair. Ye ken, it reminded me o' the village dances at the Auchentogle Fermers' Institute we used tae hae afore the war, when the Eightsome Reels used tae get completely oota hand wi' fowk birlin' and skitin' oota control wi' a' the coo an' horse shit comin' aff the fermers' brogues... an' the flair was like dancin' on the local ice rink. In thae days the lassies were nae sae much daein' the pas-de-ba as jist hittin' the wa'!

Onyway, I digress (a guid word that!) ... the hale thing descended intae farce an' naebody got tae hear onything I said. Fred McAwful, the publican, just shooed a'body oot, rollin' the fallen oot the door on a carpet o' tatties an' ingins and pool balls. When a'thing returned tae something like normal, Tam Auchterlonie managed tae get his gemme o' pool efter a', but wi' some o' the ba's missin', he had tae use a couple o' roond tatties and a red ingin. Gave a hale new meaning tae pottin' the last ba' in the "ingin bag".

When the pub was cleared there was aboot a hunner drams left on the bar that had been bocht for me. We pit them a' in some empty bottles an' donated them tae a local gairdenin' charity... the Friday Night Allotment Swally Club tae be honest.

And ye'll need tae wait yet anither week tae hear a' aboot ma shed. It's worth waitin' for.

Cheers! Slainthe! Bottoms up (like Lizzie Small on Tuesday nicht!)

Gairdener Broon

Tools

These pictures fae Thompson micht remind me.

Tools I must find for ma new shed

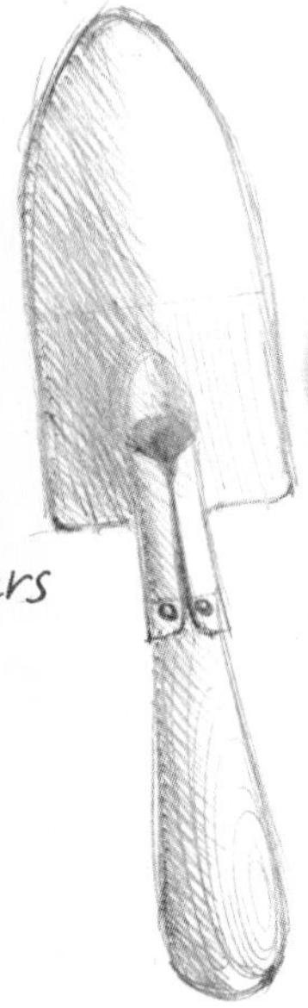

Bill hook
Edge cutter
Fork
Hoe
Kettle
Loppers
Rake

Secateurs
Shears
Spade
Teapot
Trowel
Waterin' can

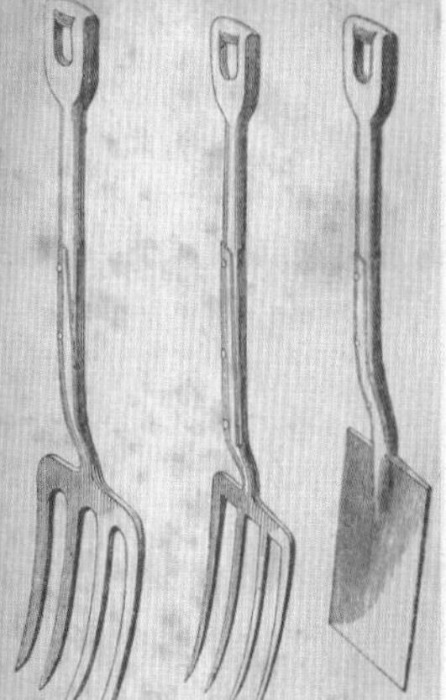

Steel Digging Forks.

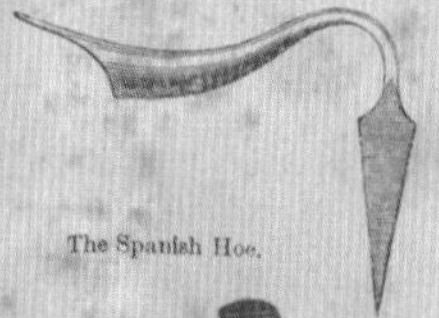

The Spanish Hoe.

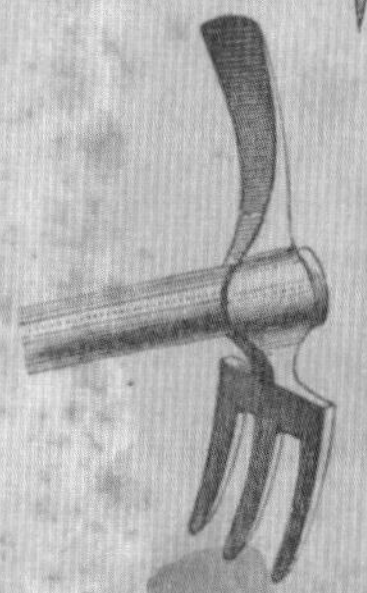

Pickfork.

Pruning Saw.

Fig. 45.

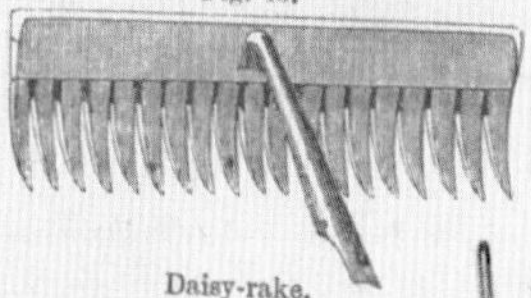

Daisy-rake.

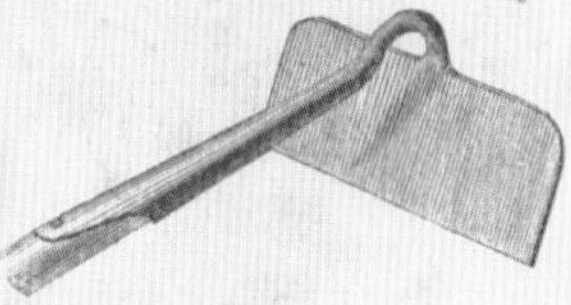

Crane-necked Hoe.

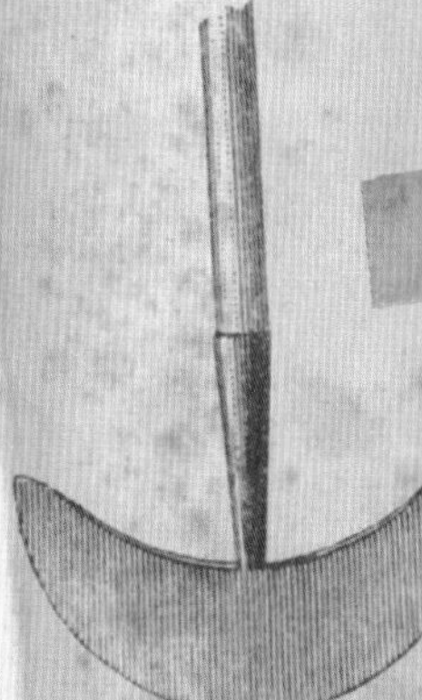

Verge-cutter.

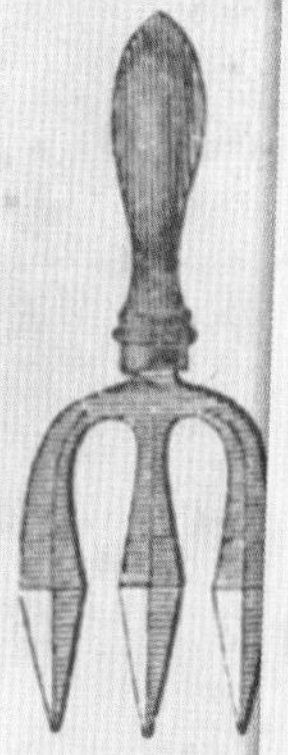

Tau-fork.

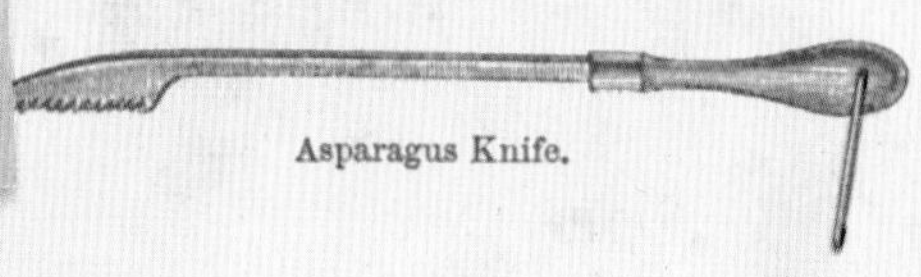

Asparagus Knife.

Noo I'm a writer, ma only tools are paper, baccy, food an' whisky (well, some writer callt William Faulkner said it first).

I always keep some o' the Bairn's plasticine handy - grand for supportin' a bent plant. Bind it roon' wi' a bit o' it.

Pruning.

Pruning.

Pruning.

PRUNING

If you have any trees in your own garden, these tips on pruning and removing them will be useful.

1. Do not prune trees merely by lopping off branches halfway. This can usually be avoided and always looks graceless. Instead, saw from beneath the branch, say 6-12 in. from the trunk of the tree and finish the cut from the top – this prevents the bark tearing back. Then, having removed the main weight, saw off flush with the trunk. It is not necessary to paint wounds.

2. When removing trees altogether, avoid simply sawing them off at ground level if at all possible. Remove stumps completely by the root if you can; rotting wood can create problems by encouraging fungus. Stumps left in the ground reduce planting possibilities unless used to support climbers.

3. With large trees, call in the experts to fell or cut them back. Check with the Council that the tree is not covered by a preservation order.

The oldest and tallest trees in Britain

THE OLDEST TREE in Britain (and probably Europe) is a yew by the kirk at Fortingall, near Aberfeldy in Perthshire. It is estimated to be between 2,500 and 5,000 years old. Its trunk had a girth of 52 ft in 1769, although this is now less obvious to see as the surviving growth is around the edge of the tree and all the wood has vanished from its centre. It is a local tradition that Pontius Pilate was born nearby and may have played in the shadow of the yew.

The tallest tree in Britain is the Stronardon Douglas fir near Dunans Castle in Argyll, coming in at 209 ft. tall – that's about 40 ft. taller than Nelson's Column in Trafalgar Square in London.

The best time to plant a tree was 20 years ago. The second-best time is now.

Small specimen trees make a great addition to a garden, but you need to take a lot of care in selecting and deciding where to plant a tree. There are a number of important factors to remember.

- Find out how tall and wide the tree will grow. A tree should be planted at least its maximum height away from your house (and your neighbours' houses). For most gardens this should rule out planting a traditional woodland tree, such as an oak, which can grow to 80 ft and more.

- Do not plant any tree close enough to your house to disturb its foundations or its drains. There is as much growth below the ground as above.

- Do not plant trees too close together. As they grow their branches will interfere with each other and you will constantly have to prune them.

- Do not plant a tree where, in future years, it will shade your flower beds or conservatory.

- Select a specimen tree that is designed for garden use and will add real interest to the garden

When looking for trees, consider the smaller varieties of maple (Acer), birch (Betula), flowering cherries (Prunus), Judas tree (Cercis), crab apples (Malus), hawthorn (Crataegeus), weeping pear (Pyrus), rowan or mountain ash (Sorbus).

Ginkgo or Maidenhair Tree
This tree is referred to a s a living fossil. It is the only survivor of a group of trees that flourished over 250 million years ago – fossils of the tree dating back this far have been found. In the wild it survives in China, but it has become a popular cultivated tree, and, having lived that long, it will not be surprising to learn that it can be grown quite easily and will put up well with urban pollution – some even survived the atomic blast at Hiroshima. Ginkgo extracts have been used as a traditional medicine, but there is no evidence that it helps to delay memory loss. The tree will reach a height of around 10 ft after 10 years and can then grow up to 80 ft and more. It has very distinctive fan-shaped leaves.

Use trees comin' intae leaf as a weather forecast:
Oak afore ash, we're in for a splash;
Ash afore oak, we're in for a soak.

The twins tellt me tae plant a ginkgo tree as I'd like havin' anither auld fossil aroond.

Vegetables

The next few pages tell ye a' aboot the best veg tae grow in yer gairden or allotment.

FIG. 306. EARLY YORK CABBAGE.

Why Grow Vegetables?

Whether it is on your allotment, in your back garden or even in whatever space you have in a back green or balcony, growing your own vegetables is one of the most satisfying of activities – as well as one which will provide your family with cheap, wholesome and wonderfully fresh food.

Homegrown vegetables are really fresh. The lettuces you will grow and cut will be crisp and runner beans will be firm – better than most of those in the shops which have had to be picked some time before. During the journey to the shop flavour is unavoidably lost. Wait until you pick and eat your own garden-grown peas. Then you will know just how fresh peas taste when they are really fresh.

MAKING A VEGETABLE PLOT

Like all living things vegetables have special requirements. Most vegetables are quick growers so they need the right conditions for healthy growth. Try to have the plot in a sunny part of the garden, with well-drained soil. Never try growing vegetables under a large, spreading tree. Not only will the tree cast a lot of shade but its roots rob other plants of soil foods.

In very windy places, a low wall, a hedge or a fence will break the force of strong winds which can damage growing vegetables. But an old hedge, like a large tree, has long, hungry roots so try to keep vegetables at least 4 ft. away.

Nearly all vegetables should be grown in a three-year rotation. This means dividing the vegetable garden into three plots and growing different groups of vegetables in each plot each year in a three-year cycle. Rotation helps break the disease cycle and avoids starving areas of the garden of particular trace elements.
A notable exception to the rotational scheme is the runner bean. These replenish the soil with nitrogen from the air and will feed the ground in this way from late summer to the first frosts. They can be grown year after year in the same spot, so there is every reason to erect a permanent supporting structure, not just temporary bean-poles.

RAISED BEDS

The best way of growing vegetables is to make raised beds. These are beds which are raised a minimum of 6 in. above the ground and are between 3 and 4 ft. wide. The edges of the beds are supported by wooden or concrete frames. The soil in the beds requires much compost to be added. Once the beds are made the soil does not have to be dug over every year as it is not walked on and does not become compressed. Plants are usually grown more closely together than in a traditional vegetable patch, and yields are higher.

Thinin' seedlins seems awfy wasteful, but it means the plants left can grow big an' strong.

160

Beetroot

LONG YELLOW BEETROOT.

GROWING BEETROOT

Beetroot is becoming more popular again – it's both tasty and very nutritious (and its purple colour brightens up any dish).

1. Sow beetroots seed directly into the ground, any time between April and July.

2. Plant to a depth of about ¾ in. As beetroot seeds are in clusters, space these out to 3 in. apart in the drill. The rows should be about 15 in. apart.

3. When the small plants have three or four leaves, thin down to one plant in each cluster.

4. Harvest some while they are young – about 1 in. in diameter. They then have a first-class flavour. Do not dig beetroot. Grasp the leaves, twist and pull.

5. Those you do not pull will grow larger and may be pulled later on.

6. All beetroot should be harvested by early October. To store beetroot cut off the tops, leaving about 2 in. of stalk attached to the crown. If stored in sand or dry earth in a shed, it should remain usable until early next summer.

If you are very limited for space, you can grow beetroot in pots.

Remember that you can exhibit your beetroot at the Annual Show, but don't go mad about getting the biggest. Really big beetroot are not good for eating, and you won't beat the world record anyway – a Dutch grower produced a 156 lb beetroot.

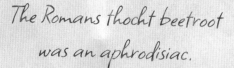

The Romans thocht beetroot was an aphrodisiac.

WHITE LEAF BEETROOT.

Here's a bonnie young beetroot I pulled this mornin'!

Brussels Sprouts

GROWING BRUSSELS SPROUTS

Brussels sprout plants may not look much like cabbages but the plant it-self is a form of cabbage and each individual Brussels sprout is like a miniature cabbage. You may grow your own from seeds or buy plants in May.

1. Seeds should be planted in a cold frame in early March. Sow the seeds in rows 3 in. apart. Thin out the plants to 2 in. apart when they are big enough to handle.

2. From late April, start planting out your seedlings. They are planted like cabbage plants but they grow large and leafy and need more space than cabbages. Leave 2½ ft between the plants in each row and 2½ ft between the rows.

3. Consider sowing crops like radishes and lettuce between the rows in early summer.

4. The sprouts form on the tall stem. Those nearest the ground are picked first, usually in November or early December. Sprouts higher up the stem then get larger and are picked in December and in January. The top of the plant looks like a loose cabbage. These plant tops are good for cooking like cabbage, and are the last part to be cut.

Brussels sprouts did indeed come from Brussels and in Victorian times seeds were always imported from Belgium.

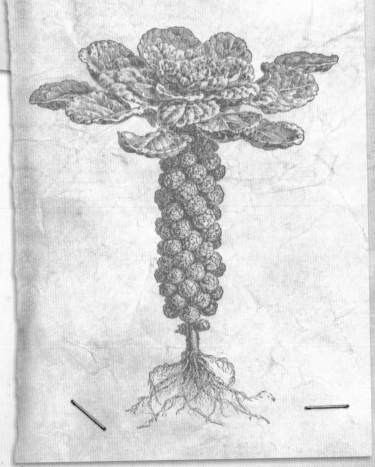

Wha's The maist popular wine at Christmas?

"Do I ha' tae eat ma Brussels sprouts?"

I really like these baby cabbages!

SMALL WHITE CABBAGE BUTTERFLY AND CATERPILLAR.

Dinnae plant strawberries next tae Brussels sprouts, they dinna like each ither!

Cabbages

LARGE WHITE CABBAGE BUTTERFLY.

GROWING CABBAGES

Spring is the time to buy your cabbage plants for summer and autumn harvesting. Some sorts of cabbages grow quickly; others slowly. Cabbage plants do not grow well in loose soil. If you have dug the garden recently, tread on the area where you aim to grow cabbages. Slow, even treading firms the soil. Then rake the surface so that it is once again neat and level. Make sure that the ground has been well composted.

1. Mark the position of the first row with the garden line. If you are going to plant several rows leave 18 in. between each row.

2. Make holes about 3 in. deep at 15 in. apart alongside the garden line. Unless the ground is very wet, fill the holes with water. Wait for the water to drain away before you start planting.

3. Take a cabbage plant in your left hand and place it in the first hole so that lowest leaf of the plant is in line with the surface of the ground. Use your right hand to press some soil up to and tightly against the root of the cabbage plant and fills the first dibber hole with soil.

4. Carry on planting the rest of the cabbage plants in this way. Make sure that the plants are firmly planted. Pull gently at one of the leaves of a plant to check this.

5. If the weather is hot and dry fill the depression beside each plant with water on the first and second evenings after planting.

6. Hoe around the plants now and then to kill any weed seedlings. Hoe carefully to avoid damaging any plants.

7. Cabbages are ready to cut when they have tight round or tight cone-shaped heads.

8. In August remove any caterpillars that you see.

9. Sow spring cabbage seeds in late August directly into the soil or plant seedlings you have bought by mid-September.

Watch out for the cabbage root fly maggot - see page 119

A drop o' beer helps ma' cabbages grow better

Babe Ruth, the baseball player, kept his head cool wi' a cabbage leaf under his bunnet.

USING A DIBBER
Gardeners often use a dibber when planting cabbage plants. Instead of buying a cabbage dibber, make one from the handle of an old spade or garden fork, or from a piece of wood of similar thickness—like a broom handle or cricket stump.

Spring cabbage is planted in summer, summer cabbage in spring, is that dear!

Carrots

Carrot seeds are awfy wee. So that ye dinna sow them too thickly, put some dry sand intae a wee tin or jam jar. Empty a packet o' seeds intae the sand and shake well tae mix the sand and seeds. Use yer thumb an' forefinger tae sprinkle the mixture intae the seed drill.

Carrot—James's Intermediate

A few strange lookin' carrots.

Carrot flies can make your crop unusable and you need to protect your plants. As carrot flies seldom fly higher than 18 in., surround the carrot plot with a thick impenetrable mesh or cover the plants with fleece.

This 'scarred' ane was grown too close tae anither!

```
CARROTS

You can enjoy carrots for much of the year. Early
(quick growing) varieties can be planted in March, the
main crop in April and further 'early' varieties in
July.

1. Sow in 1-in. deep seed drills. Cover the seeds with
soil using a rake. Use a plant label, on which you
have written the name of the vegetable and the date
you sowed the seeds, to mark each row.

2. When sowing more than one row of carrots allow 1ft.
between rows.

3. Weeds have to be removed now and then. Those
growing very near the seedlings are best pulled out by
hand.

4. Pull young carrots now and then when large enough
for eating.

5. Stop pulling them in late July and do any final
thinning so that each carrot left has about 2 in. of
room.

6. The carrots left will grow larger and may be dug in
September or October. Cut the tops off the carrots and
they can be stored in the shed in boxes of sand or dry
soil for use over winter.
```

Just cos we're used to orange carrots, it disnae mean they've aye been orange. Years ago ye could get black and purple carrots - ye can still buy thae varieties th'day.

Carrots help ye see in the dark, ma auld Air Force mates tellt me!

GROWING LETTUCE

Sow seeds in 1-in. deep drills. Wait until the seedlings are about 2 in. high and have four or five leaves before you thin them. Thin them, leaving those left to grow on at 12 in. apart in the row. If you dig up a cluster of seedlings with the trowel you may plant them 12 in. apart somewhere else. Sow seeds every two weeks or so to keep a regular supply of lettuce.

CABBAGE LETTUCE.

Marrows –
TRAP THE HEAT OF THE SUN

Some vegetable seeds germinate in quite cool weather; others rot if sown in cold soil. Marrow seeds, for example, are not sown in the garden until summery weather may be expected. Here is a way of trapping some heat from the sun to give your marrow plants an early start. An early start means earlier growth and earlier harvesting. You will need a packet of seeds and a few jam jars.

There are two kinds of marrow plants. One, the bush marrow, makes a bushy plant. The other, the trailer or trailing marrow, makes a long, spreading vine. Bush plants need almost 1 sq yd. of ground for each plant. Trailers need much more room if you let the plants roam around on top of the soil. But trailing marrows may be trained upwards as you will see later.

Wait until early May before sowing seeds. Before you sow, rake the soil level. Then make 1-in. deep holes where you intend to sow the seeds. If the soil is very dry fill the holes with water and wait for it to sink into the ground. Put two seeds in each hole and then fill them with fine soil. Stand a jam jar, open end downwards, over each spot.

It takes about a week for marrow seeds to germinate and push through the soil. If both seeds germinate under each jam jar there will not be enough room for both of them as they grow. Wait for a week and then pinch off the stem of one of them. Pinch through the stem at soil level. Do not try pulling out the unwanted seedlings. If you do, you may loosen the roots of the ones you wish to keep.

Marrow seedlings grow rapidly. Remove the jam jars when the leaves of the plants touch the glass. In warm, dry weather give the plants some water occasionally. Hold the spout of the can near the ground so that you do not splash the plants.

Marrow plants need a lot of water in dry weather. Cut marrows when they are still young and tender. They will be about 10–12 in. long. If you cut marrows regularly, more and more will be produced until September when the plants start to die.

Vegetable Marrow

COS LETTUCE.

If ye only have space for pots, plant 'cut an' come agin' varieties. Jist pick the leaves ye need and the plant carries on growin'.

The heaviest marra weighed more than oor Maggie!

Onions

*They used tae say that the juice o' ingins rubbed
on a bald heid would mak' the hair grow agin.*

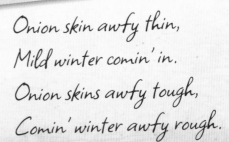

CULTIVATION OF ONIONS

Those usually grown are spring or
salad onions and main crop onions.
With both, no thinning is necessary
until some are large enough to eat
in salads.

Spring onions: Pull them on and off
all summer for use when wanted. In
very dry weather you may find it
easier to use a hand fork to get
them out of the soil. Do not leave
any to get really large or they
will be 'hot' to eat.

Main crop onions: These are the
large bulb onions used in stews and
soups and for frying. When some of
the seedlings are large enough pull
some for salads. Stop pulling them
in the middle of July and leave
strong seedlings at 8 in. apart
in the row. These will swell into
full-sized onions by September.

AN EASY WAY WITH ONIONS

Main crop onions may be grown from
seeds but many gardeners grow them
from miniature onions known as sets.
Unless you can make room for a lot
do not buy more than 1 lb. Leave
them in a cool place like a garage
or shed until you wish to plant them.

Late March and early April are
good times for planting onion sets.
There are two ways of doing this.
If the soil is quite loose fix the
garden line in position so that
you have a straight row and then
push the sets in the soil at 10 in.
apart all along the row. If you are
planting a lot of sets leave 12 in.
between rows. Push the bulbs into
the ground so that they are buried
with just the tip of each showing
at soil level.

The other way of planting is used
if the soil is hard. Lay the garden
line in position and use a draw
hoe to make a 1-in. deep drill
or furrow. Plant the sets 10 in.
apart in the drill and then cover
carefully with soil to fill the
drill. When planting sets this way
make sure that they are sitting
upright in the drill. Later on
when a few leaves show, scoop a
little soil away from the plants.
This helps them to swell. Do it
carefully so that the plants are
not damaged.

In late August the leaves will
topple over and lie on the ground.
Here and there the leaves of a
plant may not do so. Bend these
carefully and wait for the leaves
to shrivel and die, it will then
be time to harvest. Harvesting
main crop onions is easy, just walk
along the row and pick them up.

STORING ONIONS

You won't use all your onions
straight away, so prepare them
for storing. Only dry, well-
ripened onions store well. Leave
them in a sunny position, but take
them indoors at night or if rain
threatens.

Within a week or two the roots
and leaves will be very dry. Rub
off the dead roots. Don't worry
if some pieces of dry, loose onion
skin fall off when you are doing
this. Onions may be stored in
single layers in trays, but why
not rope them? The best place to
hang your onions is in a cool
garage or a garden shed.

Onions

*Onion skin awfy thin,
Mild winter comin' in.
Onion skins awfy tough,
Comin' winter awfy rough.*

Gairdenin' Wisdoms

with GAIRDENER BROON

❋❋❋❋❋❋❋❋❋❋❋❋❋❋❋❋❋❋❋❋❋❋❋❋❋

ME AGAIN. Bit fragile the day efter The Boolin' Club smoker last nicht. Had maybe a smidgeon ower much o' ma favourite …

Onions! What wid ye dae withoot them? Every meal I've ever had wi' the family at 10 Glebe Street or at the But an' Ben has had at least a DOZEN onions in it.

Onions are aboot the easiest things tae grow. The Bairn likes tae help me wi' growin' onions in the wee garden at the But an' Ben. Biggest problem wi' the But an' Ben is keepin' the rabbits aff the gairden. We once got the loan o' a big Monsterlander Dug (some name like that) fae Farmer Gray at the farm. Tae keep the rabbits aff oor "greens" ye understand. Ferocious-lookin brute. But turned oot it was a big safty … and what's worse, it was a VEGETARIAN and ate a' the lettuces it wiz supposed tae guard. Found it ae day asleep in the gairden wi' a carrot stickin' oot its mooth and three rabbits wi' full bellies fast asleep on its back.

But back tae the onions. Me and the Bairn have rare fun plantin' them oot at a' times o' the year. Ye will hae tae try really hard tae mak' a hash o' this. Mind an' gie them plenty watter tae get them roond and juicy. A nice onion bed is aboot as satisfying as a big saft four-poster, an eiderdown and a guid book.

An' ye ken this, oor local chip shop sells mair PICKLED onions than it does haddock. I widna be surprised tae hear fowk occasionally asking for a pickled onion supper and a wee fish on the side. Onions grow best in a raised firm bed, a bit like masel'. I aye think tae get a guid onion, ye need tae prepare its bed well in advance o' plantin', a bit like yer best friend comin' tae stay. Nuthin' worse than makin' up their bed at the last meenit while they're watchin' ye, as if ye didna really want them tae bide overnight. They like light soil, nice and firm … the onions that is, no' yer friends … so ye need tae dae a bit o' rakin' and hoeing an' sieving.

My favourite method o' eating onions is tae fry them wi' a wee drappie lard and eat them wi' a roll an' sausage. Onions are guid for the blood, guid for yer heart and mak' ye strong … like me. We have a saying at the allotment that "three a week keeps the doctor away … three a day keeps A'BODY away".

I aye laugh when I hear yon story aboot Dundee, whaur they sell braw pies and bridies and onions are aye ca'd INGINS. Something aboot a lad wanting tae buy a plain bridie and an onion bridie in an Auld Dundee Pie Shoppe … "A PLEN BRIDIE AN' ANINGIN ANE AN' A' … PLEASE!!"

And as fowk are wont tae say when they want to be complimentary aboot their best pal … "Aye, he really kens his onions!"

I'm awa' for an onion bridie richt this very minute.

Cheers, fowks,

Aye Yours,

Gairdener Broon

x

GREETINGS FROM AUCHENTOGLE

AUCHENTOGLE Twinned with St Brun, Belgium

GROSSET'S FILTERLESS

169

Peas

GROWING PEAS

There are many different varieties of garden peas. Some make short plants and others are very tall. Some grow quickly, others slowly. Peas that grow quickly are known as "first early"; most of them do not grow taller than 2 ft. Peas where you can eat the pod as well as the peas within are called "mange tout" or "sugar peas".

There are also many different ways of sowing and growing peas. Here is one method:

1. Mark the row with the garden line then make a 10-in. wide, 2-in. deep trench with the draw hoe.

2. Sow the pea seeds in three rows on the bottom of the trench so that each seed is about 3 in. from its neighbour.

3. After sowing the seeds use a draw hoe or rake to fill in the trench.

4. Many kinds of birds like pea seeds. Prevent them from eating the seeds you have just sown by caging the row with black cotton. Get some lengths of wood or bamboo canes about 30 in. long. Push these into the ground here and there on either side of the row. Tie black cotton to one of the sticks and run it around all of the sticks several times and across the top. You will then have a black cotton cage into which no birds will venture.

5. Pea plants like to climb, and you can use garden canes, twigs or cuttings from trees or shrubs as pea sticks (sections of trellis are also ideal). To help them climb, the plants produce tender, twisting growths. These tendrils will grasp the support and grow on it. Pea plants grown in this way look like a neat, low hedge.

6. Hoe around the row to prevent weeds from growing. Do not worry if a lot of small weed seedlings appear among the peas. Most of these weeds will be smothered by the pea plants. If you try to pull out these weeds you may also uproot some of the pea plants.

7. If the weather is dry when the pea plants are flowering and when the pods are swelling give them some water. Evening is the best time.

8. Pick a pod now and then to sample the peas inside. Never leave peapods to swell out until they are as tight as a drum. By that time the peas inside will have lost their sugary taste. They will also be tough.

Pea, Dwarf Variety

The Twins are as like as twa peas in a pod.

170

Potatoes

When ye hear the cuckoo shout
Tis time tae plant yer tatties oot

RECORD   VIRUS-FREE KING EDWARD   RUA   AVENIR

MAJESTIC   MARIS PIPER   PENTLAND CROWN   PENTLAND DELL

30

GROWING POTATOES

Potatoes are planted in April. To be able to dig them as quickly as possible, plant quick-growing "first earlies". Slightly later varieties are called "second earlies" and there are also "main crop" varieties that produce bigger potatoes later in the year. You can buy seed potatoes from early in the New Year from garden centres. There are many different types of potato with distinctive flavours and textures when cooked.

1. Stand your seed potatoes in a tray so that they may sprout. This is called "chitting". Keep the tray of potatoes near a window to give them plenty of light. Keep the potatoes indoors because they can be damaged by frost.

2. Choose a dry day during the second half of April for planting or whenever local gardeners advise. As young plants are damaged by frost, you need to avoid late frosts. Use a garden line to make straight rows. With the spade, make a 6-in. trench along the garden line.

3. Always plant potatoes with the young sprouts on them pointing upwards. Leave 12 in. between each potato in the row (18 in. for main crop varieties). Use a rake to fill in the trench, furrow or hole after planting.

4. If you plant more than one row leave 2 ft. between the rows.

5. Wait for the potato shoots to come up. When the plants are about 8 in. high move some earth to support the stem ("earthing up").

6. After the plants have flowered dig up a plant, trying not to spike a potato on your fork. If the potatoes are not large wait another two weeks.

7. Dig up new early potatoes as needed. Cut off the potato plant once its leaves begins to die back

8. Main crop potatoes should be harvested once the plant has died back.

Dinnae eat tatties that have turned green in the sun. Ye can boil them up and then use the water as a general insecticide.

I found this auld seed tattie at the back o' ma shed - looks like the potato fae the Planet X!

Maw's tip:
Add a sprig o' mint tae yer boiling o' new tatties

171

French Beans

Plant kidney beans, if ye be sae willin'
When elm leaves are as big as a shillin'.
When elm leaves are as big as a penny
Ye must plant beans if ye mean tae have any.

GROWING FRENCH BEANS

Make a seed drill for dwarf French beans

French beans are always expensive in the shops, but they are not difficult to grow. You can grow climbing French beans, which grow up bean poles, rather like runner beans, or dwarf French beans, which are short, bushy plants.

GROWING DWARF FRENCH BEANS

1. Use the garden line to make a straight seed drill. Make the drill 2 in. deep and 10 in. wide with a draw hoe. If the ground is very dry, fill the furrow with water.

2. When the water has drained away, sow the seeds in two rows about 8 in. apart. After sowing, fill the seed drill with soil. Rake the surface level so that it is neat and tidy.

3. Pull out any weeds you see growing near the bean plants. Hoe around the row occasionally to prevent weeds growing there.

4. Give the bean plants some water in dry weather.

5. The pods are ready to pick when they are about 6 in. long and quite flat. Do not leave any pods to swell and get tough.

Some dwarf French bean varieties have green pods. They are also varieties with yellow pods. These are easily seen and picking them is much simpler. French beans originally came from India. they are also called kidney beans, because of the shape of the beans in the pods.

Runner Beans

Knock, knock
Who's there?
Bean.
Bean who?
Bean a while
since I saw ye

GROWING RUNNER BEANS

A wigwam is ideal for runner bean growing.

1. Push four tall poles or canes into the ground 2 ft. apart.

2. Tie a piece of soft wire near the bottom of one of the poles and wind it round all four poles only once. To this wire tie 24 lengths of soft wire or string. Tie their loose ends to the top of the wigwam.

3. Use a draw hoe to make a 2-in. deep furrow around the wigwam and quite close to it.

4. If the soil is very dry, fill the furrow with water before you sow the seeds.

5. Sow the runner bean seeds about 4 in. apart in the furrow and then fill it with soil.

6. The bean plants will grasp the wire or strings and climb up them.

7. When the plants reach the top of the wigwam, pinch out the tip of each plant.

8. There will be a fine summer display of red or white flowers, depending on the variety sown, and plenty of long straight beans.

9. The runner beans will need watering if August is hot and sunny.

10. Pick your beans before the seeds start to swell when the pods toughen. Pick the pods regularly and more pods will form quickly.

Whit's the
fastest veggie?
Runner beans!
HA HA!

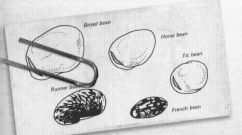

Tomatoes

GROWING TOMATOES

If you can have the space in the greenhouse use it to grow your own tomatoes. Tomatoes don't like cold weather and can only be grown outside where summers are hot. Tomato plants are on sale in May and early June. You can use growbags to grow them in. Do not plant tomato plants deeply. Plant so that the top of the soil ball is in line with the surface of the ground. After planting firm the soil around each plant with your hands.

Tomato plants in a greenhouse grow to height of around 5 ft. Tie tall plants to bamboo cane supports.

Although tomato plants like the sun-trapped warmth in the greenhouse, they do not like stuffy conditions. One greenhouse ventilator at least should always be open unless you expect the night temperatures to be very low. In warm weather the greenhouse door should be left open all day and closed each evening. Unless they have lots of fresh air, tomato plants become 'sick'.

Tomato plants also need plenty of water. At first they may not need much but in hot summer weather they must be watered each evening.

Tomato plants make two different kinds of side shoots. Those on the main stem are flower shoots. First there are buds, then small yellow flowers and later on green tomatoes which swell and turn red or yellow, depending on the variety.

The other side shoots appear at the point where the large leaves and the main stem meet. These side shoots are not wanted so pinch them out between your finger and thumb when they are quite small.

At some time in August the plants will be as tall as the bamboo canes. It is now time to stop the plants growing any taller so that they put energy into ripening the green fruits. To stop them growing just pinch out the top of each of them. Bunches of tomatoes are called 'trusses'. Pick ripe tomatoes from the trusses during August and September. Not all the tomatoes may have ripened by late September but they will ripen more quickly indoors. Pick them all and store them in a tray or in a drawer in a warm room. The tiny hard green tomatoes seldom ripen well. They can be used to make tomato chutney.

JORDAN'S
PRIME QUALITY
SEEDS

CHERRY TOMATO
"HIGH MAINTENANCE"

FROM JORDAN'S GARDEN RETREAT, NORFOLK

If ye've got loads o' green tomatoes, the cauld weather's comin' an' there's nae sun tae ripen them, ye can try puttin' them in a brown paper bag wi' some banana skins. Otherwise gie them tae Maw tae mak' chutney.

Other Veg

GROWING PARSNIPS

From late March onwards sow seeds. Choose a calm day as parsnip seeds are easily blown by the wind. Sow quite thickly as parsnips are not the best at germinating. Thin the seedlings twice. When they are quite tiny, thin them to 1 in. apart. In late June thin again so that those seedlings left to grow on are about 8 in. apart in a single row. Your parsnips will be ready for digging at any time between November and February.

GROWING NEEPS

Called Swedes by the English and the only accompaniment for haggis. Sow seeds in drills 18 in. apart at the start of June. Thin to about 1 ft. apart, and then harvest from late autumn onwards.

GROWING KAIL

The hardy stalwart of the kailyard. Sow seeds in April and May in drills 9 in. apart. Thin plants in individual drills to 6 in. apart, and can be further thinned by transplanting plants later. Harvest the kail head early in the New Year and many side shoots will then grow. It is a very hardy plant and will grow in almost any soil. It is improved by frosts. It is not to everyone's taste.

Turnip—Early White Dutch

A pumpkin floo'er maks a grand snack if ye fry it in a light batter - get them afore they open!

There are lots mair vegetables tae grow. Ye can easily find oot more in books aboot growin' vegetables

Artichokes	Endive
Asparagus	Garlic
Aubergine	Kohlrabi
(in a greenhouse)	Leek
Broad beans	Pumpkins
Broccoli	Radish
Cauliflower	Rocket
Celeriac	Spinach
Celery	Spinach beet (perpetual
Chicory	spinach)
Courgette	Squash
Cucumber	Sweetcorn

Maggie tried the garlic diet - fae a distance her friends thocht she looked thinner.

Gairdenin' Wisdoms

with

GAIRDENER BROON

✣✣✣✣✣✣✣✣✣✣✣✣✣✣✣✣✣✣✣✣✣✣✣✣✣

THE HISTORY OF THE SHED, PART 2

HELLO, HELLO. It's me again ... "Gairdener" Broon, yer number one greenfinger columnist.

A'thing on the home front seems tae have calmed doon now and life at "The Volunteer Arms" has got back tae what passes for normal efter Tuesday nicht's "debauchle". "The Bugle" editor has tellt me tae concentrate on gairdening metters and leave ither things tae ither fowk ... or I'm fired. I jist laughed at that. He widna dare fire me ... the newspaper's circulation has soared since I started writin' for them.

There must be a copy o' "The Bugle" in every hoose, garden shed and allotment "privy" in Auchentogle. Some fowk say it's the CDs the paper is gi'en awa' free that's boostin' the sales ... the recordings o' the Auchentogle Pipe Band at the Braemar Gathering in the presence o' Her Majesty. That's according tae whether ye believe Pipe Major Davie Marr' s offeeshal story ... or whether ye believe Willie McLeod wha drove the band bus that day.

I've kent Willie since we were pals at Primary and I've never heard him tell a lie ... well, that's no' strictly true. There was yon time he tellt his Missus he'd been workin' nichts, when in fact he'd been wi' me playin' three-card-brag in the Boolin' Club wi' the fowk fae Freuchie wi' loads o' money and nae idea how tae play cairds ... oh, aye an' there wiz that business wi' Effie McLary fae Ballingry, aye, but anyway, he's a stickler for the truth fifty per cent o' the time.

As for Major Marr, nae wonder he can play the 'pipes. He's fu' o' mair wind than a hale case o' Heinz Beans. Braemar Gathering my Aunty Fanny, and Her Majesty? HER MAJESTY? Jist havers, nuthin' but havers. Accordin' tae Willie McLeod, this partic'lar Braemar Gathering was in October and the band was in a big lay-by just ootside Braemar on the A93 and the only "Her Majesty" present was Davie's ain missus and ye ken fine how he aye refers tae her as "Her Majesty wants this, Her Majesty says that, Her Majesty winna like that ... ".

So no, I dinna think the free CDs have sellt a single extra copy. It's ma magnetic personality, unique gairdening tips (wha else kens how tae grow tatties like neeps?) and my modesty that shines through the writing. That's what's makin' "The Bugle" circulation grow like sunfloo'ers.

Now, I'd better tell ye a' aboot the Allotment Shed withoot mair ado afore the editor nips me in the bud like he's threatened. Are ye sittin' comfortably? Then I'll begin ...

Efter the collapse o' the auld shed, I had the best bonfire Auchentogle had seen since the end o' the Boer War. Then I cleared the space at the back o' the allotment and borrowed shuttering fae Willie ower the wa'. Shuttering's like big planks o' wood that ye stake oot like a dam, markin' oot the floor area o' yer shed. If ye want tae dae this yersel' mak' it a big floor area ... big sheds are the biz. Ye need a lot mair room than ye'd ever imagine for a' the essential gairdening things ... the card table, the stove an' coffee pot, lots o' shelves for the tea cups an' biscuit tins an' whisky an' sherry bottles, sweetie jars for the bairns, tins for soor plooms and grannie sookers ... an' spades an' forks an' hoes as weel, of course.

Once a' the shuttering was pinned in place me an' Willie McLeod mixed up a' the cement tae pour in tae the hole. Back-breaking business that I can tell ye. I was sair jist watchin' Willie dae it!

Then there was the fun bit, slooshing the cement aboot in the shuttering, wading aboot in it in oor wellies and stampin' it intae the corners tae mak' the foundation jist richt. Had tae dae that in case we mebbe had a wee dance in the shed on occasion ... an' we did. There's nuthin' quite like the dancin' for gettin' tae haud a bonnie lassie roond the waist ... jist in case she stumbles, ye understand! I had a brainwave when a' the wet cement was poured up tae the brim o' the shuttering. I buried a' ma auld love letters deep in the cement so they'd no' embarrass onybody when I shuffle aff fae this life.

Unfortunately, while I was bendin' ower tae sink ma letters in the cement, I drapped ma wallet richt deep PLOP! intae the cement, an' it sank withoot trace. I got sic a shock, my false teeth fell oot as weel and that's whaur they are tae this very day. I faked aboot in the cement for a bit trying tae pit hands on ma wallet, but nae luck and it's doon there now forever alang wi' ma false teeth and love letters. Losin' the wallet was bad enough what wi' ma pension book and some stamps in it, but there was fifteen shillin's and thruppence in it as weel. I sometimes wake up in the nicht dreamin' aboot it ... no' that it wid buy ye much nowadays ... a packet o' tattie crisps if ye're lucky ...

An' I'll finish the story the next time ...

Aye Yours,

Gairdener Broon

x

TWO GIANT WEEDS

Japanese knotweed and giant hogweed are two unwelcome plants that you should look out for. Japanese knotweed, a tall, invasive and tough plant was originally was brought to Britain as an ornamental garden plant, which then escaped into the countryside. It can grow 3 ft in four weeks and reaches over 10 ft. tall, while its roots can reach down 18 ft. Biological control with species of Japanese plant lice is being considered as eradication is proving almost impossible.

The perennial giant hogweed originally came from the Caucasus mountains and was also introduced as an ornamental garden plant; indeed, it is the largest European herbaceous plant. It can have leaves that are more than 3 ft wide and its enormous white flower heads are at the top of hollow stalks that can be 12 ft high. One plant can produce up to 100,000 seeds. As well as being so large, contact with the plant releases sap which can cause severe rashes and blisters when exposed to sunlight. If some sap gets on you, wash it off immediately and stay out of the sunlight and seek medical advice if any rash or blister develops. If you have the plant in your garden take professional advice on how to destroy it, as it is very tenacious.

Weeds

Some weeds are easier to get rid of than others – annual weeds die at the end of the season, but if they have seeded, they will return. Perennial weeds can be very difficult to eradicate because they will keep growing back from their roots. If part of your garden is infested with them, you cannot hope to plant anything new there and expect it will thrive until you have dealt with the weeds. They will choke your precious plant.

ANNUAL WEEDS

There is an old warning dictum on annual weeds: 'one year's weed, seven years' seed', which points towards the obvious truth that it's better to get rid of these weeds before they seed. One way to do this is by hoeing the earth between your plants. Use a sharp bladed hoe that severs the leaves from the roots of the plant. This will destroy all weed seedlings before they get established, after which time it might be necessary to pull the weeds out by hand or use a weed killer (one containing diquat or fatty acids should do the trick).

PERENNIAL WEEDS

Weeds like bell vine, oxalis, ground elder, couch and bindweed are difficult to dig out entirely; sometimes the only way to eradicate them effectively is with systemic weedkillers, applied to avoid damage to desirable plants. Bindweed can be killed with glyphosate, applied to the leaves every two or three weeks during the summer. However, glyphosate kills all green plants, and therefore should be applied very carefully to the leaves of weeds only. Couch can be eliminated by one application of glyphosate in the late summer, but this is only possible when clearing the ground completely as all neighbouring plants are likely to be affected.

Avoid digging or rotovating the ground until all these perennial weeds have been eradicated, otherwise each little section of root may produce a new plant. Where a garden is particularly overgrown, you may need to allow it to lie fallow for at least a year, applying weedkiller again in the following year to ensure the weed is entirely eradicated. If the weed reappears after you have planted, you may find it impossible to destroy it without destroying your plants as well.

PREVENTION

Once you have cleared the ground of weeds, cover the soil with a mulch of bark chippings, or cover with black plastic.

When weeding, the best way to mak' sure ye're removing a weed and not a precious plant is tae pull on't. If it comes oot o' the ground easily, it's a precious plant!

A weed is jist a plant growin' in the wrang place that wants tae stay.

IDENTIFYING WEEDS

It can be difficult to identify weeds when they are small. Here are some sketches of some of the worst offenders when they are seedlings.

APPEARANCE OF WEED SEEDLINGS

black bindweed
perennial

groundsel
annual

buttercup
perennial

knotgrass
annual

charlock, wild mustard
annual

mayweed
annual

chickweed
annual

nettle
perennial

dandelion
perennial

prickly sow-thistle
annual

docken
perennial

shepherd's purse
annual

fat hen
annual

speedwell
annual

field bindweed
perennial

Other weeds you need to look out for are the perennials:
bracken, brambles, couch grass, ground elder (bishop's weed), horse-tail, nettles, ragwort;
and the annuals hairy bittercress, which frequently gets into gardens from garden centre plants, sticky willie (cleavers).

Inflorescence of Dandelion

HORSETAIL (MARESTAIL)
Horsetail is a weed that really has survived – it is one of the few plants that dinosaurs would still recognise. It certainly looks unlike any other plant in the garden. Its stem is coated with abrasive silicates and it was traditionally used to clean pots and pans.

NETTLES
The Romans brought nettles to Britain – and can you believe that they used to whip themselves with nettles to help keep themselves warm in damp and cold Britain?

177

Gettin' Rid o' Weeds

If ye jist turn yer back on the gairden for a moment, weeds seem tae spring oot o' nowhere. Whit are the best ways o' gettin' rid o' them? Usin' yer hoe an' gettin' doon tae weed by hand. You'll need tae mak sure ye remove a' the roots o' those wi' lang tap roots (such as dandelion an' docken) an' try not tae be stung by nettle leaves. Rub any sting wi' a dock leaf. There are lots o' ither ways to help get rid o' weeds. Here are some ideas.

Weeds spoil the look of paved areas and their roots are troublesome to remove. An effective check to their growth is to apply – in early spring – a saturated solution of rock salt.

A traditional way of getting rid of couch grass is to sow turnip seeds in an area of the grass. Turnip seedlings will make the couch wither and die – and lupins can have the same effect. To get rid of horsetail and ivy, plant Mexican marigolds (Tagetes minuta).

How Tae Kill a Marestail

Even a systemic weedkiller willnae affect the marestail - its skin is ower tough...

If ye've no' too many, gie them a guid dunt atweeen twa stanes

Noo the weedkiller can get intae the pant and kill the roots.

Guid riddance!

Tae get rid o' weeds in a gravel path that wasn't lined wi' plastic sheetin', pour boilin' water over the gravel and leave for 24 hours, then rake and remove the dead weeds.

Weedkillers

If you just don't have time to get down and clear weeds by hand and don't mind using garden chemicals, there's help at hand. You can find weedkillers in garden centres, DIY shops and even supermarkets. There's lots of choice, but there are really only a few different sorts.

SELECTIVE weedkillers kill specific plants – very useful for killing weeds in a lawn, but don't put grass cuttings from treated lawns onto the compost heap; leave them to rot separately, turning to aerate, for a couple of years first.

There are **NON-SELECTIVE** weedkillers which work in specific ways. Choose the right one for the job in hand:

- **CONTACT** weedkillers act quickly to kill leaves – useful for getting rid of small annual weeds. There is no residual effect on the soil.
- **SYSTEMIC** weedkillers are taken into the plant through the leaf, killing the plant over the course of several days – useful for eradicating perennial weeds and brushwood. There is no residual effect on the soil.
- **RESIDUAL** weedkillers – used to keep paths and driveways clear of weeds.

Here is a list of chemical names to look out for on packets of weedkillers, with a description of what they do:

- selective weedkiller used on lawns: 2,4-D, dicamba, dichlorprop-P, MCPA, mecoprop-P
- selective weedkiller used on lawn to kill moss: ferrous sulphate
- non-selective, contact weedkiller used on annual weeds: diquat, fatty acids (inc. pelargonic acid), gluphosinate-ammonium
- non-selective, systemic weedkiller used on perennial weeds: glyphosate
- non-selective, residual weedkiller used on paths and driveways: diflufenican, flufenacet, metosulam, oxadiazon
- selective, systemic weedkiller used on brushwood: triclopyr

A Shoe-Horn Weed Puller
High Speed Weeding Simplified

THE somewhat tiresome job of weeding between close-spaced plants can be lightened by using a shoe-horn as a weed-puller. This simple garden gadget will double the speed of your weeding, and prevent sore fingers. The sketch illustrates how the shoe-horn is used.

PRECAUTIONS WHEN USING WEEDKILLERS

You've got to be careful with weedkillers. Read the label on the packet to find out how to use them safely.

Most weedkillers have to be sprayed onto the leaves of the weeds. You need to listen to the weather forecast to make sure it's not going to be windy. You don't want to be spraying any of your (or anyone else's) precious plants by mistake. Make sure it's not going to rain straight after you spray the weeds. That would be a waste of weedkiller.

You can buy weedkillers ready mixed in a handy sprayer. You can also buy weedkiller in bottles, but you need to mix it carefully with water and use in a watering can or a sprayer. If you are doing this mixing, make sure you read the instructions (don't make it stronger than it says) and do it somewhere safe. Make sure your sprayer works properly and isn't leaky. If you use a watering can, make sure it's a special one you only use for weedkiller. You really don't want to find you've used it to water your prize leeks.

Wear gloves when you're using them and wash your hands when you have finished.

Make sure you keep the weans and the pets away from where you have sprayed until it has dried. Keep weedkillers in the packets they came in, in a safe place. Only buy enough weedkiller for one season at a time. You don't want to be left with lots of half used packets. They don't get better for being left, and those scientists keep finding better and safer products anyway, so you don't want to be stuck with the old ones.

Ask the Council if you need to throw any weedkiller away; you can't just chuck it out.

Cut thistles May,
they'll be back in a day;
Cut thistles in June,
they'll be back soon;
Cut thistles in July,
they'll surely die.

Wild Gairdenin'

Gairdenin' at the But an' Ben is a bit different from in toon. Plants there have tae survive by thersel's as I'm nae there tae look efter them ower much, an' old Maw Nature, wi' the help o' rabbits, is only too keen tae reclaim the gairden. Ye need fences an' rabbit netting tae keep the beggars oot an' still they get in at times. Rabbit wire has tae be dug in deep a' roond yer fences. I've kent rabbits tae get in at nicht an' eat a' yer lettuce plants tae the ground an' still be back for breakfast in the mornin'. Thae teeth go through the firmest carrots like hot knives through butter.

We grow some veg there. Tatties grow well - and rabbits dinnae like them. There's nothing like fresh new tatties cooked with a sprig o' mint, another plant that needs nae tender care (and which will tak ower if no' kept under control). Turnips and beetroot dae fine as well, but forget aboot lettuce (what the slugs dinnae get, the rabbits will). Kail grows well an' a', specially with a dressing of farmyard manure from farmer Wilson.

As for floo'ers, ye need to look what grows roond aboot and then it may grow for ye (that's ma tip for wherever you stay). I've made a note in ma book of some plants to try.

Horace's thoughts on guerrilla gairdenin'

Reports from New York City and various cities in the UK show that guerrilla gardeners are using seed bombs, and deft planting methods, to transform forlorn, waste-strewn and unused pieces of ground into flower beds and little allotments for the benefit of the community. Sometimes neighbours approach owners of little-used gardens and take them over for the pleasure of all, and sometimes they use Council land that is not looked after, which can be popular with local residents but not with the Council!

Horace is a hippie gorilla

Plants tae grow at the But an' Ben

Broom
Daffodils
Foxgloves
Heathers
(lots o' choice here; some flower in
Spring and some in Autumn)
Lupins
Primroses
Rhododendrons
Wild roses

To join wire netting, insert a muckle nail and twist the strands. One turn is enough, but if you want rid o' bulges in your fence - just gie it another few twists, then pull oot yer nail. Better than string or fiddly wire.

I canna agree wi' Thompson's description of a bothy, though:

There's ay plenty o' guid advice fae the ne'ebors!

BOTHY. A residence for under-gardeners, usually built behind the hot-houses, or some high wall, in what is called a back shed. The place is too frequently a cramped, ill-ventilated hovel. A bothy proper should be an independent structure, and fitted with modern conveniences; for , of all people, gardeners are most susceptible to colds, etc. A library of standard horticultural and botanical works, as well as a few on other scientific subjects , and a moderate number of high-class books of fiction, one or more weekly gardening and other papers, should be supplied by the employer. During the winter months, for mutual improvement, lectures should be delivered, or papers read, by each gardener, on various subjects, after which a free discussion should take place upon the paper or lecture, by which means a great amount of good would be accomplished.

Windae Boxes

And there's aye windae boxes, dinna forget. A hale tenement wi' windae boxes wi' geraniums looks bonnie ... continental even. Mak's me feel like playin' a puckle o' French tunes on ma accordion. Ye've tae be awfy careful an' mak' sure yer boxes are weel anchored. A windae box fu' o' earth and floo'ers hurtlin' doon fae fower flairs up and landin' on somebody's napper is no' recommended. Ground floor boxes need a Rottweiler tae guard them unless ye want them fu' o' cigarette butts. Fowk jist use them as ashtrays sadly.

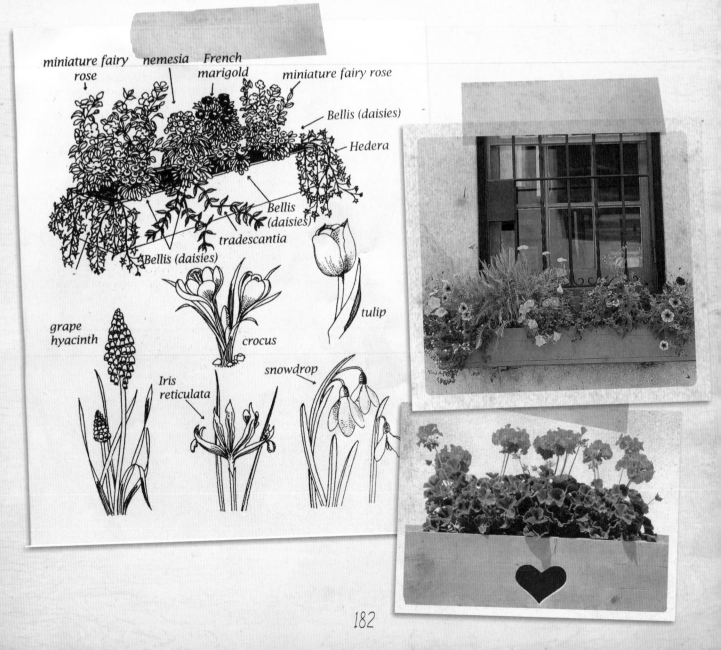

miniature fairy rose
nemesia
French marigold
miniature fairy rose
Bellis (daisies)
Hedera
Bellis (daisies)
tradescantia
Bellis (daisies)
tulip
grape hyacinth
crocus
Iris reticulata
snowdrop

Window Boxes

Window boxes make very attractive additions to the appearance of a house, but they need to be tough as they will have to stand up the heavy weight of wet soil for years. A wide range of plastic boxes are available from garden centres, and if you have a little skill in carpentry you could make your own

wooden box. Whichever route you chose to follow be careful about the size of window box. A box as big as 3 ft. long will be very heavy when filled with wet soil, and if it is less than 1 ft. long or narrower than 6 in. wide, it will not hold enough plants to make a show. The depth should be between 6 and 12 in. to allow plants to make deep enough roots.

Wooden boxes will rot in a few years if not protected with a wood preservative before soil is added. A good preservative is Cuprinol, which is painted over the inside. The outside can be decorated as you wish. Paint it in one or more colours or fix strips of wood cross-wise to look like a cottage fence. Avoid being too colourful or you will spoil the effect of the real flowers.
A final piece of advice if the window box is to go on a narrow upstairs window ledge — it must be held in place in case it falls and injures someone. Fix metal braces between the box and the window frame or wall.

PLANTING A WINDOW BOX

The same general rules apply to the preparation of window boxes as to pots, bowls and bottles for planting. There are drainage holes so the layer of material to collect run-off water need not be deep. Half an inch of gravel, pebbles or broken pieces of flowerpot spread evenly over the bottom will be enough. To stop from choking this layer, add protective cover of partly rotted leaves.

The rest of the box will contain soil. Plants will be close together in the box with many roots in the soil, so a fairly rich compost is needed. John Innes No. 2 potting compost from garden centres is the best to use because it has the right amount of plant food and a suitable mixture of soil (loam) and sand. Add this compost until the box is just over half full, then begin to put in the plants.

The window box will be an outdoor garden tended from indoors. This means that you can grow many things that would not be happy inside the window. But at the same time some tender indoor plants would find it too cold.

WHAT TO PLANT

Let us say that you are ready to start planting in May. This is a good time because it is when summer bedding plants can be obtained. These are very colourful but are intended to last only until the autumn. They can be bought as young plants in strips from garden centres and will soon come into bloom. Suitable compact ones for a window box include ageratum, lobelia, annual phlox, petunias, nemesia and tagetes. Petunias are the tallest and should be planted at the back of the box (looking from the outside). Lobelia will hang over the front edge and look very pretty with its blue flowers. From these annuals you can make a good display in a box about 3 ft. long and 9 in. deep by planting at 6-in. intervals. Stagger the position of plants in each row so that they have as much space as possible.
From May onwards it is safe to plant geraniums (pelargoniums) outside. These need

to be 9 in. apart, and there will be room for only one other smaller flower in front in an average window box. Other plants can go in the window box — but only for the summer, after which they must return indoors. These are tradescantia, chlorophytum and coleus. Hedera, the ivy, can also be used and encouraged to hang over the edge.

PLANTING BULBS

When these plants must be removed in autumn it is time to stir the soil with a hand fork, remove any weeds and then plant spring flowering bulbs. The secret of success here is to choose compact-flowering bulbs that will not get blown over in spring gales. By careful selection, you can get flowers from February until May. First to flower are snowdrops and beautiful blue flowering miniature iris. Another good blue one is muscari, the grape hyacinth. At the same time the earliest crocuses appear, and then the miniature yellow narcissi and short-stemmed tulips which are mostly red. These are on sale in garden centres from September onwards, but many people buy them by sending away an order from a catalogue. Bulbs have no roots when you plant them, but you can tell the right way up because the top is more pointed than the base. A guide when planting is to set them as far below the surface as the height of the bulb. A good thing to do during the winter when the soil is bare is to cover the bulb box with coloured gravel or chippings. This looks well and prevents rain splashing soil onto the window.

PLANTING HERBS

If you wish to try other things in the window box another time (or if you make more than one) — what about a herb garden? Sprigs can be cut from it to use in the kitchen. Ask gardening friends for a piece of mint root and small rooted pieces of parsley (an annual) and thyme. These will soon spread. Remember to firm the soil after planting and to give the box plenty of water (it may not catch much rain). Remove weeds when you see them, and nip off dead flower heads to encourage more flowers and to keep the window-box garden looking trim.

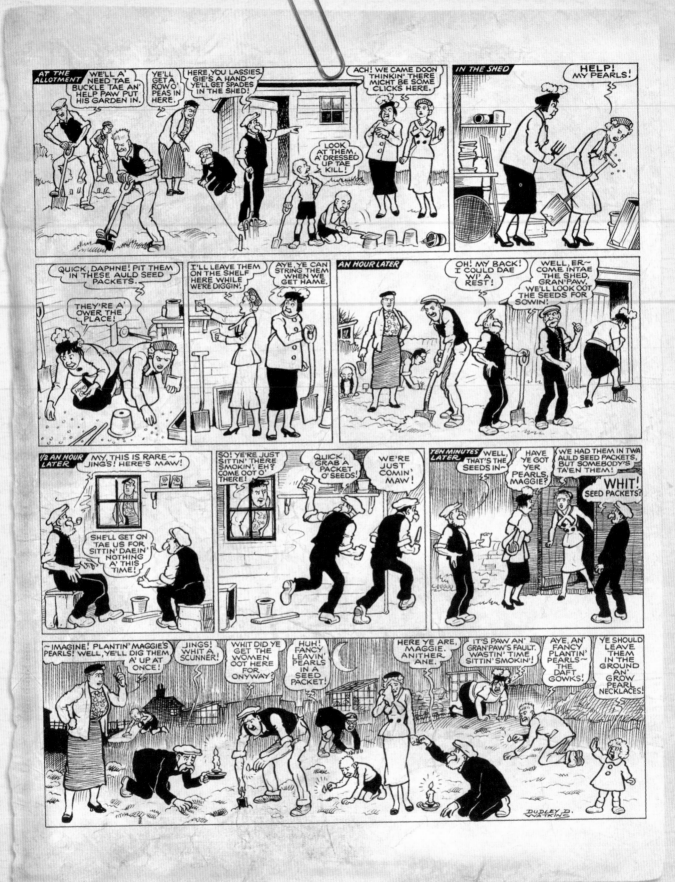

Gairdenin' Wisdoms

with
GAIRDENER BROON

✣✣✣✣✣✣✣✣✣✣✣✣✣✣✣✣✣✣✣✣

THE HISTORY OF THE SHED, PART 3

AN' NOO FOR THE END o' ma shed story.

Ye'd think a man had suffered enough bad luck on sic a day, but not a bit o' it. Naw, mair was in store for "Gairdener" Broon. I'd been standin' that lang trying tae fish oot ma wallet that the cement had set aboot ma wellies and I was stuck in the foundations. Can ye credit that?? Wellies, wallies AND wallet a' stuck fast in the cement. The ither fowk in the allotments had tae sling a rope ower an overhangin' branch and tie it tae ma waist tae haul me oota ma wellies. Broon? I was BLACK affrontit!!

Buildin' the shed itsel' was a dawdle efter a' that trouble. It wisnae new but had been the heid gairdener's wooden "cabin" on Balmoral Estate. It came wi' the fower walls in sections and the original pot belly stove and the lum and a' the fittings ... really a shed by Royal Appointment. I aye think when I'm heatin' up ma coffee pot on the iron stove that this is the same stove that biled up Queen Victoria's tea when she had her elevenses wi' ma Uncle John Broon wha wiz the gamekeeper at the time. Ye'll hae heard o' Uncle John ... John BROWN as Queen Vic probably kent him. Fowk say she had a fancy for Oor John, but ye ken fowk ... they say that aboot Annie Lennox and me. Chance wid be a fine thing.

There's no' a lot mair tae tell ... oh, apart fae the fact that when we had three walls up, the heavens opened. I hauled ma auld Norton Dominator (it's a motorbike) intae the shed oot o' the rain and watched the rain wattering my tatties through the open gable end. Aince the rain was aff, we nailed on the last gable wall ... and sealed in the bloomin' motorbike!! It was ower big tae ride oot the door, and here it bides. I polish it every so often and let oor Bairn sit on it.

My intention was tae get the pot belly stove glowin' and ask Annie in tae start aff whaur we'd left aff when I near proposed tae her jist as the auld shed collapsed aboot oor ears. But that's when I got a letter fae my auld flame Clarinda MacClure, newly back in this country fae Canada ... but I darena SHED ony light on that business. Wid hae been better if I'd been able tae bury THAT letter in the cement wi' the rest o' them! Ha ha. What a life! If Maw Broon ever kent the half o' it ...

Well, that's aboot it ... the shed's still goin' strong, so is the stove and the coffee and so am I. Drap in on me ane o' thae times ye're passin'.

Aye Yours,

Gairdener Broon

x

I meant to do some work the day,
But a butterfly fluttered across the way
An' a broon bird sang in the old pear tree,
The leaves on the trees were calling me.
So I just sat doon.

Horace's Guide tae Gairdenin' Words

annual A plant that grows from seed, flowers, produces seed and dies all in one year.

bedding plant An annual that is grown under glass and is planted out in the garden when the danger of frost is over.

biennial A plant which grows from seed one year, flowers, produces seed and dies the following year.

biological control The use of natural predators to control pests.

bud Part of a plant from which either a leaf shoot or a flower will appear.

bulb Part of a perennial plant, protected by fleshy scales, which can usually be lifted, dried and stored ready for propagation of a new plant following replanting — examples include narcissi and tulips.

cloche A temporary, portable transparent cover, used to shelter tender plants in cold weather, acting like a small greenhouse.

companion plants Plants which, when grown near others, can help them in different ways — by deterring insects (summer savory deters insects from runner beans; marigolds are said to deter carrot root flies), improving plant nutrition (beans and other leguminous plants such as clover fix nitrogen in the soil, beneficial to many other plants) or by sheltering tender plants.

composting The practice of encouraging garden, and some kitchen, waste to decompose. The resulting material is used to improve garden soil.

compost, potting Two main types. Loam-based — a mixture of loam, peat (or substitute), sand and fertiliser used to fill pots and seed trays. Different ratios of these components are used for different types and sizes of plant.

Soil-less — based on peat or peat substitutes. Provides less support and nutrients than loam-based composts.

corm Solid, swollen part of the stem of some perennial plants — examples include crocus — which can usually be lifted, dried and stored ready for propagation of a new plant following replanting.

damping off A fungal infection which can cause young plants to die, usually occurring in damp conditions, particularly if plants are close together, preventing air circulation.

dead heading Removing the dead flowers from a plant to prevent formation of seed; it extends the flowering period.

deciduous A shrub or tree which grows leaves in the spring and loses them in the autumn.

dormant period A period during which a plant is not actively growing.

evergreen A shrub or tree which retains its leaves all year.

fungicide A substance used to kill fungi.

germination The process by which seeds start to grow into small plants.

ha ha A wall set in a ditch so that the view from a garden can be enjoyed without a visible fence.

half hardy A plant that requires protection from low winter temperatures.

hardening off The preparation of plants grown under glass in relatively warm conditions to cooler conditions, before being transplanted outdoors.

hardy A plant that can survive outdoor conditions.

herbicide A substance used to kill weeds.

humus	A dark brown or black substance found in soil which improves fertility and water retention; it is a product of the decomposition of organic material.
insecticide	A substance used to kill insects.
loam	Rich, well-drained soil, consisting of sand, decomposed organic material and clay.
mulch	Material used to cover the bare earth between plants. It can be bark chippings, grass cuttings, small stones or plastic sheeting. A mulch improves moisture retention and suppresses weeds.
organic gardening	A way of gardening without using manufactured chemicals such as pesticides and fertilisers.
peat	Organic material formed in bogs. Traditionally used to improve soil, and in potting compost, alternatives to peat, such as coconut fibre and garden compost are now used to prevent further destruction of fragile peat bogs.
perennial	A plant that is dormant during the winter, grows in the spring, flowers and then dies back in the late autumn.
pesticide	A substance used to control pests — insects (insecticide), fungi (fungicide), weeds (herbicide or weed killer).
pinching out	Removing the bud at the end of a branch to encourage the formation of side shoots lower down the branch.
pot bound	A pot plant which has grown so that its roots fill its pot almost entirely.
potting on	Repotting a pot-bound plant into a larger pot and topping it up with fresh potting compost.
pricking out	The separating out individual plant seedlings from the seed tray in which they have germinated and transferring them to a container which allows them space to grow.
propagation	Formation of a new plant; there is a range of methods for different types of plant.
rhizome	The thickened part at the base of some perennial plants which grows horizontally — examples include some iris. It can usually be lifted and replanted to propagate a new plant.
scarify	Vigorous raking of a lawn in autumn with a spring-tined rake to remove the layer of accumulated moss and dead vegetation that builds up during the growing season.
tilth	Soil which has been prepared for the planting of seeds or small plants. It has a crumbly texture and a level surface.
tuber	Part of a perennial plant, growing underground — it can be a swollen stem or a fleshy root, (dahlia) — which can usually be lifted and stored ready for propagation of a new plant following replanting.
turf	Grass which is grown in one place then carefully removed and placed on prepared ground in order to form a high-quality lawn quickly.
variegated leaf	A green leaf which is bordered or spotted with another colour such as white, cream or yellow.
volunteer	A useful plant which arrives in the garden by chance — propagated from a seed blown by the wind or dropped by a bird. (It has to be said that most plants arriving in this way are weeds.)
weed	A plant which the gardener considers to be in the wrong place.

Horace's useful index

PLATE VIII.

Drawn by Mrs Withers.

Eng.^d by J.W. Lowry.

1 *Gompholobium splendens*   2 *Hemiandra pungens*

3 *Grevillia elegans*

BLACKIE & SON; GLASGOW EDINBURGH & LONDON.